# LOYAL and ANCIENT CITY

# LOYAL
and
# ANCIENT CITY

## Lichfield in the Civil Wars

*by*
HOWARD CLAYTON

"Sir, your most humble and loyal subjects, the Bailiffs,
Sheriff, and their maces &c. citizens of this your city
of Lichfield, do humbly according to their duty, surrender
into your Majestys hands these ensigns of their authority,
which they are resolved to bear from you and under you
or not at all; and whether they live or die, to live and
die your Majestys most faithful and loyal subjects."

*Address of the Bailiffs of Lichfield
to King Charles I after the
Battle of Naseby.*

ISBN 0 9503563 2 8

Published by the author at
2a Brownsfield Road, Lichfield, Staffordshire

Printed by J. M. Tatler & Son Ltd., Abbey Street Works, Derby

# Contents

# *City of Lichfield*

Mayor

*Councillor John Russell*

Secretary

*Mrs. P. Eggington*  Lichfield 54031/57503

Mayor's Parlour,
Guildhall,
Lichfield,
Staffs.
WS13 6LX.

## FOREWORD

Anyone who has lived in Lichfield for a while will have a skeletal knowledge of the part played by the City in the Civil War and I welcome this book which adds flesh to those bones and brings to life the stirring events of that lively time in our history.

The names of many parts of the City owe their origin to the battles fought as the control of the Close swung from Royalist to Parliamentarian hands and back again and I feel sure that no-one could be unmoved by this opportunity to savour life as it was in those desperate times.

Perhaps the most surprising part of the book to modern generations is the gentlemanly way in which war was conducted - one does not always find such fair play in even our day to day living these days.

I am sure that this book will be both interesting and informative reading for students of history and anyone with just an interest in life in bygone days.

I know that a lot of research went into this book and I am pleased to add this foreword in my capacity as Mayor of the City of Lichfield and congratulate the author on an excellent addition to the knowledge of our colourful past.

John Russell
The Right Worshipful Mayor of Lichfield

# Author's Preface

THIS is a book about Lichfield people of the past for Lichfield people of today and, one hopes, those of the future.

In a community such as that of the 'Loyal and Ancient' city a strong thread of continuity runs through its past and present, and as we go about our daily lives it is impossible not to wonder how our predecessors, living in much the same environment and with many of the same manners and customs as ourselves, faced up to the major upheavals of history. This is especially so when one considers the Civil War of 1642-46, for in this struggle Lichfield played a strategic part and the war became a major event in the lives of the citizens. In few places in England were the fundamental issues of the war more evident. A city whose Lord of the Manor, the Earl of Essex, became Commander-in-Chief of the Parliamentary army on the outbreak of war and which experienced the fury of siege and battery by Prince Rupert and his forces, followed by an impressive display of might by Queen Henrietta and her army, and some years later the sight of Charles I straight from his defeat at Naseby — for such a community the political aspect of the war was brought literally to their doorsteps. As for the religious aspect of the conflict, this was even more prominent in their lives, for the ancient cathedral, around which so much of the life of the city had centred for centuries, was left in ruin by Oliver Cromwell's revolution. Centuries of religious custom disappeared and the cathedral close became for fourteen years a place of ruin, inhabited by squatters and haunted by owls at night. And yet, within six years of the restoration of the monarchy the city had returned to its old vigorous self and went on, in the succeeding century, to flourish as a centre of intellectual activity, producing such names as Addison, Johnson, Garrick and Darwin.

Reading the letters and documents of the war period, one is struck by the similarity between the Lichfield people of that time and those of today. English people have not changed a great deal in 300 years.

This book is a study of a small 17th century cathedral town under the stress of civil war. As such I hope it will be of interest to others beside the present citizens of Lichfield for many of whom, I know, the events recorded are of absorbing interest.

# Acknowledgements

I would like to acknowledge the help given to me in producing this work by the following persons:

Nancy, Lady Bagot, for access to her archives of the Bagot family and for permission to photograph her portrait of Colonel Richard Bagot; Mr. Paul Barker, Curator of Warwick Castle, for permission to photograph the armour of Lord Brooke; Mr. Dace, of Lichfield Public Library for assistance on numerous occasions from his vast store of information on Lichfield history; Mr. George Deacon of Lichfield, for the loan of papers relating to the metallurgical analysis of a cannon ball found on the site of Sir William Brereton's camp; Mr. R. N. Dore, authority on the Letter Books of Sir William Brereton, for advice on this subject; Mrs. J. Hampertumian, Archivist, Lichfield Joint Record Office, for advice on possible sources of information; Prebendary E. E. C. Hill, Librarian, Lichfield Cathedral Library and Mr. Godfrey Hives, Head Verger of the Cathedral, for their help in research and the Very Reverend John Lang, Dean of Lichfield for permission to publish the results; Mr. Geoff Morgan, Birmingham Reference Library, for his ready assistance, Mr. and Mrs. Ted Simpson for information on the story of the "Marching Men"; Mr. Jack Salford for local information; Dr. Nigel Tringham, for information and advice following his research into the fortifications of Lichfield Close; Mr. John Warner-Davies, Head of Archives Department, Birmingham Reference Library, for assistance in research; Mr. Ian Wren, Headmaster, St. Chad's Cathedral School, Lichfield, for permission to photograph, and Brigadier Peter Young, whose help enabled me to track down, the paintings of the colours of Bagot's Foot Regiment.

Last, but by no means least, my thanks to my son John for designing and painting the cover of this book and also for reproducing the illustrations of the colours and standards inside it.

My thanks must also go to the following public bodies whose facilities I have used:
Birmingham Reference Library (Archives Section); Lichfield Cathedral Library; Lichfield City Council (for permission to reproduce illustrations of one of their maces and also of the Ashmole Cup); Lichfield Joint Record Office; Lichfield Public Libary; Nantwich Public Library; The National Army Museum; The Public Record Office; The William Salt Library, Stafford and Dr. Williams' Library, London.

# Introduction

THE middle of the 17th Century saw Britain racked by civil war — referred to at the time and since as The Civil War, The Great Rebellion and The War without an Enemy.

This is not the place for a close analysis of the causes of the war; it is sufficient to say that the antagonism between Charles I and Parliament rested on two main differences. The first of these was the question of who should rule the country, King or Parliament. Charles believed implicitly in the Divine Right of Kings, and when, after twenty-four years of struggle with Parliament, he stood on the scaffold about to be executed, he uttered these words, 'I must tell you liberty and freedom consist in having government . . . it is not having a share in government. That is nothing pertaining to them [the people]. A subject and a sovereign are clean different things.'

Parliament, on the other hand, believed that 'the liberties, franchises, privileges and jurisdiction of Parliament are the ancient and undoubted birthright and inheritance of the subjects of England', and their opposition to Charles took the form of refusing to vote him money.

The second difference between the two parties was a religious one; Charles ended his speech on the scaffold with the words, 'I die a Christian according to the profession of the Church of England, as I found it left to me by my father.' But to many of his subjects, with memories of the excesses of the reign of "Bloody Mary" and of the wars with Spain and of the Inquisition, the doctrines of the Church of England were too close to those of Rome and redolent of Popery and superstition. Thus, throughout the struggle, the forces of Parliament expressed their Puritanism by tearing down altars and altar rails and by the destruction of images, stained glass windows and church ornaments of all kinds. Nowhere was this more evident than in Lichfield where a beautiful cathedral, the principal one in England to suffer, became the target of religious hatred and bigotry.

These two differences came to the fore early in Charles's reign when in 1629 Parliament refused for the third time to grant the King the customs duty known as Tonnage and Poundage, a right enjoyed by every previous monarch but restricted in Charles's case to annual votes. At the same time

Parliament attacked the King's appointment of William Laud as Bishop of London. Laud was a High Churchman who later was to end his life on the scaffold for his support of Charles.

In Lichfield, as elsewhere in the country, each faction had its supporters. The tragedy of the Great Rebellion was that it set Englishman against Englishman, citizen against citizen and even divided families. This was the background against which the events recorded in this book are set and against which one must consider the effects of the Civil War in one small town in England.

\*  \*  \*  \*  \*

# List of Illustrations

**LICHFIELD**

ST CHAD'S CH.

STOW STREET

STOW POOL

MILL CROFTS

BURTON ROAD

ST MICHAEL'S CHURCH

TAMWORTH ROAD

MINSTER POOL

ST MARY'S

SADLER ST

BORE ST

FROG LANE

NORTH ST

ST JOHN ST

BRIDGE ST

SANDFORD ST

FRIERY

BISHOP'S POOL

BACUN STREET

Pases

40  80  120  160  200  240  280

*(Based on a map by John Speed, 1610)*

*Lichfield at the beginning of the 17th century*

*Chapter I*

# Lichfield in 1642

LICHFIELD in the year of the Great Rebellion was a community of less than 3,000 souls. It lay in a gentle valley along which slow-running streams formed pools and marshlands. On the north side of one of these pools, where the ground rose sharply, stood the cathedral, a jewel of gothic architecture with its three slender spires dominating the scene for miles around and its superb west front richly decorated with statues of prophets, priests and kings. Bishop Walter de Langton*, Treasurer to Edward I and II, and probably the richest man ever to live in Lichfield, completed the cathedral by building the Lady Chapel. He also built a new and splendid Bishop's Palace in the north east corner of the Close. Included in it was a Great Hall one hundred feet long and fifty-six feet wide, the walls of which were painted with frescoes showing the coronation, marriages, wars and funeral of his patron Edward I. These were still remaining in 1603 when Erdeswicke made his survey[1] and were therefore probably still in existence in 1642. Like so many other things, they were to disappear in the catastrophe of the next few years.

Langton fortified the Close by surrounding the whole of it with stone walls, built in a handsome manner and strengthened with towers and turrets. To the west and south of these fortifications were gates, each furnished with a portcullis and a drawbridge to give access over a moat. In this way, with the best of intentions, he made the Close secure from any enemy. He could not forsee that three centuries later his work would ensure that the cathedral on which he had lavished so much care and money would be visited by death, destruction and the most wanton and sacrilegious desecration.

On the south side of the pools, opposite the cathedral, lay the city of Lichfield — a large village by modern standards. Practically the whole of it was situated in the confines of the ancient fortifications built by

*Bishop 1296-1321

Bishop Roger de Clinton* in the twelfth century. These consisted of a ditch and an inner earth rampart, bounding the city on the east, south and west (the pools provided security to the north). At four places these ramparts were pierced by roads, and at these places were gates or "barrs".

However effective these defences may have been when built, by the year 1642 they had long ceased to have any military significance, the gates having gone and the only trace of the ramparts being a shallow ditch. Even this had disappeared on the south side, where, in the reign of Queen Elizabeth I, it had been let by the Corporation as a common muck-hill at a rent of sixpence a year.

The line of the fortifications still formed an effective boundary, however, and within it the streets still followed the plan laid out by Clinton, as indeed they do today. But in 1642 the houses which lined those streets were almost all timber-framed wattle-and-daub structures with thatched roofs. Buildings of brick and stone were few and far between — the Hospital of St. John the Baptist just outside the southernmost gate of the city, a fifteenth century brick building with an impressive row of chimneys (probably the first ones ever seen in Lichfield) which served as an almshouse for old men; Dr. Milley's Hospital in Bacun Street which performed a similar function for old women; the Guildhall in Borde Street, home of Lichfield Corporation, and St. Mary's, a handsome gothic parish church by the Market Place. Also in the Market Place was the stone Market Cross, erected by Dean Denton in 1530, around which the market traders cried their wares every Tuesday and Friday. This consisted of a vaulted roof supported on eight pillars, above each of which stood a stone figure of an apostle, while two crucifixes were fixed on the east and west side. Above the roof was a turret containing the market bell and at ground level, between two of the pillars, were fixed the stocks in which malefactors were confined.

In spite of its small size Lichfield was a well-appointed town. In addition to his work in the Close, Bishop Langton had paved the city streets and built a stone causeway and bridge across the pools, thus bringing Close and City nearer to each other and dispensing with the ferry across the Minster Pool which had formerly connected them. The Conduit Lands Trust, formed in 1545, supplied the city with pure water from springs at Aldershaw, just outside Lichfield, bringing it in pipes to conduits at various points where it was available to all.

Two parish churches stood outside the city — St. Chad's in the little hamlet of Stow, to the east, and St. Michael's on Greenhill to the south-east. Along the line of the streams that flowed out of the west and through the city stood four water mills. The first, at Leomansley, provided power for

---

*Bishop 1129-1148

weaving worsted cloth, while the other three, at Dam Street, Stow and Ponesfield ground the corn that was grown on the rich agricultural land that surrounded Lichfield.

Once upon a time these mills had belonged to the Lord of the Manor, the Bishop of Lichfield, but in 1597 the Lordship of the Manor passed from the Bishop to the Crown, in the person of Queen Elizabeth I. By her it was assigned to the Corporation of Lichfield, through the good offices of the Earl of Essex, a close friend of the Queen. Since at that time nobody at court was expected to negotiate a favour of this sort without getting something in return, the Earl received from the Corporation as his *quid pro quo* a lease of the Lordship of the Manor for the duration of his own life and that of his son.

But even in those days the wheels of local government turned slowly, and by 1604, when the Earl died,* the lease had not been completed. Three years later the Countess of Essex, on behalf of her infant son, the new Earl, petitioned the Privy Council, who sent the following letter[2] to the Corporation of Lichfield.

After our hartie commendacions.

We are given to understand that by an agreement made by the late Earle of Essex, and the Corporacion of Lichfield, the sayd Earle was to procure from the Bishopp of Lichfield (first to the late Queen and then by an assignment to the sayd Corporacion) the ffee ffarm of the Mannour and Lordshipp of Lichfield; and that in consideracion thereof there should a lease be made from them unto him and the now Earle his sonne of the sayd Mannour during their lives; which agreement (as wee likewise understand) was accordingly performed on the late Earle's part; but dyinge before the lease coulde be mayde from them to him and his sonne, the same remains yet unperformed on your part though you have been mooved thereto by letters from the Countess of Essex that is mother to the now Earle; we have therefore thought good to write these our letters unto you to that effect, and to let you know the evill requitall you make unto the late Earle's honourable regard of you in procuring you so good a benefit with such easy condicions, and the wrong you do your own reputacions in seeking to violate your own word and promise made with such reservacions of advantage to your corporacion. And therefore, as you shall but do yourselves right to keep your worde with him that observed his so well towards you, so do we pray and require you to make the nowe Earle (according to your promise and agreement) a lease of the sayde Mannour and Lordshippe of Lichfield during his life; which not doubting but that you will out of hand perform and give satisfaccion to ye Earle, we bid you hartie farewell. From the courte at Whitehall, the last of July, 1604, your loving friends

| | |
|---|---|
| ELLESMERE, Canc.† | THOS. BURGHLEY |
| NORTHUMBERLAND | NOTTINGHAM |
| RO. CECYLL | SUFFOLK |
| L. STANHOPE | T. DORSET |
| F. WORCESTER | H. NORTHAMPTON |
| GILB. SHREWSBURY | W. KNOLLYS |
| DEVONSHIRE | H. BINY |
| J. HERBERT | |

---

*He was executed for high treason
†Cancellarius. Ellesmere was Lord Chancellor

The letter was superscribed, 'This letter was delyvered to Mr. Bayliffe Ashmole by John Swynfen, Gent., att Tameworthe on Saturday the xiiij daye of October, after the date of the same.'

Thomas Ashmole, Senior Bailiff (Mayor) of Lichfield, on whom the Privy Council had trained this formidable battery of big guns, was a saddler by trade and a member of the Company of Corvisors (shoe-makers) of Lichfield. The records of this company, one of the ancient trade guilds of the city, are now in the Chetam Library in Manchester,* and from them can be gleaned some insights into the character of Thomas Ashmole. A memorandum dated 22nd December 1625 records that a meeting of the company was held about a very contumacious brother, Thomas Ashmole, 'keepeing his brother and not enroleing nor byndinge him'. A short time later, on the 8th of May 1626, there is a note that 'Thomas Ashmole made a forfeiture against John Warde, iij shillings and iiij pence, being absent at the meeting xij pence, likewise the said Thomas Ashmole did abuse the said John Warde at the Hall doore in the open street & called him a Cobling Clown; iij shillings and iiij pence.'

From these extracts it would appear that Ashmole was a person of fiery temperament and one who did not suffer fools gladly. John Warde was probably the Master of the Corvisors on that occasion, perhaps not a very good chairman, and the irritation of Ashmole at being fined and admonished, leading to his "words" with Warde as they left the Guildhall after the meeting is easy to understand. Thomas Ashmole was a man of some substance in the city; by 1626 he had been Sheriff, Junior Bailiff and twice Senior Bailiff. He and his son between them held the office of Bailiff no less than seven times, but as they were both named Thomas Ashmole and both saddlers by trade there is no way of distinguishing from the records who was which. Their chief claim to fame, however, was as grand-father and uncle respectively of Elias Ashmole, Windsor Herald to Charles II. But that story belongs to a later chapter.

However, in 1604, when Thomas Ashmole senior, as Bailiff of Lichfield, received from John Swynfen the letter of the Privy Council about the Earl of Essex's lease he and the Corporation wisely held their tongues and did as they were told. Without further delay the lease was completed and the Lordship of the Manor of Lichfield handed over to the young Earl to be held for the rest of his life. Under the terms of the lease he now became entitled to all the rents and dues payable to the Lord of the Manor, and to collect these and to look after the affairs of the Earl in general his mother appointed a steward, one Richard Drafgate.

Drafgate settled in Lichfield and remained there until his death in

*They were placed there by an antiquary of that city, who, passing through Lichfield in or about the year 1870, was in a local hostelry and was approached by the last of the Lichfield Corvisors, who sold him the records for five shillings — to buy himself a drink. Sic transit gloria!

1657, and during this time he played a considerable part in its life, holding the office of Sheriff* in 1623, Junior Bailiff in 1629 and Senior Bailiff in 1638.

The significance of Drafgate's place in the public life of Lichfield was that his master, Robert Devereux, third Earl of Essex (1591-1646) was in due course to become a prominent Parliamentarian and on the 13th of July 1642, just before the outbreak of war, he was commissioned by Parliament as Captain-General of their forces and given power to raise an army. In Drafgate he had a powerful agent in Lichfield and a leader for the local faction.

Others in the city who supported the Parliamentary cause were Michael Noble, the Town Clerk, Michael Biddulph of Curborough, Zachary Babbington of Elmhurst and last but not least Thomas Minors, a mercer of Lichfield who was to become Member of Parliament for the city under the Commonwealth. None of these gentlemen, with the possible exception of Minors, was possessed of any great initiative; certainly none of them had any capacity or desire to lead in battle.

This was not the case with the Royalists, however. Their cause was supported in Lichfield by several families, foremost among them being the Dyotts, a name which stands conspicuously in the annals of the City of Lichfield from the earliest period of its incorporation right up to the present day. The Dyott estate, in 1642, was at Stichbrooke, to the north of the city, and they also had a town house in Sadler Street (now Market Street), about half way down on the north side. Like all the houses in Sadler Street, it had a garden running down to Minster Pool, and at this time was occupied by Sir Richard Dyott, head of the family. A lawyer by profession, he had been chosen by Charles I in 1637 to act as one of his Counsel in the North on the 'Commission to divers of Our loving Subjects within the Counties of Westmorland and Cumberland for the regulating of the disorders within our Middle Shires, with powers of Oyer and Terminer, (and) to holde Gaol Delivery as there was occasion.' For this service he had received his knighthood, and since then he had represented Lichfield in Parliament and was now Steward and Recorder of the city.

Although too old for military service, Sir Richard was to play a prominent part in raising support for the King. His brother and four of Sir Richard's six sons all played their parts in the fighting for Lichfield.

Others who supported the Royalist cause were Henry Mott, Junior Bailiff of Lichfield for that year, Sir Walter Littleton, the Chancellor of the Diocese and Henry Archbold, Registrar of the Diocese.

---

*Lichfield is one of the select number of towns and cities in England and Wales which have their own Sheriff, though this is now an "office of dignity" without any legal function. The Sheriff of Lichfield is appointed annually under the terms of a charter of 1553.

*Portrait of Sir Richard Dyott*

*Chapter II*

# The First Siege

THE Civil War aroused conflicting passions in all parts of the kingdom; we have already seen how communities and even families were divided in their loyalties. Nevertheless, support for one side or the other tended to concentrate in certain regions, and we find that while the North, Wales and the Borders, and the West Country were predominently Royalist, London, the Eastern Counties and the South-East favoured the cause of Parliament.

Staffordshire was a borderline county, both geographically and politically. At the beginning of the war it raised two regiments of foot for the King, as well as numerous cavalry, but as the war progressed the supporters of Parliament increased their control and towards the end of 1643 set up a committee at Stafford to administer the county. To the east, Derbyshire was Parliamentary territory from early on, and so Lichfield, as a border garrison, became strategically important to both sides.

Derbyshire came under the influence of Parliament in the early stages of the war largely through the efforts of Sir John Gell (a name that was to become very familiar to the citizens of Lichfield). Gell was a country landowner living at Hopton, and a man who obviously enjoyed exercising authority over others. In 1635, as High Sheriff of Derbyshire, it had fallen to him to collect ship money throughout the county on behalf of Charles I, a task which he undertook with vigour and the utmost relish. In the process he made quite a few enemies, including Sir John Stanhope of Bretby Park, near Burton-on-Trent, who refused to pay up the £3,000 demanded of him. Gell threatened him with the full rigour of the law, and would have marched to Bretby to arrest him had not Stanhope forstalled him by dying.

On the outbreak of war in 1642, Sir John Gell immediately declared himself for Parliament; for what reason is not obvious, though one suspects that he saw it as an opportunity to secure for himself a position of power. A contemporary writer, Mrs. Hutchinson, had this to say about him.[1]

[Neither] himself nor no man knows for what reason he chose that side, for he had not understanding enough to judge the equity of the cause, nor piety nor holiness, being a foul adulterer all the time he served the Parliament, and so unjust that without any remorse he suffered his men to plunder both honest men and cavaliers.

But whatever his character, Gell appears to have been a very effective military commander. In October 1642 he received a commission from Parliament to raise a regiment of foot soldiers, which he proceeded to do without delay. The sort of recruit that he chose mirrored very closely his own character, for according to Lucy Hutchinson they were 'good, stout fighting men, but the most licentious, ungovernable wretches that belonged to the Parliament.'

As soon as he had enough troops ready, Gell proceeded to occupy the town of Derby, of which he later became Governor. Very soon he was exercising his authority over the whole of Derbyshire by mopping up any pockets of Royalist forces. These usually consisted of small detachments raised by Royalist landowners who had fortified their homes and armed their retainers.

Not surprisingly, one of the first of these garrisons to come under attack was Bretby Park, the home of Philip Stanhope, son of the late Sir John, who had been created Earl of Chesterfield by Charles I and remained a most loyal subject of that monarch throughout the war. In October 1642, shortly after the Battle of Edgehill, he had been commissioned by King Charles to raise a regiment of dragoons. What followed is described in a manuscript belonging to the Gell family quoted by Stebbing Shaw in his *History and Antiquities of Staffordshire*.[2]

The Earl of Chesterfield had sent for his sonne Ferdyando from Oxford, who brought with him a troop of horse, his father met him at Burton and theyre publiquely in the town swoare that within fewe days he would have Derby, but this was nether the first nor the last time the earles oath hath been broken. But the better to serve ourselves, we presently marched to the earles house, Bretby, then furnished with about 120 souldiers, horse and foote, well provided of all necessities; the house was too strong for our small ordinance, but our foote came desperately up to the walls, which the earle perceiving presently fled with his sonne and all his horse; we tooke the house and should have done no more hurt, but only taken the arms and ammunition, if the countess would have given the common souldiers £20 for drinke, which she refusing, part of the house was plundered, to which act the souldiers were more inclined when they understood that some of their fellowes taken prisoner at the first onsett had received hard usage, some of them having had the honour to be beaten by the earle himself, whom his servants had first disarmed and then held fast from styrring: but night comeing on, the wayes foule, and we having no nearer quarter than Burton, were forced to make haste away.

The Countess of Chesterfield appears to have displayed more valour than her husband and son, for after disengaging from the action they made their way westward to Lichfield. Not only did Sir John Gell's men plunder the house, but according to Lucy Hutchinson, Gell persued his malice to Sir John Stanhope, upon the aforementioned account, with such barbarisms after his death that he, pretending to search for arms and plate, came into the church [i.e. at Bretby] and defaced his monument that cost £600, breaking off the nose and other parts of it; he digged up a garden of flowers, the only delight of his widow, upon the same pretence.

The Earl of Chesterfield arrived in Lichfield in time for Christmas and settled down with his thirty dragoons to do nothing as inconspicuously as possible. But in January 1643 the arrival back in Lichfield of Sir Richard Dyott, released from his imprisonment at Coventry, stirred the Royalists into action. No doubt orders from the King's headquarters at Oxford had a similar effect.

The city of Lichfield had no special defensive features and its mediaeval fortifications had long since crumbled away. But the cathedral close still had the walls built by Bishop Langton three hundred years ago. On the south side was the stretch of water known as Minster Pool, which at that time extended some distance northward on either side of the Close in the form of a moat. It was not possible to carry this moat right around the Close because of the fact that the ground rose steeply to the north; instead a separate moat at a higher level guarded this part of the fortification. This separate moat is sometimes referred to as a "dimble" or dry ditch, but from the prevalence of springs in the high ground to the north of the cathedral it is likely that at certain times in the year it would fill with water. This would certainly be the case in March and April.

Inside the moats the Close was surrounded on all sides by a massive stone wall with a tower at each corner*, that at the south-west corner being larger than the others. In this wall were two gate houses; one facing west-wards towards Beacon Street and one southwards towards Dam Street. Each was furnished with a double gate and portcullis, and outside each gate was a drawbridge over the moat.

The Close was the obvious place to garrison, and the Royalist leaders made the decision and moved in. There was no triumphant entry or show of force; the garrison entered in small groups, those from the city being joined by reinforcements of two or three at a time from the surrounding country. One morning the inhabitants of Lichfield woke up to find the gates of the Close shut and a red† banner flying from the centre tower of the cathedral.

The garrison consisted of some three hundred men, mostly local gentry with their retainers. As the senior officer present the Earl of Chesterfield took command. At this time he was 59, a man without military experience and a sufferer from gout. Now it is quite possible to have a disability such as a missing eye or limb and still maintain one's military credibility (Nelson is the supreme example), but a man with gout, which is

---

*The remains of the north-east tower can still be seen.

†Red was the colour used by the Royalists to distinguish their troops, e.g. Royalist officers wore red sashes. The Parliamentary forces used orange in the same way.

*Portrait of Lord Robert Brooke*

caused by an excess of protein, that is, too much good living, does not inspire confidence as a commander. Moreover, the troops under his command were ill-armed, ill-trained and unused to fighting together, and little thought appears to have been given to the provisioning of the garrison, an important point as many of the men had brought their wives and children with them. All in all, prospects for holding out against a determined attack did not look good.

News of the garrisoning of Lichfield Close was soon carried to the headquarters of the Earl of Essex, and within a very short time a force under the command of Lord Brooke was ordered to Lichfield to take the Royalist stronghold.

Robert Greville, 2nd Lord Brooke, was a relative of the Earl of Warwick. He was born in 1608, and when four years old was adopted by his cousin, Fulke Greville, 1st Lord Brooke, by whom he was educated, partly in England and partly abroad. He was brought up with strict dissenting principles where religion was concerned and became so great a zealot against the established church that nothing less than the extirpation of episcopacy and abolition of all traditional forms of worship would satisfy him.

In 1627, at the age of 19, he became Member of Parliament for the Borough of Warwick, but a year later gave this up on succeeding his cousin to the barony of Brooke of Beauchamp Court in the County of Warwick. Part of his inheritance was Warwick Castle, and on his marriage to Lady Catherine Russell they made this their home and there brought up their five sons.

An able man, Lord Brooke became a member of one of the early trading companies, the Company of Adventurers for the Plantations of Providence and Henrietta Islands. He took an active part in its management and with Lord Saye and Sele helped to found the settlement of Sayebrooke in New England in 1635.

His religious principles led him to oppose King Charles, and in 1639 when he was ordered to take part in the King's expedition against the Scots, he refused and was imprisoned at York. In spite of this Charles nominated him one of the Commissioners appointed to negotiate with the Scots for the Treaty of Ripon.

In July 1642 when war was imminent Lord Brooke garrisoned Warwick Castle, and on the outbreak of hostilities he offered his services to Parliament, being appointed Lord Lieutenant of Militia for the counties of Warwick and Stafford. He was also given a commission as a colonel in the Parliamentary army and ordered to raise a regiment of foot. This he did with impressive speed in London, and in September 1642 Brooke's Regiment marched out of the city 1,000 strong, wearing their coats of purple and with their colours of purple bearing the arms of England and seven stars in the field. They were organised in ten companies, each commanded by an officer who had been elected by the troops under him. The most senior of these company commanders, and second in command to Lord Brooke, was Lieutenant Colonel Sir Edward Peyto, Lord of the Manor of Chesterton in Warwickshire.

Chesterton lies at the end of a side-track off the Warwick to Banbury road. Set in the depths of rural Warwickshire, it is little different today from what it was in the time of Sir Edward. The first sight a visitor will see is the windmill he erected to the design of Inigo Jones, surely one of the most elegant examples of such a machine anywhere in Britain. Inigo Jones also designed a manor house for Sir Edward and a triumphal arch for the Lord of the Manor's private entrance into the churchyard of St. Giles Church. Inside the church Sir Edward Peyto and his wife face each other on their marble memorial, the latin inscription of which describes him as a man of letters and a mathematician. One cannot help wondering what impelled him, at the age of 54, to take up arms in such a cause. From his memorial, and those of other members of his family, one would consider him to be a loyal member of the established church, and the Protestant fanaticism of Lord Brooke must have been difficult for him to come to terms with. But if his dispute with the King was political, it certainly did not go to the lengths pursued by some of his fellow officers — for example, Captain John Lilburne, who also commanded a company in Lord Brooke's Regiment. "Honest John" Lilburne was later to form the extreme republican group known as the Levellers. It is hard to imagine Sir Edward Peyto, Lord of the Manor of Chesterton with his triumphal arch, as a Leveller. But whatever his motivation, he found himself plunged into war from the very first days, for Lord Brooke appointed him Governor of Warwick Castle which he had to defend from a Royalist attack in August 1642. Now he was back with his regiment and marching to attack Lichfield.

Lord Brooke's Regiment joined the army of the Earl of Essex in time to take part in the Battle of Edgehill, where it suffered heavy casualties which reduced its numbers to under 500. After the battle Lord Brooke employed his men to secure the county of Warwickshire for Parliament, a process which culminated in the capture of Stratford-on-Avon in February 1643.

Following this success he was appointed General of the Midland Counties and ordered to attack Lichfield and Stafford with the object of taking over the county of Staffordshire for Parliament, and for this purpose his regiment was reinforced with 700 men from Warwick, Coventry and Birmingham. He was also allocated a piece of artillery, a demi-culverin, and a number of drakes (small cannon).

With this force of 1,200 troops he set out for Lichfield, arriving there on March 1st. At a spot known today as 'Cromwell's Meadow'*, about a mile south of the city, he drew up his troops and before bivouacking for the night prayed for God's blessing on their work, earnestly requesting some sign of Divine approbation.

The following morning Lord Brooke's forces entered the city. The Royalist troops resisted fiercely, falling back to the Close as they did so. The Parliamentarians took over the town and Lord Brooke set up his headquarters in the house of Michael Biddulph, in Sadler (now Market) Street.

With the two sides now confronting each other, it is perhaps appropriate to take a quick look at the opposing commanders. They make an interesting contrast.

The fortunes of the Royalists rested in the hands of Lord Chesterfield, 59, gout-ridden, lacking any warlike qualities or military experience and in command of 300 men whose principal merit was their loyalty to King Charles.

Against him stood Lord Brooke, 35, able and adventurous, with 1,200 men, many of whom he had already led in battle, all of them fired with a zeal to destroy the place they were attacking — Lichfield Cathedral — which to them symbolised everything that they hated. The contrast between the two men is striking.

Having arrived at the south side of the Close, and any further progress being barred, Lord Brooke decided to open his offensive against the South Gate. It does not seem to have occurred to him that there might have been an easier way elsewhere.

The demi-culverin, nick-named 'Black Bess' by the soldiers, was brought into Dam Street and manoeuvred into a position just south of the causeway which led to the South Gate on the other side of Minster Pool. The range was about 100 yards, so 'Black Bess' was firing point-blank at the gate. It was well within musket shot from the Close, and some form of earth work to protect the gunners would have been necessary. To overcome this, two members of the Royalist garrison climbed the winding staircase to the top of the central tower of the cathedral and took up positions behind the battlements at the base of the spire. From here they would be able to fire over the barricades.

Early on the morning of March 2nd the bombardment against the South Gate began, but produced little effect apart from smashing the woodwork of the drawbridge and gates. After some time Lord Brooke

*On the general principle that anything to do with the Parliamentary cause in the Civil Wars must be connected with Oliver Cromwell. In fact, at that particular moment in time Cromwell, recently promoted from Captain to Lieutenant Colonel, was busy in his native Huntingdonshire recruiting men to expand his troop of horse into a regiment, and came nowhere near Lichfield.

decided to make an assessment of the situation and left his headquarters in Sadler Street. Making his way across the Market Place he went through the house of Richard Newbole and passed under cover along the backs of the houses until he came to that of Walter Francey. Here he passed through an entry which led into Dam Street close to the gun position of 'Black Bess'.

Lord Brooke was wearing a purple plush cassock (tunic) 'with a head-piece of steele, having before his face five barrs of gilt steele.'[3] He stood there watching while the gunners fired twice and then, the better to observe the effect of their fire, leaned forward of the porch behind which he was taking cover.

The two men on the cathedral tower were watching. One of them, a deaf and dumb man, was a brother of Richard Dyott.* He was armed with a fowling piece or punt gun, the sort of firearm that was usually loaded with small shot and used for shooting ducks. A fearsome-looking weapon of iron, about seven feet long, with a calibre of about an inch and a half, it still exists in the possession of the Dyott family at Lichfield.

On this occasion it had been loaded with a lead ball made from some of the lead taken from the cathedral roof. John Dyott was watching as the Roundhead general issued from the entry; he took careful aim and as Lord Brooke leaned forward he fired. The shot struck Robert Brooke in the left eye and he fell down dead.

The event caused much jubilation amongst the defenders of the Close and was hailed as a sign of Divine displeasure with the victim, the more so because it had taken place on March 2nd, St. Chad's day. Lichfield Cathedral is dedicated to St. Chad; the inference was clear.

The feelings of one of the besiegers are contained in the following report, published in one of the Parliamentary Diurnals:[4]

> Sir, I pray take of me in this strait of time a short and rude relation of our proceedings since our coming. Our General the Lord Brooke having cleared Warwickshire of all the Forces of the Enemy, resolved to advance to Staffordshire, the other Countie in his Commission, and understanding that the Enemy was possessed of Litchfield and Stafford, he resolved to go first to Litchfield, and after to the other. The Forces in Litchfield, under the Lord of Chesterfield, were about 300. My Lord took with him about 1200, that is to say a troop of Reformadoes, and about 400 Foot which he had from London, and to them added 100 out of Warwick Castle and 200 out of Coven-trie, and about 300 of the most forward of the Countie came and offered themselves (for he had not raised any in the ordinary way); besides these one Gentleman brought him an 100 Dragooners and at least·100 came from Brumegeom to him; Sir John Gell also sent him a troop of Horse, with these a demi-culverin and some small Drakes. He advanced and came before the town on Wednesday morning and after some hot but short service the Enemy left the town and retired into the Close, which is a kind of castle; in which first action my Lord was too forward rather than [the] other way. But when they came to assault the Close the Commanders desired his

---

*John Dyott and his wife Katherine were both deaf and dumb from birth.

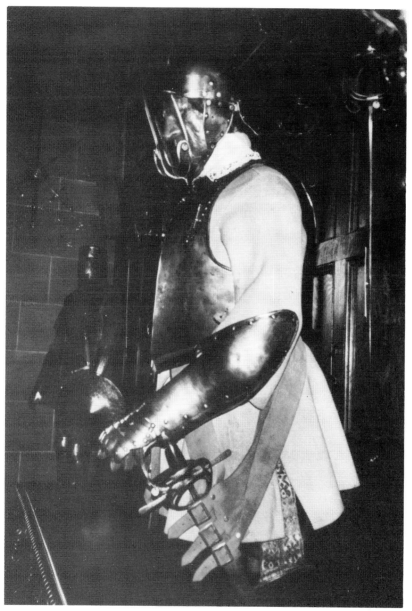

*Armour of Robert, Lord Brooke, displayed at Warwick Castle*
*worn by Lord Brooke at the first siege of Lichfield*

Honour to go into a House where he might see and give direction but be in less danger. For the life of the General is to be accounted equall with all the lives of all the rest in all service. My Lord thus disposed of we fell to it with our musquets. After a while we had a parlee, my Lord Chesterfield was willing to leave the place with 100 Musketeers with him for his Guard, but that My Lord would not consent to, nor did the Commanders think fit, and so they set to it again. My Lord observing some thing that he liked not in the fight, put forth his head out of the window to direct, which he had no sooner done but unhappily a Bullet stroke him in the left eye, which instantly put an end to his life, without speaking one word. This much enraged us and put this resolution into us, that we would die every man, but we would take the place and put every man to the sword in it. We have made a breach in the walls and driven all of them from the Wall, and are now ready to put the Petard to the Gate when this bearer* came away.

The Lord of Heaven give us victory, and revenge the blood of that Noble Lord his Servant now in Heaven with Him. I will say no more of him than this, for in courage, good discipline and zeal to the cause, I do not feel he would have fallen short of any. Wee sent poste to Sir John Gell to come to us untill my Lord Generall shall send us a head; whom God grant may be as right as he that went before him. From Litchfield is thus written: that those Forces that were brought thither by the Lord Brooke are by the coming of Sir John Gell the present Commander in Chief and the people of the Counties increased to 2,000. Sir John has made Proclamation that he will either gaine the Close and revenge the losse of that Noble Lord, or loose his life in that Service; at which they all promised to do the like. They want great Cannon and a Mortar peece to blow up the Wall, which is going to them. They in the Close have victuals for a fortnight and expect help. Which to prevent, the besiegers have made work to defend themselves, cut off all release from the Close, and turned the water from them; and as soon as the Mortar peece comes they intend to blow up the wall. Sir John Gell has promised a large reward to him that brings the Lord of Chesterfield, dead or alive, and fourtie shillings a man to the first ten that shall enter the Breach. They have likewise taken thought how they may get another Generall in the place of the Lord Brooke, and thereupon have despatched a Captain poste with a letter to which all the Commanders hands are, and Sir John Gell's also.

Historians have sometimes expressed doubt as to who actually shot Lord Brooke, for Clarendon's account describes the marksman as being "a common soldier". But this description could well have applied to "Dumb" Dyott, for a person with his disability could hardly have carried out the duties of an officer. In any case there were many examples of men of good families fighting in the ranks of the Royalist armies. In the Dyott family, and amongst Lichfield people generally, the tradition has always been maintained that the fatal shot was fired by "Dumb" Dyott.

With the death of Lord Brooke the control of his forces passed to his second-in-command, Lieutenant Colonel Sir Edward Peyto. He called together the council of war and they hastily assembled in the house of Michael Biddulph. They decided to keep the news of Lord Brooke's death from the troops as long as possible and to give out that it was his servant that had been killed. It was also decided to send a messenger to Derby as fast as he could ride to find Sir John Gell and tell him what had

---

*i.e. the bearer of the letter.

happened. The officer chosen for this duty was a Captain Fox, a local man who knew the area.

This was done, and in the words of one of Sir John Gell's family[5] 'Whylst part of our forces were thus engaged at Newarke, Captain Fox came post from Lichfield, and brought the sadd news of the noble lord Brooke's death, whereupon our colonell [i.e. Sir John Gell] went immediately with the captain to Lichfield and kept together those forces ready to disband.'

From these remarks it is evident that the news of Lord Brooke's death, in spite of the efforts to keep it secret, had already leaked out and as a result morale amongst his troops was at a low ebb, 'being a great part of the souldiers' courage was wrapped up in the life of their generall' as an eye-witness put it.

There can be little doubt, however, that Sir John Gell received the news with relish, for it opened up all sorts of opportunities for him — the opportunity to make a name for himself and for his exploits to be recorded in the Parliamentary diurnalls (the journals or newspapers of the day). Lucy Hutchinson had stated of Sir John, 'This man kept the diurnal makers in pension so that whatsoever was done in the neighbouring counties against the enemy was attributed to him and thus he hath purchased for himself a name in history which he never merited.' Now he had a chance to make real history. There was also the opportunity to pursue his feud against the Stanhopes; the Earl of Chesterfield was boxed up in Lichfield Close and Gell now had the chance to assault him with 2,000 men and a heavy cannon. Without wasting a minute he set out for Lichfield and arrived towards the end the day.

That day must have seemed a long one for the inhabitants of the city. They had awoken to find themselves invaded by Lord Brooke's soldiers who had rapidly taken over the town — some had even occupied St. Chad's Church at Stowe, to the east of the city, where they had caused considerable damage. Others lost no time in destroying Dean Denton's Market Cross, because it was adorned with crucifixes and figures of the Apostles. From an early hour the town had echoed to the sound of musketry, the boom of cannon and the crash of cannon balls against the defences of the Close, while smoke drifted and eddied around the streets.

In the morning there had been the coming and going after the death of Lord Brooke, and then, while they waited for the arrival of Sir John Gell, the members of the council of war put into operation a scheme which they had devised earlier.

From Parliamentary supporters in the city they had obtained a list of those citizens who had joined the Royalist garrison in the Close. A party of soldiers was detailed to go around the houses of these people and arrest their wives and relatives, as well as anyone who had sons, apprentices or servants in the Close. The body of citizens thus assembled was kept under armed guard until they were required.

The purpose of this was soon made clear as an assault on Lichfield Close got under way. At this period in the war neither side had many officers trained in military tactics. For this reason Lord Brooke, and after him Sir Edward Peyto, attacked Lichfield Close from the south for no better reason, it would appear, than the fact that their approach march had brought them to that side of the city. In doing so they had chosen the most difficult side to attack, for the whole of the south side was protected by water, crossed at only two points by narrow causeways. That from Bridge (Bird) Street was only seven feet wide, and the Dam Street way was probably little wider. Both could be raked by gunfire from the Close without any possibility of cover for the attackers. It was now apparent to the band of citizens who had been collected together that it was to be their function to provide that cover. The full horror of the situation gradually dawned on them — Colonel Peyto had put them at the front of the troops in the hope that their presence would force the Royalists in the Close to hold their fire.

Accounts of the siege do not tell us which causeway was used in the attack, but it is reasonable to suppose that it was the one from Dam Street which led to the South Gate. This had been under fire all morning and so would be the logical one to attack.

As the defenders in the Close saw the advancing force charge up Dam Street, over the causeway and past the watermill, and recognised their own families at its head, hustled on by the Parliamentary soldiers from behind, they had little time to make up their minds as to their course of action. They did not hesitate however, and as soon as the enemy were within range they opened fire, aiming to avoid, as far as possible, the civilians. They succeeded so well that the attackers withdrew and the captive citizens were allowed to return to their homes. We do not know if any of them were casualties, but certainly their captors suffered. Among those wounded was Sir Edward Peyto, and so badly that a rumour spread that he had been killed. In fact he died some weeks later at his home at Chesterton. His Lieutenant Major was also wounded and reported killed.

As darkness fell and the sound of cannon and musket fire died away the citizens of Lichfield emerged from their hiding places breathing sighs of relief that the long day was over. Or so they thought.

However, seven miles away at Rushall Hall, near Walsall, a small Royalist garrison had received in the course of the day a visit from Colonel Henry Hastings of Ashby-de-la-Zouch. Colonel Hastings was a swashbuckling Royalist leader who had already lost an eye in this war and wore a patch which added to his fighting image. He moved around the Midlands with his troop of cavalry looking for Roundhead forces to harry. At Rushall he was told of the siege of Lichfield Close and set off immediately to see if he could bring any help to the Royalist defenders.

At Pipe Hill, overlooking the city, he split his force into two, sending one body round to enter the city from the north-west via Beacon Street and the other to attack from the south-west via St. John Street. The weary citizens of Lichfield, recovering from a day which had consisted of nothing but alarms and excursions, now had to face another. As the drums beat the call to arms the cry went round among the soldiers of Parliament, "Blind Hastings is here with his Popish cavaliers."

For many of them it was the last straw. With the arrival of Sir John Gell the news was finally confirmed of the death of Lord Brooke. On top of this their attack on the Close had been repulsed and they were in no mood to resist a surprise attack. Had Colonel Hastings pressed his action and held the town for a couple of hours the Parliamentary forces might well have given in. But instead, having caused what he considered to be a satisfactory number of casualties, he drew off his troops and retired to Rushall.

The following morning, that of Friday, March 3rd, the body of Lord Brooke started its last journey to Warwick Castle. With the cortege went several waggons carrying those wounded in the fighting of the previous day.

As soon as the waggon train had left Lichfield the new commander, Sir John Gell, 'in a buff coat garded with silver lace' rode round the streets of the city showing himself to his troops, 'incouraging the souldiers, some with small gifts,* others with good words and large promises.'

Having thus restored the morale of his men he called a council of war at which the following three decisions were made:

(a) A request should be made immediately to Coventry for heavy mortars which were kept there, in order to bombard the Close.

(b) Another assault should be made, this time against the West Gate.

(c) If this were not successful, an attack to be made on the north walls.

A messenger was despatched to Coventry forthwith and preparations put in hand for the assaults.

Soon afterwards the spirits of the troops were raised by the arrival of 3,000 reinforcements, both horse and foot, under the command of Colonel Sir William Brereton with Lieutenant Colonel Simon Rudgeley as second in command. Rudgeley was a local man, a member of the family which took its name from the town of Rugeley. Sir William Brereton came from Brereton in Cheshire, not the village of that name near Rugeley. A competent soldier, he later became one of the Parliamentary Committee for Staffordshire, a body set up to administer the county for the prosecution of the war.

---

* Those readers who, like the author, served under Field Marshall Bernard Montgomery during the 1939-45 War will recall that he adopted the same method of keeping up morale, the gifts in this case being cigarettes.

During Friday morning parties of soldiers were detailed to go round houses in the city searching for pitch, rozen, tar and hurds of hemp or flax, requisitioning what they found for the assault on the West Gate. At the same time a proclamation was made throughout the city that they should forthwith bring their long ladders on carts to Stow Church (situated to the east of the city) where the Roundheads kept a garrison.

The 'long ladders' referred to were probably the ones kept under the charge of the dozeners, or constables, in each ward for use in case of house fires. Together with long poles, tipped with iron hooks for pulling down burning thatch, these formed the fire-fighting equipment, very necessary when most houses were roofed with thatch.

The ladders were loaded into a cart which was driven round to Stowe Church as ordered. St. Chad's Church at Stowe had been occupied by Lord Brooke's soldiers from the time of their arrival in Lichfield and now, when the driver of the cart arrived outside the ancient thirteenth century building he found the troops on parade and officers detailing a section which was to form the assault party on the north side of the Close. Instead of unloading his ladders as he had hoped the driver was told to join the attackers with his cart.

Meanwhile, back in the city, the main assault against the West Gate was getting under way. The inflammable materials which had been collected were ready in iron pots and buckets, bundles of flax and hemp had been prepared and the wretched families of the townsmen in the Close were assembled once again to head the approach across the causeway.

In this way the attackers reached the gateway with their firebombs and attempted to lay them against the raised drawbridge, by this time under heavy fire from the Royalists lining the walls of the Close. As they did so the drawbridge was suddenly lowered and over it surged a party of Royalist troops who laid into the attackers, beating them back and breaking their iron pots. Once again a direct assault had failed and both sides withdrew.

Orders were now sent back to the troops at Stowe Church to make their attack on the north side of the Close. They set out along what today is known as St. Chad's Road, but at that time was referred to as Dark Lane. With them went the waggon carrying the ladders, still in charge of its civilian driver, no doubt quaking in his shoes at this unexpected incursion into the battle scene. They turned into Gaia Lane, a narrow, winding road with banks on either side, a perfect setting for an ambush. Experienced troops would have put out scouts on either side, but the relatively untrained Roundhead soldiers marched straight up the lane and straight into the fire of an enemy force waiting for them.

From their many observation points high on the roofs of the cathedral building the Royalist defenders of the Close must have had plenty of opportunity to watch the activities of their opponents. The preparations outside St. Chad's Church, the arrival of the ladders and the setting out of the attacking column would all have been observed, and long before any move was made from the church a party of Royalist troops would have been despatched to intercept them.

These now poured their fire into the soldiers trapped in the narrow defile. The driver of the waggon pulled up his horses, leapt from his seat and made off as fast as his legs would carry him. A soldier jumped up to take his place, but he had scarcely picked up the reins before he was shot dead. Pandemonium followed; then panic, and those still unhurt turned tail and fled.

The Cavaliers descended into the roadway, unhitched the horses from the waggon, and then set fire to it and its contents. Later that evening, under cover of darkness, they returned to the scene and recovered all the ironwork from the waggon and ladders for use in the Close. That they should go to this trouble and risk is an indication of the lack of almost every munition of war within the garrison. The iron, one would imagine, would be used for making pike heads.

There was no further activity from the Parliamentary side that day, though during the night Colonel Hastings' men from Rushall made another attack on them just to keep them on their toes. So far the Royalist garrison within the Close had every reason to congratulate themselves. They had beaten off every attack, taking the initiative on more than one occasion; they had killed the enemy's commander-in-chief and, as they believed, two other senior officers, and they had continuing help from their friends at Rushall. The battle seemed to be going their way. In contrast, morale on the other side must have been low indeed. Yet within the next twenty-four hours the whole situation was to change.

Saturday the fourth of March began quietly, no further attempt on the Close being made by the despirited besiegers. During the day, however, their spirits rose with the arrival of the mortar from Coventry. An eye-witness described this event in these words.[6]

> This day came their morter-piece, which struck the poor citizens into an ague-fit of trembling and gazing at the strangeness thereof, having not ever seen the like before, and hearing the round-head soldiers making such bragging bravadoes, and thundering out soe many terrible threats, crying nothing but fire and sword would reconcile them.

Like all mortars, this one was a smooth-bore weapon which fired its missiles up into the air with a very high trajectory so that they came down on the heads of the enemy — in other words, it lobbed them. We know its size, because a number of the projectiles still exist in Lichfield. These are spherical in shape and ten inches in diameter and are made of cast iron. The interior is hollow, with the shell about one inch in thickness, and into this cavity is packed gunpowder. A small hole in the shell is fitted with a

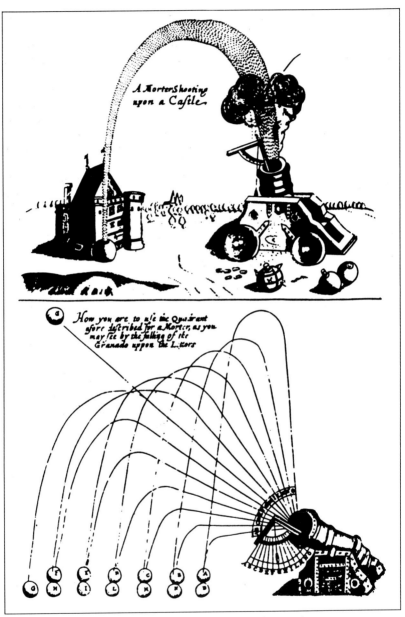

*Diagrams illustrating the use of a mortar to fire granadoes.*
From Captain Thomas Venn's 'Military and Maritime Discipline', 1672

short length of tow which was probably soaked in saltpetre so that it would smoulder when a light was applied.

> On its arrival in the city, Sir John Gell ordered that this gun, called the morter-piece, should forthwith be drawn into the high street (alias Sadler Street) and so unto Sir Richard Dyott's house and in his garden to be mounted or placed according to Mr. Gunner's instructions, which was done accordingly.

Sir Richard Dyott's house was on the north side of Sadler (i.e. Market) Street, and the garden ran down to the edge of the Minster Pool. Here, no doubt, behind suitable earthworks to protect the gunners, the mortar was sited, its target being the houses of the Prebendaries and Canons on the south side of the Close which the Cavaliers and their families occupied. Our eye-witness described the scene as follows.

> This thundering piece of destruction being placed, the gunner prepared his mischievous discomfitures, the fire balls, to scare true subjects out of their known allegience, and charging his gunn made several shoots with his granadoes but little execution, either they were too wyd of the place or too short, and some fell into the poole that was between them and the Close, commonly called the mill-poole, which put a stop at present to their brazen-faced rashness in boasting.

The shells, or granadoes, which fell short into the Minster Pool, were recovered two hundred years later by the Victorian engineers who turned the pool into a reservoir. Still full of gunpowder and with the tow intact, they were placed in Lichfield Museum and now provide us with valuable information about the siege. That other shells fell 'wyd' and short is hardly surprising. Gun sights at that time were very rudimentary, gunpowder varied in quality from batch to batch, and getting on to the target was very much a matter of hit or miss. By the next day, however, the mortar team had got things sorted out.

> Sunday, the 5th of March, the gunners, not minding prayer, but the better day the better deed, fell to their warlike destructive trade again . . . [and] upon better notice being taken there were several granadoes shot into the Close, but the besieged prevented the hurt that might have happened in their bursting.

From these last words one can only infer that some brave men among the besiegers risked their lives to defuse the shells that fell in the Close, either by throwing water on the smouldering tow or, if it was long enough, snuffing it out. Some did explode, however, for the fragments of these still exist in the Cathedral today, frightening shards of iron that must have wreaked havoc.

A determined garrison could have minimised the effect of the bursting granadoes by moving the women and children to the north east corner of the Close, out of range of fire and by digging trenches to protect the troops. But the granadoes seem to have had a profound psychological effect upon the members of the garrison — hardly surprising when one considers the violence of the explosion. It requires little imagination to visualise the shattering effect of the granadoes and the terror they would produce in those nearby.

It was indeed traumatic, and before long some of the women were gathered around Lord Chesterfield, imploring him to surrender. He himself, crippled by gout, had little stomach for further resistance. During the evening he called a council of war and, 'in view of the shortage of provisions and ammunition, and no relief being at hand it was decided that further resistance was useless.' With the benefit of hindsight, which every historian enjoys, none of these excuses sounds very convincing. A commander who has prepared for a siege over several months and runs out of food and ammunition in three days shows a remarkable lack of foresight, while the help available from Colonel Hastings seems to have been ignored. One suspects that the real reason for the surrender was the devastating effect of the granadoes.

On the following day, Sunday, March 5th, the red flag of defiance which flew from the central spire of the cathedral was taken down, and to quote our eye-witness once again —

> The Earle of Chesterfield caused a parlee by his trumpiter to be sounded, desiring a treaty with Lorde Brooke, commander in chief of the Parliamentary forces now against the Close of Lichfield, taking no notice of the Lord Brookes death, although they all knew of it. It was agreed that the said Earle of Chesterfield, Governor of the Close, should have leave to send forth from thence an officer or two to treat with the Lord Brooke, safe to come and safely guarded back with his (or their) answer.

Accordingly a messenger, clothed in white, was sent out into Dam Street to contact the opposing forces. There he was received and after being blindfolded with a napkin around his head he was led to Michael Biddulph's house in Market Street where, he was told, Lord Brooke lodged.

Robert Brooke, of course, was not there, but amongst the reception committee headed by Sir John Gell were Colonel Simon Rudgley and Colonel Sir William Brereton.

> So, with many jeers and shouts, he was brought into a room where they said Lord Brooke was. He heard many strange voices but he directed his speech to the Lorde Brooke, Commander in chief, according to the earle's orders, on behalf of the besieged, craving articles of agreement for the rendition of the Close, as follows:
>
> First, that a safe and free passage (or conduct) may be granted to the Earle of Chesterfield to any of his majestie's garrisons where he be pleased to goe, with his proper goods, horse and arms, for himself and his retained servants without any violence, plunder or prejudice from any of your souldiery.
>
> Secondly, that all gentlemen voluntaries whatsoever, all civilians belonging to the civil law, all officers and souldiers, with their servants, should have the like privilege.
>
> Thirdly, that all divines, the clerkes, vicars and all other officers belonging to the cathedral church [should] enjoy their places and profits as freely as formerly they ever did, and their goods without any spoyle or embezzlement.
>
> Fourthly, that all housekeepers inhabiting within the said Close should peaceably enjoye their estates, proper goods and cattle, liberties and privileges without being pillaged or plundered by any of your souldiery, or by any others of the Parliamentary party.

These requests, not surprisingly, were rejected out of hand by the council of war. Instead they offered the besieged garrison the following terms:

> First, that the Earl of Chesterfield should forthwith surrender the garrison called the Close of Lichfield, upon conditions of free quarter to all those within the Close. For all other terms they were to throw themselves upon the mercy of Parliament.
>
> Second, that if the Earl would not yield up the garrison on these terms, it would be taken by force of arms.

"Free quarter" meant simply exemption from being put to death.

The messenger, still blindfolded, returned to the Close with these terms. There being little hope of carrying on the battle, the garrison decided to accept the conditions. This message was conveyed to the commander of the Parliamentary forces and the gates of the Close opened for him to march in his troops, while the Royalist forces laid down their arms. Thus ended the first siege of Lichfield Close.

The news was reported to Parliament in the following despatches which appeared in the Diurnal a few days later.

> By letters out of Warwickshire it is signified that Sir Edward Peto [sic] who is made Commander in cheife of those forces which went forth under the command of that renowned lord, the lord Brooke, hath taken the minster at Litchfield, and all the cavaliers, with the earl of Chesterfield himselfe, prisoners; but as for Mr. Hastings, it was reported that he was not there.
>
> Along with the earl of Chesterfield his sonne Ferdinando, Sir John Harper of Swaston, Sir John Harper of Caulke, Sir John Tichaber, Sir Edward Moseley and Sir Edward Deering were taken prisoners.
>
> Friday, March 10th.
>
> In the last weeks intelligence, mention was made that the Parliaments souldiers at Litchfield had taken the Minster, giving the Cavaliers quarter for their lives, and took the earl of Chesterfield prisoner; since that time it is further signified by letters that not long after the taking of these, together with all their horses, arms and ammunition, plate and money, which they had gotten into the Minister, the earl of Northampton and Mr. Hastings came with forces intending to besiege the town, but the said earl was quickly forced to fly away, with the loss of about 60 horse; but to fly is not to escape, it is many times to increase the danger.
>
> Monday, March 15th [13th?]

The concern of the Parliamentarians for the whereabouts of Henry Hastings is a measure of the extent to which they feared him. There is little doubt that if he had been in the Close, as they believed, it would not have been rendered up as easily as it was.

A Royalist description of the siege, one which is often quoted, perhaps because of its character accords closely with the romantic idea of the dashing cavalier, is contained in a letter from James Audley, one of the defenders of Lichfield Close, to Lady Dyer.[8]

> To the fair hands of my ever honoured lady Dyer, at the White Unicorn in the Old Bailey.
>
> Madam,
>
> My last letter (dated February 25th) and your ladyship's precious answer, are part of the plunder which I have every day more and more, but I can meete no day to

revenge it in. Since I came from home four men and five horses I have lost; thrice have I been actually taken, besides other close pursuits, but yet I live to service your ladyship next to God and my king. And hitherto I can number as many escapes as dangers. We have had the honour in these parts to bring my lord Brooke into a quiet condition. That enemie to our church (March 2nd) was slaine in his quarrell against our church, by the God of our church, with a shott out of the cathedrall, by a bullet made of church lead, through the mouth which reviled our church. And (if this be worth your reading) this cathedral being dedicated to an old Saxon holy man, (called Ceadda, commonly Chad), the blow of death came from St. Chadd's church, upon St. Chadd's day. This being a veritie is fitt for a lady of rare worth. His lieutenant (thought to be Sir Edward Peto), and his lieutenant major, both slain. Several loads of hurt men and dead men carried away to be privately buried. After all this, the place poorley and basely yielded up. But we have more blood ready to purchase it withall. Your noble friend and I made out several summons into Cheshire, Leicestershire, Oxfordshire and Staffordshire. And the numbers (I hope) are growing on to a full service. I was twice prisoner in half an hower; but I am still a free man. Bonds cannot hold mee; only your noble favours have power to bind mee in a perpetual service, where I am happy to bee the thrall of your kindness, in beeing the admirer of your virtue.

March 11th, 1643.                                            James Audley

A comparison of the two accounts reveals some discrepancies, perhaps deliberate, perhaps the result of the "fog of war". While the Parliamentarian report credits Sir Edward Peyto with the capture of the Close, the Royalist letter gives news of his death. The truth was, of course, that he had been badly wounded on the first day and had been invalided home, where he died some weeks later. On this same matter, one cannot help wondering how Sir John Gell, that assiduous cultivator of the diurnals, felt when he saw that his capture of the Close had been attributed to someone else!

For the next fortnight, however, Sir John was too busy with other matters to have any time for reading journals. The Earl of Chesterfield, presumably on orders from Parliament, was sent under escort to London where he was imprisoned in the Tower for the remainder of the war. The members of his force were disarmed and allowed to go. Many of them made their way to Stafford where there was a strong Royalist garrison. Their place in Lichfield Close was taken over by a force of Parliamentary troops under the command of Lieutenant Colonel Russel.

Having thus dealt with Lichfield, Sir John Gell then turned his attentions to Stafford, towards which town he marched his troops, flushed with success. But here he found not only a strong garrison, but arrived also at the same time as a reinforcement group under the Earl of Northampton. This had been on its way to relieve Lichfield Close, but arriving too late to achieve this purpose had moved on to Stafford. Heavily outnumbered, Sir John Gell fell back to Hopton, about three miles north-east of Stafford. Here he linked up with a force under the command of Sir William Brereton, which had marched that morning, Sunday, March 19th, from Newcastle-under-Lyme. So the victors of Lichfield were united once more and on Hopton Heath, at two o'clock in the afternoon, they turned and faced a determined attack by the Earl of Northampton's cavalry, consisting of two regiments of horse of his own, one of which included the Prince of Wales's troop, and another regiment under Colonel Hastings.

Overwhelmed by the sudden onslaught, most of the Roundheads fled, with the exception of 240 men of the late Lord Brooke's Reformado Troop* who stood their ground with great gallantry.

Sir John Gell, according to an eye-witness account,[9] quit his horse and went to the foote, being taken in great feare and disorder, many of them ready to rune, and standing with their pikes advanced; the colonel with his own hands put down their pykes, encouraged both them and the musquetyers, who were all disorderly, crowded together; he speedily got them into order and gave the enemy such a vollie of shott upon their charge that they first wheeled and much discouraged by the death of the earle of Northampton, Captain Middleton and dyvers others, gentlemen and officers, they presently fled.

The Royalists lost their commander and had greater casualties, but captured four of the enemy's drakes (small cannon) and took 40 prisoners. Among the casualties on the Parliamentary side was Sir John Gell, who received a wound in the neck (probably a sword cut), which kept him out of active service for some time. Writing 150 years later,[10] Stebbing Shaw recalls having seen the doublet worn by Sir John on this occasion, with the slash made by the sword near the neck, and also the surgeon's bill for £10 for attention. Both these relics were at that time in the possession of Sir John's descendants.

Back in Lichfield, Colonel Russel and his garrison had taken over the Close. Colonel Hastings, that thorn in the flesh of the Parliamentary forces, estimated Russel's men to be about 150 horse and 400 foot. A quick attack on these, before they had time to get settled in, might redress the defeat of the Earl of Chesterfield. So on March 21st, two days after Hopton Heath, he led three companies of dragoons in an attack on Lichfield from the north. But the Parliamentary commander got wind of their coming and, we are told:

Colonel Russel drew forth 100 musqueteers and one frame of musquet cannon and let fly at them, causing them to flee.

Having beaten off this attack, the Parliamentarians set to and strengthened the Close against further assault. Having done this they set about a systematic destruction of the furnishings of the cathedral. Sir William Dugdale describes it as follows:

They set up courts of guard in the cross aisles; broke up the pavements; every day hunted a cat with hounds through the church, delighting themselves with the echoe from the goodly vaulted roof; and to add to their wickedness brought a calf into it,

---

*Reformadoes were officers who were professionally trained soldiers and who had been retained on half-pay by Parliament in 1642, ostensibly for service in Ireland, but actually in case of the outbreak of civil war. The only Reformado officer in Lord Brooke's Regiment was Sergeant-Major (i.e. Major) Walter Ailworth, so presumably it was his troop that is referred to.

wrapt in linen, carried it to the font, sprinkled it with water and gave it a name in
scorn and derision of the holy sacrament of baptism.

These actions, of course, were not the wanton vandalism of undisciplined troops, but rather the carrying out of a deliberate policy ordered by Parliament. Similar destruction was effected at the cathedrals of Hereford, Peterborough, Lincoln and Ely. The war, it must be remembered, was religious as well as political and it was an article of faith with the Puritans that worship should be confined to preaching, catechising and prayer. Beauty, whether in the form of music (except, perhaps, for metrical psalms), painting, sculpture or needlework was regarded as a distraction from worship and therefore to be ruthlessly eliminated. So at Lichfield Colonel Russel's men destroyed the two organs owned by the cathedral, smashed the stained glass windows, and in the strict interpretation of the commandment 'Thou shalt not make unto thyself any graven image, nor the likeness of anything that is in the heaven above, or in the earth beneath or in the waters under the earth', they broke up every image they could find; crucifixes, figures of saints and even the effigies on the tombs (especially when these were of former bishops). The great west front screen decorated with 113 statues of 'Kings, Prophets, Fathers and Martyrs' was an especial target for their destruction. Those figures low enough to be reached were pulled down with ropes and those too high for such treatment were battered with gunfire from muskets and drakes.

The books of the cathedral library were burnt except for a few of the more precious which the cathedral clergy had hidden beforehand. Among these was the now famous manuscript known as the Textus St. Cedde or St. Chad's Gospels, though it has no direct connection with St. Chad. It is written on vellum, the text being in Latin, and contains the gospels of Matthew, Mark and a portion of Luke. It came into the possession of Lichfield in the tenth century, during the episcopacy of either Bishop Wynsey or Kinsey, having formerly been at Llandaff.

This precious relic of early Christianity was preserved by the foresight of Prebendary William Higgins, Precentor of the cathedral, who carried it off before the siege and hid it until the war was over and it was safe to return it to its home. To him we owe its present existence as one of the treasures of Lichfield Cathedral, for it would certainly have been destroyed had Colonel Russel's men found it.

The cathedral linen and plate was carefully put aside on the Colonel's orders, to be taken away and sold, or in the case of the silver melted down, to provide the sinews of war.

Having thus dealt with the cathedral church and having strengthened the defences wherever possible, Colonel Russel and his troops awaited the almost inevitable counter attack from the Royalists. They had not long to wait.

# SOURCE NOTES
## *Chapter II*

1. Lucy Hutchinson, Memoirs of the Life of Colonel Hutchinson (1810)
2. Stebbing Shaw, History and Antiquities of Staffordshire, p.54. "A True Accounte of the Raysing and employing of one Foot Regiment under Sir John Gell"
3. Clarendon, History of the Rebellion and the Civil Wars in England (1759)
4. Special Passages and Certain Information from Severall Places, Collected for the Use of All that desire to be truly informed. No. 30, page 243
5. Stebbing Shaw, History and Antiquities of Staffordshire, p.55
6. Ibid, p.240
7. A Perfect Diurnal of Some Passages in Parliament, and from Other Parts of the Kingdom, 1643, No. 38
8. Stebbing Shaw, History of Staffordshire, p.53
9. Ibid, p.57
10. Ibid, p.54
11. Sir William Dugdale, A short View of the late Troubles in England

*Prince Rupert*

*Chapter III*

# The Second Siege

FOLLOWING the Battle of Edgehill and the retreat from Turnham Green, the Royalist army at the end of 1642 made its headquarters at Oxford which King Charles turned into his temporary capital.

The position throughout the country at this time was that the Royalists held the north of England, including the Border Counties, part of Lancashire, Yorkshire and Nottinghamshire and in addition Wales and the West Country.

Parliament controlled London, the Eastern Counties and the South East, with a narrow corridor stretching across the Midlands into Cheshire and the south of Lancashire, thus dividing Royalist territory into two parts.

In the middle of this corridor was the city of Lichfield, standing on the highroad from Leeds to Bristol and thus controlling the main line of communication between the two parts of the kingdom still loyal to the King. It was vital to the Royalists to keep this line open, and so the loss of Lichfield must have caused great dismay in the Royalist camp.

On the 22nd of February 1643, the King's wife, Queen Henrietta Maria, landed at Bridlington in Yorkshire, bringing with her from Holland a large quantity of much-needed arms, stores and ammunition. The need to open up a line of communication by which these could be delivered to the army was urgent, and so it was decided that a strong force should be sent north from Oxford to Lichfield, 'and settle there a garrison for the King [which] lay most convenient for that northern communication and would with it dissolve other little adjacent holds of the enemy which contributed much to the interruption.'[1]

The King's Council of War assigned this task to one of the ablest commanders in the Royalist forces, Prince Rupert, General of the Horse.

Rupert, Prince Palatine of the Rhine, was a nephew of Charles I, his mother being Charles's sister Elizabeth. Although only twenty-two years of age at the beginning of the war, he had made a name for himself already as a military commander. He was a born leader of men, tall and commanding in mien, trained in the skill of arms and experienced in war. At his own request he had begun his military career as an ordinary soldier in the ranks and had seen service when the Duke of Orange invaded Brabant in 1635. He had been in the famous siege of Breda in 1637, and there had learnt something of the art of military engineering, including the use of landmines, knowledge which he was to put to good use at Lichfield.

Rupert was the professional soldier *par excellance*, and among the enemy he became a legend nationally in much the same way as Colonel Hastings had in the Midlands. Stories about him were legion; on the Royalist side they usually extolled his skill at arms, daring and dash in battle and deception of the enemy, for in the eyes of those who fought under him, Rupert could do no wrong. Many of these stories were apocryphal, as is usually the case, but the story of his exploit at Stafford early in the war, already mentioned, was confirmed by Dr. Plot, writing forty-four years later.[2]

> It may also be looked upon as an Art not altogether foreign to fire, that Prince Rupert showed at Stafford in the time of the Civil warr, *temp. Car I*, when standing in Captain Richard Sneyd's garden at the High-House there, at about sixty yards distance, he made a shot at the weather-cock upon the steeple of the Collegiat Church of St. Mary with a screwed Horsman's pistol and single bullet, which pierced its taile, the hole plainly appearing to all that were below: which the King then present judging as a casualty* only, the Prince presently proved the contrary by a second shoot to the same effect: the two holes through the weather-cock taile (as an ample testimony of the the thing) remaining there to this day.

When Dr. Plot refers to 'a screwed Horsman's pistol' he presumably meant a pistol with some form of rifling in its barrel.

Amongst the forces of Parliament stories of Rupert took a different aspect, some crediting him and his dog Boye with occult powers, including the power to be in two different places at once. The death of Boye, a poodle, at the hands of Roundhead troops after the Battle of Marston Moor was even the subject of a pamphlet published by the Parliamentarians afterwards, so important did they think it.

On a different level Rupert was accused of every possible crime — rape, looting, plunder, the massacre of civilians, torture and murder of prisoners of war, so much so that he was moved to publish a tract himself, styled 'Prince Rupert, His Declaration'.[3] which he ended with the following words:

> I think there is none that take me for a coward; for sure I fear not the face of any man alive, yet I should repute it the greatest victory in the world to see his Majesty enter London in peace without shedding one drop of bloud: where I dare say (God and his Majesty are witnesses I lye not) no Citizen should be plundered of a penny or a farthing; whereby that ancient and famous City would manifestly perceive how

---

*i.e. a fluke

desperately it hath been abused by most strange, false and bottomlesse untruths, for which some body (without repentance) must be ashamed at the Day of Judgement, if they escape a condigne legall punishment in this world: I therefore conclude with this open profession (and I am confident that our whole army with say *Amen* unto it) he that hath any designe against the Protestant Religion, the Lawes of England, or hopes to enrich himselfe by pillaging the City of London, let him be accursed: And so, whether Peace or Warre the Lord prosper the work of their hands who stand for GOD and King Charles.

Rupert.

On 27th March Prince Rupert received orders to take the town of Birmingham, then held by Parliament, and to re-take the city of Lichfield. For this purpose he assembled a force of 1,200 horse, comprising his own regiment (including the Lichfield Troop commanded by Anthony Dyott), Colonel Lord Digby's Regiment of Horse and Colonel James Usher's Regiment of Dragoons. In addition he had 400 foot, probably Colonel Gerrard's Regiment, and a small train of artillery.

On Easter Monday, 3rd April, he arrived at Birmingham, described by Clarendon as 'a towne of as great fame for hearty, wilful, affected disloyalty to the King as any place in England.'

The town had only a small garrison of a troop of horse and a company of foot, detached from Colonel Russel's garrison at Lichfield. It was soon captured, and Prince Rupert burnt a number of buildings in the town, to show his disapproval of their disloyalty and also to prevent the inhabitants using their skills to produce arms for Parliament. (Even at that time Birmingham had a considerable reputation for skill in metal-working). Leaving a small garrison behind him, the Prince, with the rest of his force, pressed on to Lichfield where his advanced guard arrived on Thursday, 6th April. The main body arrived on the 7th having been reinforced by the regiments of Colonel Hastings and the late Earl of Northampton, from Stafford.

Once again no attempt was made to defend the town, Colonel Russel withdrawing his forces inside the Close, where a summons to surrender left them unmoved, as might be expected. Instead, they rang the cathedral bells in defiance. But unlike Lord Brooke, Prince Rupert did not immediately attack the Close from the south. Acting on the military principle that 'time spent on reconnaissance is rarely wasted' he took the trouble to send his scouts ahead and found that, while on the south side the Close was well defended by water, to the north the ground rose steeply so that after only a short distance it was level with the battlements of the cathedral.

By Saturday, 8th April, his troops had surrounded the Close and his battery of artillery was set up on the highest piece of ground to the north of the fortress, a spot known to this day as 'Prince Rupert's Mount'.

The size and number of his guns has not been recorded, but several cannon balls have been unearthed near the site of his battery. One of these,

*Prince Rupert's Mount, showing position of gun emplacement earthworks. 1985*

in the former Lichfield Museum, was weighed and measured by the author and found to be 10 pounds in weight and 4.25 inches in diameter. From published tables[4] this would appear to be ammunition for a demi-culverin, a gun similar to 'Black Bess' used by Lord Brooke in the first siege.

Another cannon ball found by Mr. George Deacon in his garden at Nether Beacon, close to the site of Prince Rupert's battery* weighed 14.25 pounds and had a diameter of 4.92 inches. Allowing for a cavity found in the ball, which would reduce its weight, this would appear to be a projectile for a culverin. Evidence would suggest, therefore, that Prince Rupert had both culverins and demi-culverins in his artillery train.

A culverin had a barrel 11 feet long, and a demi-culverin one of 10 feet. In each case the barrel was mounted on a wooden gun-carriage with a trail, and was worked by a crew of six men — two gunners and four matrosses or assistant gunners. We know from records[5] of Prince Rupert's artillery train that when it was set up at Oxford on 28th March it had five gunners and twelve matrosses (each of them was issued with a pole-axe as a personal weapon). This would suggest no more than three guns — possibly two demi-culverins and a culverin. All these guns were

---

* This ball was the subject of a metallurgical examination by Dr. J. E. Hurst and Dr. R. V. Riley in 1948.

designed to be used on the battlefield against troops. In no way were they siege artillery, for use against fortifications. Prince Rupert would be well aware of this, but it was a case of using what was available.

On the morning of 8th April the inhabitants of Lichfield awoke once again to the sound of gunfire as the Royalist cannon opened up against the north walls of the Close. The object was to make a breach through which Prince Rupert's troops could storm the fortress, but Bishop Langton's walls were strong and well-built, and even at the point-blank range of 400 yards the guns made little impression on them. All day the artillery pounded away, but by the evening it was obvious that the ten pound and fourteen pound cannon balls did not carry enought weight to produce the desired effect. Something more drastic was required.

To Prince Rupert, with his experience of military engineering, this meant mining the walls and for this he required sappers.

A few miles away on Cannock Chase coal had been got for many years, and there were plenty of men skilled in mining. Colonel Hastings was sent to find recruits and in a short time returned with fifty miners armed with picks and shovels. The next day they set to work.

Before they could start undermining the walls the top moat had to be drained of water, and this was probably done by diverting the springs that fed the moat from the high ground on the north. As soon as this had been done it was possible to start tunnelling under the walls.

In his report of the siege to Parliament[6] Colonel Russel estimated his attackers to consist of some 4,000 troops (in fact, an over-estimate), and he stated that it soon became apparent to him and his garrison that mining was in progress — they thought in three or four different places — and so he ordered countermining to take place with the object of intercepting the Royalist sappers.

All through the week Rupert's artillery pounded away, not only from the heights to the north, but later against the South Gate which Lord Brooke had attacked with such disastrous results. Unlike Brooke, Prince Rupert kept his head down and eventually his gunners were successful in making a breach of sorts near the gate. Scaling ladders were brought and three men succeeded in getting over the wall. Two of them were killed almost immediately and a third was taken prisoner. This unfortunate man, reported Colonel Russel, was hanged 'like a sign' three yards back from the wall, while his captors shouted for Prince Rupert to shoot him down, a reference no doubt to the Prince's shooting episode at Stafford. The reaction of Rupert to this was to swear 'God d--- him, he would not give one man quarter!'[7]

The following day, Sunday 16th, the two sides clashed again as one of Prince Rupert's tunnels broke through into the defenders' countermine workings. A grim subterranean fight by the light of candles ensued when, in Colonel Russel's words, 'they discharged upon each other'. After this savage encounter the Royalist sappers withdrew and abandoned the tunnel. Two other tunnels were discovered in a like manner and also abandoned.

Work continued on a fourth tunnel however, and this one was more successful, reaching the foundations of the tower at the north-west corner of the Close without being detected. Here they enlarged the excavation into an underground chamber and began to pack it with gunpowder to explode as a landmine.

Because the Royalist resources were so stretched, and munitions so short, the gunpowder had to be brought from the army's headquarters at Oxford and the difficulties involved in organising this are brought out in the following letter from Colonel Arthur Trevor, a Royalist officer, to a friend, Major Legge, in Prince Rupert's force at Lichfield:[8]

> Deare William,
>    With noe small stir have I awakened the foggy burghers of this place to sett this ammunition going towards your close-works at Leichfield. I hope it will come seasonably to yow to doe your worke, wherein wee of this place goe a great share; for I assure yow, wee have sett all wee have to venture in this bottom. If your work be done before it comes, I pray you intercede with His Highness for a return (in part at least) . . .'

Additional gunpowder was brought from Tamworth and altogether five barrels of the explosive were assembled at Lichfield and taken down the tunnel to form the mine.

Today, when combatants all over the world seem to enjoy almost unlimited supplies of ammunition, it is difficult to appreciate the effort involved in accumulating just five barrels of explosive. But as the letter above shows, it represented a major effort by the Royalist ammunition commissary, with a request in the last sentence to return any that they didn't use. The manufacture of gunpowder was concentrated mainly in Kent, Essex and Sussex, areas outside the control of the Royalist forces and to ensure a sufficient supply all sorts of expedients were necessary as we shall see later.

Thursday, 20th April, 1642 was a day which would remain for long in the minds of the citizens of Lichfield. It was a day when history was made, a day to be set alongside the recent one in March when Lord Brooke had met his end, a day to be remembered and spoken of by parents to their children, by grandparents to their grandchildren and repeated by generations after that.

During the hours of darkness the Royalist forces had taken up positions all round the walls, ready with scaling ladders to attack the Parliamentary fortress. In the underground chamber beneath the tower at the north-east corner of the Close an officer laid the fuse to the powder; a long length of match used by the musketeer for their matchlock muskets. In the octagonal stone tower above, looking out over Beacon Street, the end of Gaia Lane and the little cul-de-sac known as Millstone Place, six Roundhead soldiers stood on sentry duty, not suspecting what was going on beneath their feet.

As the first glimmer of dawn appeared behind the spires of the cathedral a Royalist officer lit the end of the fuse and made a hasty retreat from the tunnel.

Five minutes or so later the whole tower erupted and the inhabitants of Lichfield were jerked abruptly from their sleep as the first landmine ever to be exploded in England's history tore a gaping hole in the walls of the Close, wide enough, as Colonel Russel reported later, 'for six men to enter abreast'.[9]

At seven o'clock the Royalists attacked at points all round the Close to keep the defenders engaged while a storming party, estimated by Colonel Russel as being 200 strong, rushed the newly formed breach. For the assault on the fortress the Royalist cavalry had agreed to fight on foot, and the storming party contained most of their principal officers. The Roundheads took cover in the houses of the Close and repelled the attackers with hand granadoes. These were smaller versions of the ones fired from mortars which had been used in the first siege. Each weighed about two pounds, was spherical and hollow and was filled with gunpowder. A length of match provided a fuse and the soldier using the granado lit this and then swung the granado around to fan the fuse and at the appropriate moment threw it at his opponent, hoping that the fuse would not last long enough for him to throw it back.

The fighting in the Close was fierce. In the Royalist ranks the casualties were high; Colonel Usher was killed, Colonels Gerrard and Wagstaffe wounded and Lord Digby shot in the knee. Prince Rupert himself was shot in the boot and his personal chaplain, a Scotsman named Erskin was wounded and taken prisoner. Many others were killed and wounded before the attackers withdrew under the heavy fire from Colonel Russel's troops, who estimated that they had killed some 100 men and taken 120 prisoners. Against this, they claimed, only fourteen were killed on their own side.

But the triumph was short-lived. At a council of war that evening it was found that only one barrel of powder remained and all their match was spent. Without this, their muskets were useless. In addition, like their predecessors under the Earl of Chesterfield, they were short of food and in a desperate state they sent a trumpeter to parley with Prince Rupert, saying that they could not feed their Royalist prisoners and if he did not supply provisions for them they would be forced to cut their throats or let them starve.

Prince Rupert himself was in something of a dilemma. Two days before he had received a letter from King Charles with an urgent summons to return with all the strength he had for the relief of Reading, under siege by the Parliamentary army. Time was not on his side. He sent back a message to Colonel Russel offering generous terms if he would surrender. Russel agreed, so Prince Rupert left the arrangement of the surrender in the hands of the formidable Colonel Hastings and set off immediately for Reading with most of his force.

On the same day the following articles of agreement were signed:

> It is consented by Colonel Hastings, by the authority given to him by His Highness Prince Rupert that, in consideration of the delivery and yielding up of the Close of Lichfield, Lieutenant Colonel Russel, and all the captains and officers with him, shall march out of the said Close tomorrow, being the one-and twentieth day of this instant Aprill, by ten of the clock in the morning, with four score men and musquetts with flying colours, and four score horsemen with arms belonging to them, and all others persons within the said Close to be at liberty to go whither they please; and for their better and safe conveyance, a free pass or convoy from His Highness, and eleven carts to convey away such goods as belong to any of the officers or soldiers with themselves to the Cittie of Coventrie; and that all prisoners shall be released on both sides which have been taken in the County of Stafford since the coming down of the Right Honourable Lord Brooke. In witness whereof we have put our hand and seal, this twentieth day of Aprill, Anno Domini 1643.
>
> H. Hastings

Accordingly, the following morning Colonel Russel and his men marched out of Lichfield Close with all the honours of war, carrying their arms, with drums beating and colours flying. Behind them came the eleven waggons carrying their bags and baggage. They marched over the causeway, down Bridge [Bird] Street, along St. John Street and out of the city on their way to Coventry. No doubt there were many Lichfield citizens lining the streets and looking from windows at this display of panoply and martial pride, wondering perhaps what the next similar occasion might be. One garrison was leaving, another was taking over.

Not until Colonel Russel and his men were well on their way did the Royalists discover that in one of those eleven waggons was all the silver plate and other moveable treasures of Lichfield Cathedral.

So ended the second siege of Lichfield, and once again the citizens gathered their wits together and attempted to restore life to normal.

Prince Rupert had achieved his purpose and the Royalists were elated at their success. How did the Parliamentarians take their setback?

In Coventry Thomas Ellis, one of the Parliamentary garrison there, sent the following letter to a friend in London:[10]

> Dear Brother,*
> Since my last to you, being the last week, it hath fallen out that the Close of Lichfield is lost; yet the loss to me is not so great as the joy of heart I have conceived for the safety and honour which God hath bestowed upon our friends that were there, who

---

*Used as a form of address, not of kinship.

have reaped praise and commendation for their valour and prowess, even out of the mouths of their enemies, of whom they doe affirm *that never did Souldiers so honour the Parliament as these have done.* A brief rehersall of the particulars I have here enclosed, together with the Articles on which it was surrendered, as I received them from Lieutenant Colonell Russel's own hand, whereof I think he has sent a copy to the House of Parliament; and according to the conditions, they marched forth on Friday last. Myselfe and Brother Burges rode forth to meet them, a mile beyond Merryden [Meriden] and tarryed with my brother Henry Pretty all that night at Merryden, being four miles from Coventry, it being no small joy to us to meete him who was soe deare and tender in our affections, who we had given up for lost; but God who is rich in mercy found out a way beyond our expectations, and even in the moment of difficulties, when as many, or rather more, brake in upon them than was of them in the Close, God made it his opportunity to deliver them by weake means, (as you may see by the enclosed being not above 30\*). They beat the enemy down so fast in the said breach that they made a breast-work, about a yard high of dead and wounded bodies.

Many circumstances might be added to set forth the excellencie of the mercie but time will not permit. You have the substantiall part of the Tradjedie; yet for my brother Henry Pretty, his particular, take notice (with thankfulness) of two remarkable passages of God's Providence to him. He was shot in the middle of his back, upon his belt, with a musket bullet, which struck him down yet neither pierced belt nor coat, and at the breach, when so many brake in, he and his lieutenant, with Captain Graves, lead on those 30 men, where Askin, [Dr. Erskin] Chaplain to Prince Rupert, presented a pistol to his very face, the powder whereof flew in his forehead and the bullet went through the brim of his hat and did him no hurt, so gratiously did the hand of Providence direct it. He, with the rest, came yesterday, being Saturday, with ten waynes laden with bagge and baggage. They could not prevail for their ordnance.

On Thursday night there marched forth of this town [Coventry] Colonell Barker his troop, under command of Captain Lieutenant Flower; the Minister's Commander† of Dragoons, under command of Captain Ottoway; a commander of Dragoons from Killingworth under command of Captain Peter Hunt; Captain Potter's part of a troop. Captain Pont being Commander-in-Chief of this Briggade, they marched that night to Leicester, where they have abode ever since and are expected to joyne with Lord Gray, for some design,‡ very speedily. Captain Oakey marched with them and they were well last night at 10 o'clock. I have commendations from Captain Oakey and Captain Flower, who desire to be remembered to their friends in London.

Prince Rupert is marched from Lichfield and hath left a garrison there. He lay last night at Cosill [Coleshill] and is now upon his march on Merryden Heath, within four miles of us, what his designe is we know not. We expect Father Bough to Coventry this night, if he be living, for the convoy is gone for the prisoners at Stafford, where, if he be alive, he is. I fear the post will be gone, I will therefore conclude and rest,

   Your truly loving brother till death,

Coventrie, 23rd Aprill 1643                                    Thomas Ellis

It is interesting to note that Ellis reports the arrival of only ten of the eleven waggons that left Lichfield; one cannot help speculating on whether the missing one was that containing the plate of Lichfield Cathedral and if so what happened to it, but that is likely to remain one of those mysteries that will never be solved.

---

\*i.e. the number of men who defended the breach.

†The term 'Commander' here is used to denote a military unit, c.f. the modern 'Commando'.

‡The design, as we shall see, was to counter attack Lichfield Close.

Before departing for Reading Prince Rupert had taken good care to ensure not only the future garrisoning of the close but also the organising of resistance among the Royalist supporters in and around Lichfield as the following letter[11] indicates. It was sent to him soon after he left.

Most Excellent Prince,

The many favours your Highness, of your pious and princely goodness, vouchsafed us, the gentlemen and inhabitants of the Counties of Stafford and the Citie of Lichfield* command more than a bare acknowledgement from us, your humbly devoted servants; these make us in all humility tender out bounden and demerited thanks to your Highness for the great care and hazard your Highness in person underwent for the delivery of us and our estates from the exhorbitant pressures the rebells laid upon us. And, as in all duty obliged, we render your Highness most humble thanks for the continuance of your former favours in sending Captain Trevers (a man of approved valour and fidelity) amongst us, whose care, experience and industrye give us ample hope of our future libertie by reuniting the gentlemen of our countries into a body, and by his paynes in disciplining them to preserve us from the thralldoms of the traiterous rebells. This, (a favour beyond our expression and merit) imboldens us to become humble suitors to your Highness to arm him with such powers in these countyes that he may be joined in counsell of warre and have free libertie to exercise those goode parts he is endowed with all to the furtherance of his most royall Majesties service in these countyes, which, by the means of able officers and commanders under him, may the better be effected. For this we shall infinitely bee to your Highness obliged and expresse our selves to bee, as wee are,

Your Highness's most humbly devoted servants,

| | |
|---|---|
| Francis Grosvenor | Walter Grosvenor |
| Clement Fisher | Mich. Dyot |
| Thomas Corbin | Houmfrey Mathers ⎫ ⎧ Ballivi. |
| Jeff. Glasier | Thomas Ashmole ⎭ ⎩ Lichen. |
| Thos. Wately | Roger Fleetwood |
| Richard Walmisley | Hugh Humphries |
| Thos. Underhill | Richard Harrison |
| Henry Boyleston | William Wolriche |
| Henry Baker | Jo. Hill |
| Rowland Fryth | Richard Davies |
| Edward Taylor | Bern. Terricke |
| James Wolriche | Symon Hill |

The familiar names of several Royalist sympathisers in Lichfield appear amongst the signatories: Michael Dyot, Jeffery Glasier, John Hill, Thomas Underhill and Richard Walmisley were all young men who served under the command of Colonel Richard Bagot as officers of the Lichfield garrison. Houmfrey Mathers and Thomas Ashmole were the Bailiffs of the city then in office. At that moment the Royalist party were in the ascendancy in Lichfield and were to remain so for the next three years. The supporters of Parliament such as Richard Drafgate, Thomas Minors and Michael Biddulph had disappeared from the scene, though they were to return later under the Commonwealth. Lichfield was now a Royalist garrison town and one could drink the King's health in safety. For those with different views it was prudent to keep a low profile.

---

*Until 1974 the city of Lichfield was a county, its title being 'The City and County of the City of Lichfield'.

## SOURCE NOTES
*Chapter III*

1.    Clarendon, History of the Rebellion, Vol. III, p.51
2.    Robert Plot, The Natural History of Staffordshire, p.336
3.    Prince Rupert His Declaration, 1642
4.    Hogg, O. F. G., Artillery — Its Origin, Heyday and Decline (London, Hurst 1970)
5.    Young, Edgehill, 1642, p.34
6.    Salt Library, Stafford, M.s 438
7.    Warburton, Memoirs of Prince Rupert, Vol. II, p.166
8.    Salt Library, M.s 600
9.    Ibid. M.s 596
10.   Ibid. M.s 596
11.   Ibid. M.s 596

*Colonel Richard Bagot*
*1619–1645*
*Governor of Lichfield Close Garrison 1643–1645*

*Chapter IV*

# A Royalist Garrison
## 1643–1646

BEFORE Prince Rupert departed for Oxford on 22nd April he 'committed the government of it [the Close] to Colonell Bagott, a son of a good and powerful family in that county.'[1]

The Bagot family lived at Blithfield, a country estate about six miles north of Lichfield, where they kept the famous Bagot herd of goats. These animals, reputedly descended from a number brought back from southern Europe by one of the Bagot family who had fought in the first crusade, became so much a part of the family image that a goat's head forms the crest in the family arms. The present descendants of the goats still flourish in the pleasant countryside of rural Staffordshire.

In 1642 the head of the family was Sir Hervey Bagot, the first Baronet, who had been knighted for his services to the county as High Sheriff in 1626. He had four sons, two of whom did not take any part in the war. The other two both played conspicious parts as Governor and Deputy Governor respectively of Lichfield Close. Richard, the fourth son, probably had a military training, and on the outbreak of war he joined the regiment raised by Lord Paget. This was the regiment of foot commanded by Colonel Richard Bolle, and Richard Bagot was commissioned into it as a captain and given command of a company. He saw active service at the Battles of Edgehill, Brentford and Heywood, and was with the Earl of Northampton's cavalry at Hopton Heath.

In April 1643 he was chosen by Prince Rupert to become Governor of Lichfield Close, with promotion to Colonel. At the same time he was given the task of raising a regiment of horse and another of foot, to form the Lichfield Garrison. In this task he had the help of his brother Hervey, the third son, who also was promoted to Lieutenant Colonel.

In March 1643 Parliament had issued an ordinance that the estates of all those in arms against them, or assisting the King in any way, should be sequestrated. Sir Hervey Bagot, deprived of the support of his estate at

Blithfield in this way, decided to seek refuge with his sons in Lichfield Close, though at fifty-two he felt too old to play an active part in the war. However, he and his wife settled in the Close and gave their moral support to the Royalist garrison, and this meant that there were three male Bagots present, two of them named Hervey and two of them colonels. It is hardly surprising that some confusion has been present in the minds of historians over the centuries.

As well as being Governor, Richard Bagot raised a regiment of horse which he commanded himself, and his brother Hervey raised and commanded a regiment of foot. The command structure was therefore as follows:

Colonel Richard Bagot
Governor of Lichfield Close
Garrison Commander

| Colonel Richard Bagot's | Lieut. Colonel Hervey Bagot's |
|---|---|
| Regiment of Horse | Regiment of Foot |
| (Three troops, 200 men) | (Eight companies, 500 men) |

Colonel Richard Bagot assumed command on 22nd April 1643. One of his first acts was to appoint as his Treasurer, to keep the accounts for the whole garrison, a Lichfield man by the name of Jeffery Glasier.

Glasier (1607–1672) was one of the twenty-four Staffordshire gentlemen who had written to Prince Rupert pledging loyalty. He lived in Lichfield Close where he had held the position of Chapter Clerk and Registrar (i.e. steward to the Dean and Chapter of Lichfield Cathedral), a position in which he succeeded his father Thomas Glasier in 1627.

Several of Jeffery Glasier's colleagues on the cathedral staff served under Colonel Bagot. A name which keeps cropping up is that of Michael East (or Est), one of the Vicars Choral, whose father* had been Master of the Choisters. He joined Bagot's Regiment of Foot as a lieutenent and served right through the campaign. So too did the Reverend Zachariah Turnpenny, Subchanter of the cathedral, who took up arms and became Captain Zachariah Turnpenny, Commander of the Citizens' Company of Bagot's Foot, though with a name like that one cannot help feeling that **he** should have been Treasurer.

Some of Jeffery Glasier's accounts[2] have survived, namely those covering the nine months from the embodyment of the garrison on 22nd April 1643, up till the end of that year, ands also for the last three months of 1645. From them we can obtain a very good picture of what life was like in Lichfield Close and especially, from the details of the troops' pay, of the composition of the forces there.

---

*His father, also Michael East (1580-1648) is known today as a composer of madrigals.

Early on in the accounts there is reference to the casualties suffered in the fighting:

> Payde by my Lord Loughboroughs command* for lame souldiers cure and quarters and money to officers of Colonel Ushers Regiment and others who were hurt at the entrance to the breach of the Close . . . £13 0s 0d.

Colonel Usher himself had been killed in the assault, and in the papers that form Glasier's accounts is the following letter:

> Warrant to Mr. Ashburnam, 18th December, 1643.
>
> Our will and pleasure is that you forthwith, out of such of our treasure that remaineth in your custody, pay unto Sara Usher, widow of Col. James Usher, slayne in the warre at Lichfield, the full sume of fifty pounds in part of two hundred and ninety nine pounds due unto her husband for his emoluments from the 4th of February 1642 unto the 20th April past and this warrant to you shall be your full discharge.
>
> Given on the 18th December, 1643.

The warrant is not signed, but is takes the form of pay warrants issued by King Charles at various times during the war. One hopes Sara Usher got the rest of her money.

One of the Parliamentary journals,[3] reporting the loss of Lichfield Close, had made the following observation:

> Prince Rupert, on entering the Close, thought his labour well-bestowed on the gaining of it, being a place of great strength and very advantageous for a cross passage into the north to fetch the Queene this way, and he set his men to work presently to rectify the breach and strengthen the fortifications.

The accounts give us a fascinating insight into what was involved in 'rectifying the breach and strengthening the fortifications'.

> Payde for making up the breach where the mine was sprung, and the South Gate where the batterie was made ...................................................................... £75 0s 0d
>
> Payde for making a drawbridge and chains and making good the wall in that place .................................................................................................................... £12 0s 0d
>
> Payde for making a new pair of gates and the ironwork for them ........... £8 0s 0d
>
> Payde for repayring the Inner Tower at the West Gate, makyinge a floor for it and planting a piece [i.e. a cannon] for seven-pound bulletts upon it ........... £8 10s 0d

Prince Rupert's miners, it will be recalled, had drained the upper moat of the Close in order to carry out their mining. The water now had to be restored, and so we find in the accounts an item:

> Payde for drawing the water round about the Close ................................. £10 0s 0d

While on the subject of water, it should be noted that for centuries the Close enjoyed its own piped water supply, brought from a source at Maple Hays, about a mile away to the north-east. In the first siege one of the earliest actions of Lord Brooke's troops had been to cut off this supply. But the garrison still had the use of wells which tapped the almost inexhaustible supply in the sandstone sub-stratum. Two of these at the east end of the Close, probably made for the use of the mediaeval Bishop's Palace, were uncovered during the building operations in recent years.

---

*Colonel Henry Hastings, the scourge of the Roundheads in the Midlands, had been elevated to the title of Earl Loughborough, with command of all the Royalist forces in Staffordshire.

Colonel Bagot had up to 200 cavalry quartered in the Close at times, and horses are thirsty animals. So some provision had to be made for them, too, and in the accounts we find,

> Payde for drawing the water through the Close and making up a horse-pool .................................................................................................... £15 0s 0d

The site of this horse-pond has long since vanished without trace, but as water would have to be brought from the moat on the high ground to the north by pipe or trench, one can only surmise that the horse-pool was in the lower part of the Close, possibly where the ground is now level before the west front of the Cathedral. The cost of £15 0s 0d represents a considerable sum and so we can assume that the work involved was fairly extensive.

The new garrison was short of everything and so the help of other Royalist strongholds was sought.

> Payde to the Governor of Shrewsbury for three barrells of gunpowder att our first coming ........................................................................................... £22 0s 0d

reads one item, and at first even troops had to be borrowed, as shown by the entry,

> Payde for the quartering of 200 horse of Colonell Lane's* that came into our service for the garrison ........................................................................................ £30 0s 0d

Soon, however, Richard Bagot was recruiting men for his cavalry. The nucleus of his regiment appears to have come with him, for an entry in the accounts for the whole period from April to December reads:

> Payde for quarter for those three troops at a rate of three shillings and sixpence apeece wickley, allowing but 60 horse for the first month which I [i.e. Colonel Bagot] brought in with me, and by that time raised the rest; cometh to .......... £2646 0s 0d

It would seem, therefore, that Richard Bagot brought with him into the garrison the troop which he had commanded in the Earl of Northampton's Regiment and added to it by recruitment another two troops (about 140 men) by the end of May. These would be volunteers from the surrounding district who provided their own horses and armour. They did not receive pay, but only the three and sixpence a week for quarter for themselves and their horses. They came mostly from the land-owning gentry, and were in fact the the true 'Cavaliers' though the term came to be applied generally to all who fought for the King. In the same way the term 'Roundhead' came to be applied to all those who fought for Parliament, though originally the name referred to the apprentices who made up a large part of the London trained bands and who, in the manner of the young, cropped their hair close in derision of the long-haired Cavaliers. Very few of their elders in the Parliamentary army followed their example. There is nothing new about 'Skinheads'.

---

*Colonel John Lane was Governor of Stafford and the brother of Jane Lane who in later years was to achieve fame for the part she played in helping Charles II to escape after the Battle of Worcester.

The cost of arming and equipping Colonel Bagot's men is also recorded:

> Expended for raising of three troops of horse and for carrabines, pystolls and sadlles for them ................................................................................................ £900 0s 0d

The carbines were short-barrelled muskets with a wheel-lock firing action (match-locks would be quite impractical on horseback).

Each trooper also had two wheel-lock pistols, carried in holsters on the saddle, and a sword which Jeffery Glasier's accounts show to have cost four shillings each. In a cavalry charge the troops advanced at a trot, discharged their pistols when a few yards from the enemy, and attacked with their swords before the enemy could regroup. Carbines were used for longer distance engagement, either on horseback or dismounted.

Armour, which each man supplied for himself, consisted of a breastplate, a backplate, a helmet and a steel bridle gauntlet, worn on the left hand and forearm with which a trooper controlled his horse. A coat of buff leather was standard wear for cavalry.

A sum of £13 0s 0d was paid to each troop commander for fitting out expenses; this went to 'my Lieutenant Colonel's troop', to Captain Trevers and to Captain Dymock. The fact that Colonel Bagot commanded a troop in his own regiment was not unusual, and in the same way commanding officers of foot regiments also had their own companies.

Captain Trevers has already been mentioned in conection with the letter to Prince Rupert from the twenty-four Staffordshire gentlemen. He must has spent his early days in the garrison visiting the local gentry, drumming up support and raising recruits. Of the other troop commander, Captain Dymock, we know nothing. Both he and Trevers must have moved on elsewhere as soon as the regiment was properly formed, since there is no further mention of them.

A manuscript in the Salt Library,[4] probably the work of Jeffery Glasier, lists some of the officers in Colonel Bagot's Horse. The second-in-command, and 'Major of all the Horse' was Major William Warner of Wolaston, in Warwickshire. He bore the nickname of "Crab" Warner, 'because of his cross peevishness'. Another troop commander was Captain William Ruggeley, of Dunton Hall, also in Warwickshire, of whom the writer says, 'for his loyalty towards his Prince the leeches of Goldsmiths' Hall* sucked from him the sum of £33 3s 4d besides the great loss received by plunder (as the mercenary souldiers of Coventrie called it).'

Each troop commander had under him a lieutenant and a cornet or subaltern officer. Among these was Lieutenant Adderley,† of Uttoxeter, in Major Warner's troop; he left early on to be succeeded by Cornet

---

*Goldsmiths Hall was where the Committee of Sequestrations met.

†A relative of the Bagot's. Sir Hervey Bagot's first wife was Katherine Adderley.

Humphrey Slugard, 'a man of good part and a subject faithfull to doe his colonells commands, with a willing love to serve the King at all times of need'.

The Lieutenant in Captain Ruggeley's troop was Thomas Underhill, a Lichfield man and another of the signatories of the letter to Prince Rupert. In the list of officers he is described as:

> A man known for his valour and courage, but a little now and then troubled with folly and giddiness in the braine, for once, on a march, he overshott himself verie much. Being behinde the troopes and coming a good rate after them, he found one of his troope either taking a pipe of tobacco (or imbibing some drinke) and some words passed between them which were unknown, but he forthwith drew and ran the young man through, whom he knew to be a good subject and souldier.[5]

War does strange things to men's minds, and one cannot help feeling that Lieutenant Underhill was as much a casualty of the war as the unfortunate trooper.

The cornet of the troop was John Bracebridge, of Curdworth, in Warwickshire, the black sheep of Colonel Bagot's Horse, for later on, we are told,

> He changed his opinion and fleyd, after some rough account from either captain or lieutenant, and he revolted from his true alliegance, changing his opinions and flying to Olivers gang of traytors.[6]

Here, one feels, he must have been one of Parliament's "bad bargains" in the recruiting sense.

Another cornet was Michael Dyott, sixth and youngest son of Sir Richard Dyott. As one would expect from a member of this Lichfield family, his loyalty never wavered and he laid down his life in the King's cause.

A cornet of horse, as his name implied, carried a cornet, or standard, when on parade or in action. The cornet was a flag two feet square, the colour and design being chosen by the commander to denote his regiment. Each troop had its cornet, and in action this was carried close to the troop commander to form an easily recognised rallying point. Colonel Bagot's Regiment of Horse carried 'three blue cornets without manner of badge, motto or distinction.'[7]

Turning now to the foot soldiers, we find that the very first entry in Jeffery Glasier's accounts refers to them:

> Payde unto seaven foote companies, consisting of 300 soldiers, two shillings apeece and three shillings and sixpence apeece for their quarter, is £82 10s 0d per wicke, and £1 1s 0d for the pay and quarters of the Serjeants, Drummers, Clarkes and Corporalls of the said companies, cometh to £97 11s 0d a wicke, which service the said 22nd Aprill to the 26th December cometh to £3316 14s 0d.

It would appear from this item that Bagot's Regiment of Foot, with a strength of 300 men plus officers and non-commissioned officers, already existed on 22nd April when Colonel Richard Bagot took over the command of Lichfield Close.

We know that Colonel Hervey Bagot, though he had not made such a name for himself as had his brother, had nevertheless been active in raising forces for the King. He was one of those approached by the Sheriff and Justices of Staffordshire in November 1642 to raise a force of 800 foot and 200 horse from within the county. He himself was nominated for and appointed as a captain in the force raised in the Totmanslow Hundred (the northern part of the county).[8] It was probably from this group that Bagot's Regiment of Foot was drawn, and it was very much a Staffordshire regiment. Many of the officers were Lichfield men.

In Jeffery Glasier's accounts there exists a payroll for December 1645, from which the accompanying establishment chart has been drawn up. It will be noted that after three and a half years of existence the regiment still retained its establishment of seven companies, though its numerical strength had grown from 300 to nearly 500.

In addition to its seven full-time companies the regiment also had a citizens' company of part-time soldiers — the "Home Guard" of the period. Its members lived in the city and reported for duty and training in the Close as required. The commander of this company was Captain Zachary Turnpenny, and assisting him was Lieutenant Robinson.

The members of the citizens' company were not paid, being volunteers, so they do not figure in Jeffery Glasier's payrolls and consequently we have no direct record of their number. But in the William Salt Library at Stafford there is an interesting manuscript, obviously the work of someone who was present in the Close and was closely associated with the garrison. It is entitled

> THE NAMES AND ARMES ACCORDING TO THEIR TRADS OF ALL THOSE OF THIS ANCIENT AND FAMOUS CITTIE, which according to their Oaths and Allegiance ventured their lives and fortunes in his Majesties Service, KING CHARLES the first."[9]

There follows a brief description of each of fifteen Trade, or Livery Companies of Lichfield. With each description is an illustration of its arms and also the names of members who presumably served in the Lichfield Company of Bagot's Regiment. From these names it is possible to draw up the following muster roll:

| Company Commander | Capt. Zachary Turnpenny | Sub-Chanter, Cathedral |
|---|---|---|
| Second i/c | Lieut. Robinson | |
| Serjeant | One, name not known | |
| Drummer | John Newth | Glasiers' Company |
| Soldier | Philip Unitt | Mercers' Company |
| Soldier | Edward Tayler | Vintners' Company |
| Soldier | Henry Baker | Bakers' Company |
| Soldier | John Millington | Bakers' Company |
| Soldier | Thomas Robinson | Saddlers' Company |

| Soldier | — Robinson | Son of Thomas Robinson |
| Soldier | — Robinson | Son of Thomas Robinson |
| Soldier | George Mason | Cooks' Company |
| Soldier | Richard Mason | Son of George Mason |
| Soldier | John Mason | Son of George Mason |
| Soldier | William Lambe | Smiths' Company |
| Soldier | James Morris | Farriers' Company |
| Soldier | Simon Bowering | Farriers' Company |
| Soldier | Richard ——— | |

Other Trade Companies which had members serving were the Chirurgeons, from whose members came Richard Thornton and Humphrey Spooner, but they were Chirurgeons to the garrison and were unlikely to have served under Captain Turnpenny. The Butchers', Carpenters', Shoemakers' and Joiners' Companies also provided volunteers, but their names are not given. A probable strength of about thirty is likely.

Thomas Robinson, of the Saddlers' Company, may have been the same person as Lieutenant Robinson; there is no way of telling.

Like their successors, the Home Guard of 300 years later, the members of the Citizens' Company carried on their civilian occupations and did their training and duties in their spare time. This we know because the Churchwardens' Accounts of St. Mary's Church record that John Newth (who lived in Market Street and was a member of St. Mary's congregation) was paid several times during the year 1644 for work done in the church, presumably to the windows. Likewise Will Lambe, the blacksmith, was paid during the same year for repairing the church clock and for making new gudgeons for the church bells.

Last in the list of trade companies is the Glasiers' Company; in the description of this body there is the following intriguing comment:

> There was but two in this Cittie of Lichfield who both according to their oath that every Freeman should sweare* (hath performed to their power) that they shall be good and true to their Sovereigne King Charles and to the heirs of their saide Sovereigne Lord the King. The first was a captain, and the other was a dromer [drummer] for his Neighbours and Townsmen in this service. Newth was dromer, all the siege, for the Townsmen in the Close.

There is little doubt that the captain referred to was Captain Thomas Glasier, who commanded a company of foot in Bagot's Regiment. He was probably a kinsman of Jeffery Glasier, the Treasurer. The Glasier family lived in the Close, and their name is a reminder that many people's surnames reflect an ancestor's occupation; it may not have been long since a Glasier followed that trade.

---

*As the present author can testify, having taken the same oath (to her Majesty Queen Elizabeth II) on being admitted Honorary Freeman to the Worshipful Company of Smiths of Lichfield.

The Commanding Officer, Colonel Hervey Bagot, had his own company within the regiment, as was the usual practice at that time. So too did his Second in Command, Major Roger Harsnett. The remaining six companies were commanded by Captain Anthony Dyott (eldest son of Sir Richard), Captain Baduley (or Badderley), Captain Thomas Glasier, Captain Swift, and Captain Zachary Turnpenny (Citizens' Company).

A muster of the regiment for October 1645, compiled from Jeffery Glasier's payrolls is shown on the next page. Each company, it will be noted, had under its commander a lieutenant and an ensign. The ensign, or "auncient" was a junior officer who, like the cornet in the cavalry, carried the colours. Each company had its own colour, a flag six foot square, marked in such a way as to identify the company.

The colours of Bagot's Regiment of Foot were 'azure, a mullet or, on a canton a cross'[10], or in other words a deep blue standard with a St. George's Cross in the top corner nearest the stave and carrying one or more mullets (five pointed stars) in gold.

In common with the usual practice, the colour of Colonel Bagot's Company would be plain blue with the St. George's Cross, but no mullets. Major Harsnett's would be the same with the addition of a little stream or tongue of gold issuing from the bottom outer corner of the St. George's Cross. Captain Anthony Dyott's had the St. George's Cross and on the blue field a single mullet, while Captain Baduley had two mullets and Captain Glasier three, and so on.

An unusual appointment was that of the pages, who appeared in varying numbers on the establishment of each company. Such a rank was unusual in the Royalist army, and they were probably junior members of the officers' families employed as runners (messengers). They were paid at the same rate as common soldiers.

Early on in the accounts appears the entry, 'Payde for eight drums, £9 12s 0d'. Drums were needed for use as a means of giving orders during drill and for signals in action, as well as keeping troops in step on the march. The eight drums would provide one for each company, including that of Drummer Newth of the Citizens' Company.

Drummers were quite an important part of the military establishment. Like the cavalry trumpeters, they were used by the opposing sides to communicate with each other by conveying messages, accompanying envoys or hostages and conducting parleys. Their importance was recognised by the fact that they were paid at the same rate as corporals.

At the head of the drummers was the Drum Major, one of Colonel Bagot's Company members. As well as training his charges, he would also lead them when they came together to form the Corps of Drums, and no doubt over the years Lichfield people grew accustomed to the sight and sound of the nightly tattoo. It is not difficult to picture the scene as

## BAGOT'S REGIMENT OF FOOT

### Lichfield Close Garrison, October 1645

#### Lieut. Colonel Hervey Bagot
#### Commanding Officer

**Lieut. Colonel's Company:** Lieutenant Colonel Hervey Bagot, Captain Collier, Ensign Walmsley, 1 Drum Major, 2 Serjeants, 2 Corporals, 1 Gunsmith, 2 Pages, 57 Other Ranks.

**Major's Company:** Major Roger Harsnett, Lieut. Dorington, Ensign Emmins, 2 Serjeants, 3 Corporals, 2 Drums, 1 Gunsmith, 5 Pages, 69 O.Rs.

**1st Captain's Company:** Captain Anthony Dyott, Lieut. Blencowe, Ensign Fisher, 2 Serjeants, 2 Corporals, 2 Drums, 1 Gunsmith, 1 Page, 64 O.Rs.

**2nd Captain's Company:** Captain Baduley, Lieut. Baguley, Ensign Cutler, 2 Serjeants, 2 Corporals, 1 Drum, 1 Gunsmith, 3 Pages, 31 O.Rs.

**3rd Captain's Company:** Captain Thomas Glasier, Lieutenant East, Ensign Sharpe, 2 Serjeants, 2 Corporals, 1 Gunsmith, 2 Pages, 31 O.Rs.

**4th Captain's Company:** Captain Ralph Swift, Lieutenant Burdon, Ensign Pyott, 2 Serjts, 3 Corporals, 1 Drum, 1 Gunsmith, 4 Pages, 77 O.Rs.

**5th Captain's Company:** Captain Benskin, Lieut. Johnston, Ensign Stanford, 4 Serjts, 3 Corps., 1 Gunsmith, 4 Pages, 73 O.Rs.

**Citizens' Company:** Captain Zachary Turnpenny, Lieut. Robinson, 1 Serjt., 1 Drummer, (John Newth), Other Ranks, see Page 57.

**Headquarters Staff:** Advocate General, Dr. Littleton; Treasurer, Jeffery Glasier; Quartermaster, Mr. Goodall; Chirurgeons, Mr. Thorneton and Mr. Spooner; 2 Commissaries; 1 Ammunition Commissary; 1 Muster Master.

Colonel Bagot's drums marched out of the West Gate of the Close, over the causeway and into Bird Street and the town, with the fifes playing 'Here's a Health unto his Majesty'. A brief halt in the Market Place to get the troops out of the alehouses, and then back they march up Dam Street, through the South Gate and into the Close.

Lastly we come to the rank and file, the backbone of this, as of any army. The common soldiers (the term "private soldier" had not yet been introduced) were of two kinds — musketeers and pikemen, in the ratio of two muskets to one pike.

The musketeers were armed with matchlock muskets — we know this from the large amounts of match that were purchased and recorded in Jeffery Glasier's accounts. A matchlock was a comparatively simple firearm which used a length of match, a fuse rather like a long wick, impregnated with saltpetre so that when ignited it would smoulder slowly along its length. Each musket was fired by a trigger action which brought the smouldering end of the match onto the pan, which contained fine gunpowder. This ignited and the flash passed through a touch hole and into the barrel where it ignited the main charge — though sometimes the musket misfired and all one got was a "flash in the pan".

Reloading a musket took time, perhaps half a minute, and to protect the musketeers while they were performing this operation was a function of the pikemen, who formed a cordon around the musketeers. The pikeman's weapons were a pike (a pole-arm sixteen feet long, with a plain spearhead) and a sword. They also, unlike the musketeers, wore armour to protect them from the pistols of the cavalry. This consisted of a pot helmet, breastplate and backplate.

The Lichfield garrison made their own pikes, and in the accounts we find several references to this,

To a carpenter, for felling ten ashes to make pikes, six shillings.
To the joiners, for their work in finding out ash to make pikes and cleaving it, £1 6s 8d.
To Marson, the cooper, for rounding six dozen and a half of pikes, four shillings.

The pike heads would be made by the smiths, of whom there were several in the garrison.

The troops had to be clothed, and cloth for fifty men cost £40. It was probably blue cloth, to match the Regimental colours, for the idea of a regiment wearing a uniform colour to denote their connection was just becoming fashionable.

Bagot's Regiment wore caps (probably something like the modern military beret), for the accounts have an entry 'payde for capps for my foot souldiers, £7 10s 0d'. Mr. Goodall, the Quartermaster, would not have to go very far for these, for Lichfield had a flourishing trade in the manufacture of them, centred on the worsted mill at Darnford, a fact perpetuated to this day by the name "Cappers Lane".

In addition to his horse and foot, Colonel Bagot had a small and rather motley collection of artillery. Jeffery Glasier's payroll shows two gunners at ten shillings a week and two matrosses at six shillings. These must have been on detachment from Prince Rupert's force. To begin with the only guns they had were those taken from Colonel Russel, including the seven-pounder which had been mounted in the tower of the West Gate. Nothing daunted, Colonel Bagot engaged a founder, set up a foundry, and began making his own artillery. We read in the accounts, 'Payde for brasse for making a piece of five-pound bullets, £36 0s 0d.' and later on, 'Payde for brasse more, for making of six smaller gunns and towards the making of a mortar piece, £42 0s 0d.' A mortar piece, which would fire granadoes, would be quite an achievement.

After this comes an entry 'Payde for making foure new carriages for cannon and mending olde ones, £12 0s 0d.' In the Royalist army ingenuity and a gift for improvisation counted for a lot.

But having made his guns, ammunition was then required, and we have seen how scarce this was for the Royalists. Once again the problem was tackled energetically. If gunpowder could not be purchased, then it must be made and so we find in the accounts the item 'Payde for making a corn mill and a gunpowder mill, £87 0s 0d' and 'Payde for a furnace to boil saltpetre in, and setting it up, £18 0s 0d.'

Gunpowder was made at that time to the formula:

   Saltpetre (potassium nitrate)....40%
   Brimstone (sulphur) .............. 30%
   Charcoal powder ................... 30%

Charcoal was easy enough to obtain and saltpetre could, with difficulty, be made. Only the sulphur had to be bought, for it was imported from Sicily. Jeffery Glasier paid £32 a ton for it.

So the furnace was set up and two salpetre men engaged.

The simplest, though most laborious way of obtaining saltpetre is from cattle dung. This is done by soaking it in water which is then boiled away to leave the saltpetre in crystalline form. A lot of fuel is required, and so coal had to be brought from Cannock Chase (under guard). 'Payde for coals already since our first coming for the saltpetre man, and guards, £30' writes Jeffert Glasier, and 'Payde saltpetre men, they costing us £8 a wicke, 27 wickes £216.'

When the charcoal, saltpetre and brimstone had been mixed in the right proportions it had to be fine ground. This was done in the gunpowder mill, worked by a horse. This was a fairly dangerous process which would probably have been done in a fairly secluded spot. One hopes that the entry, occuring in 1645, of 'a mill-horse and other necessaries about the mill, £1 15s 0d' was not the result of losing the previous one rather suddenly.

So guns were made and gunpowder to fire in them, and now all that was required was a supply of projectiles to fit them. These were produced by the foundry in the Close where both lead bullets and 'iron shott for all manners of cannon' were manufactured.

The matchlock muskets required a standard charge of powder, and one way of ensuring this was to make up a charge in a cartridge made of stiff paper*, a bullet being placed in one end and the other end screwed up after the cartridge had been filled with powder. These cartridges were then carried by the musketeers in there bandoliers, ready for use.

In the accounts there is an entry, 'Payde for paper for cartridges' so we know that these were made on site, and there are many payments for making match. In fact there was in the Close a complete arsenal turning out weapons and ammunition.

Troops and horses require feeding, and from the accounts we learn something of Quartermaster Goodall's work in this field:

Payde unto Thomas Hackett for a wagon load of butter and cheese, most of which he laid in at the relieving of Stafford Castle ............................................. £25 12s 0d
Payde for cheeses for store besides what I took from the rebels ............... £20 0s 0d
Payde for bacon for store ......................................................................... £39 0s 0d
Payde for salte ........................................................................................ £1 12s 0d
Payde for corn and malt for store ............................................................ £35 15s 0d
Payde upon my commissaries accompt for provisions of such things as appeareth by their accompt passed ............................................................................. £79 4s 0d

Early on there appears in the accounts an item for 'brewing vessels for the brewing of beare' and we know too, from the same source that bakers and butchers worked in the Close. Out of these items there emerges a picture of an almost self-contained community, with beer being brewed, bread baked and meat prepared, as well as the work of making munitions of war.

There was work, too, for carpenters. When the defences had been put in a state of readiness and stables built for the horses, the whole area of the Mill Crofts (the land lying between Stowe Pool and Gaia Lane) had to be fenced in so that it could provide summer pasture for the horses, all at a cost of £6 15s 0d. A payment of £58 was made 'to Mr. Green and Marmaduke Taylor for rente for safe pastures for grasse for my troope horses in the summer', and one of £25 'to Mr. Humphreys and Mr. Harvey for hay at first coming.' Later in the year £39 was spent, 'for mowing, haymaking and carriage.'

Eleven score and six load of wood from Mr. Hobler cost £8 17s 0d and the price of 'showing' (shoeing) the horses for six months came to £8 10s 0d. Oxen (used for drawing wagons) were also 'showed'.

Altogether, for the period from 22nd April to 29th December 1643, the grand total of expenditure on the garrison came to £8727 8s 6d.

---

* Hence the term 'cartridge paper'

How was this sum found?

In the first place each parish in the surrounding Hundred of Offlow had a levy made upon it through the constable of the parish, recorded as follows:

> Receaved out of the Hundred of Offlow in the County of Stafford for the use of Colonel Baggott for the maintenance of His Majesties garrison of Lichfielde and all the severall contributions since his coming the 22nd of Aprill, £384 17s 1d.
>
> Jeffery Glasier
> Hump. Baguley

Secondly, there were donations from Royalist sympathisers, often in the form of gold and silver which would go to be melted down at one of the Royal Mints that still operated at various cities in Royalist hands. An example of this in the accounts reads 'This accompt doth further acknowledge money received for plate of my Lady Blundell's the sum of £650 10s 0d.'

But the total receipts for the period were £1035 15s 5d, which fell far short of the expenditure — some £7600 in fact. Who paid? The answer would appear to be Richard Bagot. Attached to the accounts is a copy of a petition from him to King Charles. It reads:

> To the King's Most Excellent Majestie.
>
> The humble petition of Collonel Richard Bagot, Governor of Lichfield.
>
> Showeth
>
> That your petitioner hath now in the Garrison of Lichfield three hundred foote soldiers and two hundred horse wherewith he doth make good the place for your Majestie and secures your people of the neighbourhood from being spoiled by the rebells of Stafford and other garrisons thereabouts.
>
> That the contribution assigned to your petitioner* for the support of the said souldiers is so small that your petitioner is not able to pay or feed the said souldiers therewith of all that is alloted him did come in which cannot be expected by reason of the poverty of the people or that the souldiers would serve without pay which he cannot persuade them to do.
>
> That your petitioner hath issued over seven thousand four hundred pounds of his own and such other monies as he has gained from the enemy by the sword for the keeping alive and together the souldiers of the said garrison above and over all that he received in contributions for the said garrison which hath soe impoverished your petitioner that hee is not further able to support the said garrison in a condicion to advance your Majesties service in the protection of your people in these parts.
>
> May it therefore please your Majestie to recommend to your gratious Treasurer the care of the enlargement of your Petitioners quarters for his contribution to the Right Honourable Lord Loughborough, Collonel Generall under your sacred Majestie there soe as your Petitioner be not forced to be further troublesome to your Majestie in this behalf.
>
> And your Petitioner shall pray for your Majesties most happy reign over us.

The petition is undated, but the figures would appear to indicate the financial situation at the end of 1643, as shown in Glasier's summary of accounts. Indeed, it could well be that the summary was drawn up

---

*i.e. the rate product of the inhabitants of the Offlow Hundred.

especially to accompany the petition. It serves to show how poor the district around Lichfield was, and to what extent Richard Bagot was venturing his own fortune in the King's cause. Presumably the petition was successful, for the two Bagot regiments soldiered on until the end of the war.

Compared with the rural area surrounding it, the city of Lichfield would appear to have been one of those places which actually benefited financially from the war at this particular period. From the expenditure we have considered, of nearly £9,000, only a small part — the £900 for weapons — was spent outside the area. Otherwise the money went to landowners for grazing, forage, wood, etc., to local farmers for their produce, to Lichfield artisans for work of many kinds, and to local manufacturers of cloth, shoes and caps. By far the greatest item of expenditure was the pay of the troops, and most of this would find its way into the tills of local merchants, tradesmen and alehouse keepers. For the three years that Lichfield garrison was in existence it must have had a considerable and beneficial effect on the economy of the city, bringing in money which otherwise would not have been there.

\* \* \* \* \*

Colonel Bagot's garrison settled down to their work of maintaining the Royalist presence in Staffordshire and keeping open the lines of communication between north and south. The inhabitants of Lichfield soon became used to the sight of cavalry patrols riding through the streets and the sound of hooves ringing on the cobbles, the jingle of harness and the trumpet calls echoing between the houses as a troop set out on its journey.

The area they covered ranged from Stafford in the north to Tamworth in the south, westward to Rushall, near Walsall and east as far as Burton-on-Trent.

In the course of a patrol they might make contact with the enemy on the same task and a skirmish would ensue. It was in such a situation that Lieutenant Humphrey Slugard found himself near Cannock, when,

> He draws up his party and with all speed lets fly at the Parliamentary party in soe much that they had a sharpe skirmish with loss on both sides, in which dispute the said lieutenant was shot in the right arm, of which he died.[12]

It was probably in similar circumstances that the death occurred of Michael Dyott, recorded on a tablet in St. Mary's Church, Lichfield in the following words:

> Here lyeth the body of Michael Dyott, sixth son of Sir Richard Dyott, and a Cornet of Horse in the service of King Charles I, in which said service he received a shot, and dyed thereof, March 16, 1644.

But on Sir Richard Dyott's own memorial, erected close by, fifteen years later, Michael seems to have received posthumous promotion, being referred to as 'a Captain also in the said army, who died from a shot received in defence of this loyal garrison.'

Escorting convoys through the area would be another duty of the garrison, and early on in their existence they had the satisfaction of seeing one of their primary objectives achieved, when they guided through the district the army of Queen Henrietta and the convoy it accompanied. The Queen entered Staffordshire in July, attacking and capturing Burton-on-Trent on the 4th. On July 6th she was at Ashby-de-la-Zouch, and from there she moved via Croxall and Lichfield to Walsall and then on to Stratford-on-Avon where she arrived on July 11th, to be met by Prince Rupert.

Once again the people of Lichfield found themselves at the centre of national affairs, as they watched the Queen's army wind its way through their narrow streets; a vast number of people to their eyes. To the children it must have seemed like another Bower procession, on a scale hundreds of times greater. Instead of one knight on horseback there were 1,200 horse and dragoons; instead of two drummers there were two score and following them were not just eight musketeers but 2,000 of them. The place of the fourteen halberdiers was taken by 1,000 pikemen, and in the middle of all these cohorts was a convoy of six pieces of artillery, two mortars and 150 wagons of arms and stores.

It was to be many years before the Bower procession had a Bower Queen included in it, but on this occasion there **was** a queen — a real queen. Before their staring eyes the Queen of England rode past in her coach.

On one occasion Colonel Bagot, while himself out on patrol with his troop, captured the Governor of Tamworth Castle. This garrison, the nearest Parliamentary one to Lichfield, was commanded by Major Hunt, a former mercer of Coventry, who at the beginning of the war had been appointed by the Parliamentary Committee at Coventry to be Governor of Astley Castle near that city. From here he had been promoted to the Governorship of Tamworth.

On April 16th, 1644 he was taken prisoner with several of his officers and men and taken to Lichfield. As was usual, an exchange of prisoners between the two sides was made and Major Hunt soon regained his freedom. There is a well-known story of how, on his release, he wrote to Colonel Bagot in the following terms:

> Bagot, thou sonne of an Egyptian* hore, meete me half-way tomorrow morning, the half-way betwixt Tamworth and Litchfield if thou darest; if not I will whip thee when-soever I meete thee.
>
> Colonel Bagot met him and after a brisk action whipped the fellow himself into a brisk retreat and narrowly missed taking him.[13]

Generally it was Richard Bagot's Regiment of Horse which operated throughout the area, while Hervey Bagot's Foot Regiment carried out a

---

*i.e. Gypsy

static role in the Close. On at least one occasion however, a detachment of foot left Lichfield for an operation outside, as is shown by the following entries in the accounts.

> Payde to the soldiers that marched the 20th October, 3s 6d each.
> In Major Harsnetts company, 1 serjeant, 1 corporal, 18 soldiers.
> In Colonel Bagots company, 1 corporal and 4 soldiers.
> In Captain Dyotts company, 1 serjeant, 1 corporal and 14 soldiers.
> In Captain Glasiers company, 1 serjeant, 1 corporal, 6 soldiers.
> In Captain Swifts company, 1 serjeant, 2 corporals, 19 soldiers.
> In Captain Benskins company, 1 serjeant, 1 corporal, 1 drummer, 16 soldiers.
> To the waggoner and his two men ............................................................ 15 shillings.
> To the same soldiers as a largess or reward, when they returned, £3.

This detachment was probably that used in the autumn of 1645 for an attack on Burton-on-Trent, which by that time had reverted to Parliament. This attack was carried out on the orders of Lord Loughborough. The whole of Colonel Bagot's Horse, 200 in number, took part, together with the ninety men listed above.

After capturing Burton, they withdrew for the night to Lord Paget's manor house, where at four o'clock in the morning they were attacked by Parliamentary troops who had come to relieve the town. A brisk action ensued and the attackers were beaten off with heavy casualties. On the Royalist side Major 'Crab' Warner, an ensign and three troopers were killed. Colonel Bagot did not attempt to hold on to Burton but retired with his troops to Lichfield.

Jeffery Glasier refers in his accounts to payments made to men of Lichfield garrison who were prisoners at Nantwich, in Cheshire. Among these were Lieutenant Startin and Ensign Pyott, who must have been captured in one of the skirmishes in the north of the county. Such prisoners were taken to Nantwich because it was the headquarters of Colonel Sir William Brereton, Commander of the Parliamentary forces in Cheshire, and one of their strongholds. The large parish church of St. Mary's, in the centre of the town, was used as the prison, and only recently, while repair work was being carried out in the church, the remains of men, probably prisoners who had died, were found just below the floor of the nave.

Royalist prisoners captured in the south of Staffordshire, or in Warwickshire, were sent to Coventry.

In between the skirmishes and patrols there was the routine work of gathering in the money from the constables of the various parishes and chasing up the bad payers. Among these were John Heath of Weeford and his son, also John Heath, of Hammerwich. The following letters[14] give some idea of the kind of persuasion used by the Royalist garrison on these occasions.

Sir,
    The present occasion for money, for the making of such works as we have in hand, and other necessary charges for the defence of His Majestie's garrison, causeth us to desire you to lend us XX£ and pay it unto Mr. Glasier, at the Close, at Lichfield, upon Friday next, which, if youle be pleased to do, youle engage us to be your friends. We expect your answer speedily.

|  |  |
|---|---|
| Richard Bagot | Anthony Dyott |
| Hervey Bagot | William Gilton |
| Robert Harsnett | Zachary Turnpenny |

Lichfield,
November 28th, 1644.

The Heaths were Presbyterians, supporters of Parliament and notoriously bad payers. Probably as a result of this we find them the following year, being addressed by no less than Lord Loughborough himself.

Sir,
    Being intrusted by His Majestie with the command of the county and having advised with the gentlemen of His Majesties Commissioners; it is thereby consented that a present supply of moneys be raised whereby his majesties service may be most advanced, his loyal subjects secured, and be put in a faire way of obtaining a happy peace. Presuming therefore that, according to your ability you will not be wanting to soe goode a work, I have thought fit to desire you to advance the somme of fifty pounds for the said service and not to fail to bring or send the same by the ninth of September next to the Close at Lichfield to Henry Archbold, Esq. at his house there, who is the treasurer for the receipt thereof and will register the same, that it may, uppon occasion be represented to his majestie for best advantage by,
                        Your loving friend,
                          H. Loughborough

Lichfield,
30th August, 1645

Such examples of the iron hand in the velvet glove, with just a hint of a protection racket, paid off, but only just. Even when they did pay up the Heaths only paid by instalment, £20 appearing to be their limit, as the following document illustrates:

    Recieved of Mr. John Heath of Weeford, and Mr. John Heath of Hammerwich, his sonne, for his majesties service, the somme of XX£, I say, recieved the said somme per me.
Lichfield,
19th December 1645.                H. Loughborough[15]

While the Close was a military stronghold, inhabited by the King's garrison a number of civilians continued to reside there, while others came in to live, mainly for security. Among the former was William Unitt, who described himself as 'merchant, of the staple, the most ancient inhabitant of the Close of Lichfield'.[16] He appears to have carried on his business throughout the war, not without difficulty one imagines. No doubt there were others like him. Those who came into the Close were mainly members of the land owning aristocracy whose estates had been sequestrated, referred to by the Roundheads as 'grandees'. Sir Hervey Bagot was one, Sir Walter Aston of Bridgenorth another. Sir Richard

Dyott and his wife moved into the Close in August 1645; the reason he gave was that he did so in order to avoid the plague which had infected Lichfield at that time.

Usually Lichfield, unlike most mediaeval cities, was singularly free from plagues, since it had a source of pure piped water brought into the city from outside. On this occasion the plague appears to have been most prevalent in two inns near Sir Richard Dyott's house (probably the George and the Swan), which would suggest that the infection was brought in by travellers. Sir Richard lived close by, in Sadler (Market) Street and removed himself and his family into the Close, where they could not have been very welcome, the Close being free from plague.

Of the cathedral clergy, only two remained. Bishop Wright, who was one of the ten bishops imprisoned by Parliament in 1641, had retired to his castle at Eccleshall, near Stafford on the outbreak of war. Here he died in 1643 (of natural causes) while the castle was under siege by Sir William Brereton. It was some time before his body could be buried in Eccleshall Church.

His successor, Bishop Frewin, was consecrated at Oxford, but retired to Kent and never came near his see. The Dean, Griffith Higgs, also retired, in his case to Henley-on-Thames, the place of his birth, where he died. All the residentiary clergy were forcibly ejected by Colonel Russel when he occupied the Close after the first siege. They suffered various fates; the Treasurer, Thomas Lawrence, was befriended by Colonel Watson, a Parliamentarian who later was one of the judges at the trial of King Charles. Lawrence had shown some kindness to Colonel Watson when he was a prisoner of the Royalists at Oxford, and in return Watson installed him in a chapelry at Colne, in Huntingdonshire, where he died in obscurity. Another residentiary canon, George Jay, obtained leave from the Speaker of the House of Commons, Speaker Lenthall, to go to Spa for the purpose of his health. Having thus shaken the dust of England from his feet he remained abroad, dying soon after the restoration. His prebend was sequestrated from him, as were all the others.

Of the two clergy who returned to Lichfield after it had been recaptured by Prince Rupert, one, Zachary (Zacharias) Turnpenny, the Subchanter, took up the profession of arms and became Captain Turnpenny in Colonel Bagot's Regiment of Foot. He served throughout the war and after the Restoration he returned to the cathedral as Sacrist.

The other was the Precentor, William Higgins. He has already been mentioned as the person who saved the Lichfield Gospels and preserved them for posterity. When Colonel Russel ejected the clergy, Higgins, for some reason not known, was sent to Coventry where he was a prisoner for some weeks. On his release he returned to Lichfield and took up residence in the Close where he continued his ministry at the cathedral, maintaining the daily offices for the garrison and the few remaining civilians until the Close was finally surrendered to Parliament. Several times he nearly lost his life, once from the discharge of a drake, once from a ship-musket and again from a granado which exploded as he and his son were leaving the cathedral after reading morning prayers. But he continued to perform his duties, one of Lichfield's unsung heroes of the Civil War.

## SOURCE NOTES

*Chapter IV*

1.   Clarendon, History of the War, Vol. III, p.23
2.   Lichfield Cathedral Library, Ms 24
3.   A Continuation of Certain Special Remarkable Passages
     Informed to both Houses of Parliament. No. 38, 20th April 1643—27th April 1643
4.   Names and armes of the Officers of Horse within the Garrison of
     Lichfield Close, Wm. Salt Library, S.Ms 195/1
5.   Ibid
6.   Ibid
7.   Richard Symonds, Diary, p.172
8.   Staffs. Record Office, Q/SR, Special Sessions.
9.   Wm. Salt Library S.Ms
10.  Richard Symonds, Diary, p.172
11.  Wm. Salt Library, S.Ms 438
12.  Staffs. Record Office, 547
13.  Mercurius Aulicus, p.1347
14.  Harwood, History of Lichfield, p.47
15.  Ibid, p.48
16.  Shaw, History of Staffordshire, Vol. I, p.309

*Chapter V*

# King Charles in Lichfield

FOR two years the garrison of Lichfield Close, under the command of Richard Bagot, maintained effectively the Royalist cause in South Staffordshire. During that time the security of the city was assured and it enjoyed a prosperity which did much to alleviate the effects of the war; the hardships and miseries were still to come. So when Prince Rupert re-visited Lichfield in March 1644, on his way to relieve the town of Newark, they rang the bells of St. Mary's Church for him, and they rang them again on his return when his mission had been accomplished in the face of considerable odds. For these two peals the churchwardens paid the ringers one shilling and eightpence; a short time afterwards they gave them two shillings to ring in commemoration of King Charles's coronation, and a similar sum to ring 'when the Earl of Essex retreated to London'.[1] At the beginning of July they rang 'for the first news from York', referring, presumably, to the news that Rupert had raised the siege of that city, and a few days before hearing of his defeat at Marston Moor.

Marston Moor marked the beginning of a decline in the Royalist fortunes of war. It had always been Charles's strategy to march on London and take the capital, but as the war progressed his chances of doing so grew less and less. After Royalist successes in the summer of 1643, the indecisive Battle of Newbury allowed Essex and the Parliamentary army to slip away and so prevented the Royalists from moving on London.

At the same time John Pym was concluding the Solemn League and Covenant with the Scots, which brought the Scottish army of 21,000 men into the war on the side of Parliament. In return for this, Parliament had to agree to pay the Scottish army and also to introduce Presbyterianism into England as the established religion.

A joint body, the Committee of Both Kingdoms, with 14 English and 4 Scots members, was set up to take over the direction of the war. It met at Derby House, Cannon Row, in London.

The success of Parliament at Marston Moor was due in no small part to the work of Lieutenant General Oliver Cromwell, whose reputation as a cavalry commander was made on this field. From then on he occupied an increasingly important role in the direction of the war. In November 1644 he persuaded Parliament to introduce the 'Self-Denying Ordinance' which called on all members of Parliament (including members of the House of Lords) who held commissions in the army to resign them. He himself was conveniently excluded from this arrangement, but is enabled him to dispose of the Earl of Essex, his deputy the Earl of Manchester and all other of their Lordships who held commissions. Having done this, Cromwell then got Parliament to agree to the formation of a 'New Model Army' to consist of 22,000 men, trained in his own rigorous methods of discipline and commanded by his own nominee, Sir Thomas Fairfax.

On May 7th 1645 the Royalist army moved out of its winter quarters at Oxford with Charles at its head and Prince Rupert and Prince Maurice in attendance. They set out via Evesham, Droitwich and Wolverhampton and moved into Shropshire. At that time the King had only 5,000 men,[2] and he sent urgent orders to Lord Goring, his general commanding the army in the West Country, to join him. Goring never came, and Charles was forced to swell his numbers by 'drawing in' troops from the Royalist garrisons in the Midlands.

Early in May 1645, the Lichfield garrison received orders to join the King, and on the morning of May 15th the citizens of Lichfield lined the streets to see Colonel Bagot's men go to war. It must have been a brave sight as they passed through the city: first a troop of horse, 100 strong, with Richard Bagot at its head and his cornet flying behind him, followed by the foot marching to beat of drum.

Leading the foot was Lieut. Colonel Hervey Bagot, behind him his colour of plain azure blue with the St. George's Cross in the Canton, carried by Ensign Sharpe, followed by the Lieutenant Colonel's Company, in charge of Lieutenant Ward. Next came Captain Anthony Dyott with his company, including Lieutenant Baguley and Ensign Blenkcowe carrying the colour having one gold mullet.

In the centre were the baggage waggons containing all the force's *impedimenta* and then two more companies of foot — Captain Thomas Glasier, Lieutenant Johnston and Ensign Emmins with their colour showing three mullets and finally the company of Captain Ralph Swift, with Lieutenant Cowper and Ensign Thomas, whose colour bore four mullets.

The rear of the column was brought up by the second troop of horse, but we do not know the name of the officer commanding it.

They left the city they had defended for the last two years, protected now by Major Harsnett with 100 horse and 200 foot. The column marched along Sandford Street, up Pipe Hill, and at the Watling Street they turned right and headed west, following in the footsteps of the Roman legions. On May 16th they made contact with the King's army at Newport, Shropshire, providing a welcome reinforcement.

The army marched east, through Uttoxeter, Tutbury and Ashby-de-la-Zouch. On May 30th they took Leicester, and June 11th found them at Daventry where they met the advance guard of the Parliamentary forces commanded by Sir Thomas Fairfax. There was a skirmish and the King's army moved away towards Market Harborough, with Fairfax following them.

The two armies met near the village of Naseby, and on the morning of June 14th faced each other across a narrow valley. The Royalists had some 8,000 men and the Parliamentarians about 14,000.

The result was a disaster for the King's army. Rupert, with his usual impetuosity, made a charge against the enemy left flank and drove them from the field. While he was so engaged, Cromwell, on the other flank, led his cavalry against the remainder of the Royalist army and annihilated them. The infantry were killed or taken prisoner and the King, with what was left of the cavalry, fled from the battlefield and sought refuge in Ashby for the night.

Some 900 Royalists were killed and half the army taken prisoner. The Royal Standard was captured and every infantry colour taken. It was a complete victory for the Parliamentary army and marked an end to King Charles's hopes for re-establishing himself as the ruler of the country.

Bagot's Foot were in the Royalist centre, where the heaviest fighting took place. Colonel Hervey Bagot managed to escape back to Lichfield: so too did Captain Swift. All the other officers were taken prisoner. Remarkably, none were killed. The fate of the other ranks is not clear, but we know that at least one man got back to Lichfield, so perhaps others did too.

All four colours were lost. Soon after the battle Jonathan Turmile painted watercolour reproductions of some of the captured Royalist standards, and the four from Bagot's Foot were amongst these. Today the volume containing them can be seen in Dr. Williams' Library in London, a moving relic of a bloody encounter. Turmile painted them exactly as he saw them, and that of Captain Swift's Company is ripped from top to bottom as if it had been contended for furiously.

Bagot's Horse remained together as a unit after the battle, accompanying the King to Ashby and later to Lichfield. They lived to fight another day, but their valiant young commander, Richard Bagot, was wounded in the engagement. He received a bullet in his right arm, and as with Humphrey Slugard and Michael Dyott, it was to prove fatal. The heavy bullets of those days caused a gaping wound and a compound fracture, and casualties rarely recovered.

On the following day the King, with what was left of his army, moved to Lichfield where he spent the night at the former Bishop's palace in the Close. Bagot's Horse returned to their quarters and the rest of the cavalry were dispersed in the villages around Lichfield.

The news of Naseby had gone before, and this time there was no ringing of church bells. Relatives of those who had been in the action waited anxiously for news of them, and the crowds who turned out in the streets to see the King arrive were subdued.

Shortly before his arrival a small procession could be seen setting out from the ancient Guildhall in Bore Street. At its head walked the Bellman and the two Serjeants-at-Mace, carrying the silver maces granted to the city by King Edward VI. After them came the Senior Bailiff, William Bennett, and his Junior Bailiff, Talbot Edwards, wearing their scarlet gowns and followed by the Sheriff of Lichfield, John Bayley, in his robe of dark blue. They walked up Greenhill, past St. Michael's Church and out onto the Burton Road. At the city boundary they waited to meet King Charles, and the Senior Bailiff presented their loyal address.[3]

> Most Gracious Sovereign,
>
> Though the sad report of the late ill success hath so oppressed our souls with grief, that we are rendered more apt to express our loyal affections in tears than words, yet the safety and presence of your sacred person (as dear to us as our lives) hath so much revived and restored us, that we have taken the boldness, though suddenly and rudely, in a few words, to present to you the most zealous affections and loyal services that a most obliged and grateful people can possibly bear to a most gracious Sovereign.
>
> And as we are not so stupid as not to be sensible of God's corrections, where he is pleased so sharply to punish us for our sins, so we are not so unchristianlike as to despair of God's final blessing upon a most just and righteous cause, nor so unmanly as to lay down our courage and confidence for one cross event, as knowing that man's necessity is God's opportunity, and that God's power is most glorified in man's weakness.
>
> And albeit the sun may be for a time eclipsed, even by that planet which itself enlightened, and for a time be obscured even by those clouds which itself drew from the earth into an higher region, yet the light and virtue of the sun is not thereby made less though less conspicious: eclipses and clouds last not always. *Mendacia diu non fallunt*; men will not always be wicked in this sin of rebellion. Truth at last prevails: right never dieth, but will shortly, by God's blessing, (all clouds being dispelled) restore the sun of this our firmament to his former splendour and glory, and therein his faithful subjects to their former peace, plenty, and happiness which is our daily prayer, and shall be our incessant endeavour to the utmost expense of our estates and blood. *Nec plus obire possumus, nec fas est minus*. More we cannot undergo, less we may not.

And having thus delivered themselves of the rather florid sentiments which protocol and the occasion demanded, the Bailiffs ended their address with the following stirring words:

> Sir, your most humble and loyal subjects, the Bailiffs, Sheriff and their maces, etc., citizens of this your city of Lichfield, do humbly, according to their duty, surrender into your Majesty's hands these ensigns of their authority, which they are resolved to bear from you and under you, or not at all; and whether they live or die, to live and die your Majesty's most faithful and loyal subjects.

The King received this address very graciously and required Sir Richard Dyott, who was present, to return his thanks to the Bailiffs for their loyalty. The civic party then kissed hands with His Majesty and waited upon him to his quarters. The following day the King left Lichfield and proceeded to Wolverhampton.

In his quarters in the Close, Richard Bagot lay sick from his wound, looked after by his chirurgeons, Richard Thornton and Humphrey Spooner. In spite of all their efforts his health declined and on July 7th he died. He was just 27 years of age.

He had made his will earlier in the year, on May 16th. After making a number of legacies, he concluded the document with these words:

> That small estate I have is now settled and I have fitted myselfe for Deathe; and the more I think of it, the more I strive to embrace it; Especially when I think howe much my friends will be comforted with my death, that [they] may say one of their fleshe and bloode is sacrificed in doinge faithfulle service for his anoynted Sovereign whom God preserve and defend from all his enemies — my desire is wheresoever I am slayne I may be buried in the Cathedral Churche of Litchfield.[4]

Two days later he was buried in the south choir aisle of the war-shattered cathedral where a monument was erected to his memory. It reads:[5]

Juxta hic situs est
Ricardus Bagot
fil. natu min. Harvei Bagot, Barti.
flagrante nuperima fanaticorum conjuratione
hujus munitione praefectus;
qui in fatale isto Navesbiensi praelio
fortissime dimicans lethaliter vulneratus,
caelebs occabuit die m. Julii 7mo
Ao. Dom. MDCLV

[Near this place lies the body of Richard Bagot, youngest-born son of Harvey Bagot, Bart., a victim of the recent conspiracy of fanatics; Governor of this fortress, who in the fateful struggle in yonder Naseby, while fighting most bravely, was fatally wounded. He died unmarried the 7th July, 1645].

His place as Governor was taken by his brother, Hervey Bagot, who immediately set about the task of rebuilding his foot regiment. This he did with such success that by the end of 1645 all his former officers except Captain Dyott and Lieutenant Ward were back on duty, having either escaped from their captors or been exchanged. The exchange of Captain Dyott was still being negotiated, while Lieutenant Ward had probably been badly wounded and was unfit for further duty.[6] Recruiting had also made good the losses of Naseby and the strength of the regiment was up to 500 without including the citizens' company.

At the same time he set about strengthening the defences of the Close in preparation for possible attack. To this end an earthwork was thrown up against the inside of the old mediaeval walls, the earth probably being brought in from outside, for the accounts of the Constable of Mavesyn Ridware for the period contain this entry:

> June 30th, July 1st, July 2nd. Twelve teams [of horses] and 13 workmen to the raising of the bulwarks at Lichfield, £2 17s 8d.[7]

King Charles was present again in Lichfield on August 10th and 11th, on his way to Newark. His visit gave him the opportunity to express his strong feelings on the subject of the behaviour of Lord Loughborough.

Henry Hastings, Lord Loughborough, once the darling of the Cavaliers and the epitome of a fighting Royalist, had lately fallen into disfavour with Charles. Just before the Battle of Naseby he had been appointed Governor of Leicester, following its capture by the Royalist forces. A few days later came the battle and the defeat of Charles. Lord Loughborugh, when summonsed by Fairfax, had handed over Leicester on the best terms he could obtain. It was a logical decision, for the city had little in the way of defences and his garrison was small. But Charles viewed it as an act of treachery, and would have had Loughborough court martialled had circumstances permitted.

In view of this it is hardly surprising that later on in the year, when Lord Loughborough appeared before the gates of Lichfield Close, those gates were closed against him and he was refused entry. After the ensuing altercation he and his party of horse had to turn away and make for Ashby-de-la-Zouch instead.

In a civil war spies are everywhere, and it did not take long for news of this little episode to reach the ears of the Committee of Both Kingdoms, sitting in the stately splendour of Derby House* at Cannon Row, in the City of London. The following letter issued forth:

> 12th January, 1646. Committee of Both Kingdoms to Sir Richard Skeffington and Colonel Willoughby.
>
> We are informed that there is some difference lately grown at Lichfield between Lord Loughborough, Sir Richard Dyer [Dyott], and Lieut. Colonel Bagot, and that Lord Loughborough was beaten out thence and is returned to Ashby; of which difference we conceive some good use might be made by application to the party discontented. We desire you to inform yourself of the cause of that difference, and on which part the discontent is. We wish you accordingly to make trial whether, upon this occasion, one of these garrisons might not be gained for the Parliament. Certify us of what you shall understand and how you proceed therein. Sent by Craven.[8]

Sir Richard Skeffington, to whom this letter was sent, was Governor of Coventry. On January 22nd the Committee of Both Kingdoms sent a letter, in similar vein, to Colonel Bridges, Governor of Warwick. It concluded with these words:

> If you find Lieut. Colonel Bagot will deliver up that place [Lichfield] to the Parliament you may promise him that we will do our best to procure his father's reconciliation with the Parliament, as also a reward for himself not exceeding £2,000.[9]

On the same day, after the above letter had been dispatched, it was followed by another one to Colonel Bridges:

---

*Before the war, home of the College of Heralds

We wrote to you this day concerning Lichfield. We have since had conference with
this bearer, Mr. Bagot, and conceive him to be a very fit instrument to be employed
in that business and therefore recommend him to your service. You may communicate to him the instructions in your letter and let him make a trial of Lieut. Colonel
Bagot, whether he will deliver up the place or not. Sent by Mr. Bagot.[10]

One must asasume from this correspondence that attempts from the
Governor of Leicester to persuade Lord Loughborough to surrender
Ashby had met with no success, and so efforts were now concentrated on
trying to get Colonel Bagot to yield up Lichfield. In this attempt the
Committee of Both Kingdoms were fortunate in having the help of a
member of the Bagot family. The 'Mr. Bagot' referred to in the last letter
was a distant relative of Lord Bagot, living at Shrewsbury.

Unfortunately for him, and fortunately for the Royalists, his instructions from the Committee of Both Kingdoms came just too late. In the
middle of January Lichfield Close had received a visit from Sir Jacob
Astley, Serjeant-Major-General of the Royalist foot. At that time he was
trying to get together a force to raise the siege of Chester, and he wrote
two letters on this subject from Lichfield, one to the Duke of Ormonde
and the other to the Archbishop of York. Both were dated January 12th,
1646.

It can hardly have been a coincidence that immediately after Sir Jacob's
visit, the governorship of Lichfield Close changed, Colonel Bagot giving
way to Major General Sir Thomas Tyldesley, to whom he became Deputy
Governor.

Tyldesley (1592-1651) was a member of a well-known and influential
Roman Catholic family of Leigh, in Lancashire. The family motto was *Pro
Regia et Patria tantum valet amor* (Love of King and Country is worth so
much), a motto which Thomas Tyldesley certainly lived up to. He had
served as a professional soldier in the Spanish army in the Low Countries,
and when the war broke out in England he quickly raised regiments of
horse, foot and dragoons from his part of Lancashire to serve the King.
He was present at Edgehill and with his regiments took part in the convoy-
ing of Queen Henrietta's force from Bridlington to Oxford. During the
storming of Burton-on-Trent he led his cavalry in a charge across the long
36-arch bridge over the River Trent, an action for which he received the
honour of knighthood.[11]

In November 1644 he was taken prisoner at the capture of Liverpool by
the Parliamentary forces and remained captive for the next twelve
months. At the end of this time he was moved to Stafford, from where he
managed to escape, making his way to Lichfield. He joined the garrison
under Colonel Bagot and took part in garrison duties.

During one of these occasions, on January 7th, he was leading a cavalry
patrol on Cannock Chase when they encountered a body of Parliamentary troops from Stafford garrison, led by the Governor, Captain Stone.

In the ensuing skirmish Sir Thomas Tyldesley was unhorsed and only escaped re-capture by hiding. Captain Stone returned to Stafford with several prisoners and Sir Thomas Tyldesley's hat, cloak and horse.[12]

Although at the age of 53, Tyldesley might have been considered too old for command in the field, he was cast in the same mould as his predecessor, Richard Bagot — a professional soldier, experienced in war, able to communicate the military disciplines to those under his command, and an unwavering adherent to the Royalist cause. There was no possibility of a bargain with the Committee of Both Kingdoms under his governorship. Whatever lay ahead, Lichfield Close would not be yielded up lightly.

The Committee of Both Kingdoms gave up any idea of a negotiated settlement and made preparations for the capture by force of Lichfield and the other Staffordshire garrisons. The person whom they chose to carry out this task was Major General Sir William Brereton, who as Colonel had been involved, three years ago, in the first siege of Lichfield.

---

## SOURCE NOTES

*Chapter V*

1.  St. Mary's Church, Lichfield, Churchwardens' Accounts. Joint Record Office, Lichfield.
2.  Warburton, Memoirs of Prince Rupert, Vol. III, p.104
3.  Harwood, History of Lichfield, p.28
4.  Bagot, Lady Nancy, Family Archives
5.  Harwood, History of Lichfield, p.103
6.  Young, Brigadier Peter, Naseby 1645, p.88 (But see Ch.VII, Note 9, for another possible explanation)
7.  Hewitt, John, Lichfield in the Civil War, 1856
8.  Calendar of State Papers, Domestic Series, Charles I, Vol. 21
9.  Ibid
10. Ibid
11. Reid, Stuart, The Finest Knight in England, 1979
12. Ibid

*Chapter VI*

# The Great Siege
## March—July 1646

O F THE three sieges, this is the one which has received the least attention from historians, perhaps because it had little strategic significance. By the time it began it was obvious that the King's cause was lost and that Parliament had power over most of the country. All that was required, from a military point of view, was the mopping up of the remaining Royalist garrisons which still held out, and of which Lichfield was one.

But as far as the citizens of Lichfield were concerned, the impact on their lives of the third siege transcended by far that of the other two. Whereas these had been over in a few days, the final struggle for the possession of Lichfield Close went on for four months, completely disorganising the life of the city and drawing into the conflict many of the citizens. As a result of it, many parts of Lichfield changed and many familiar landmarks disappeared, and all this took place at a time when the city was suffering the worst plague in its history. Truly, 1646 was a black year for the loyal and ancient city.

The plague had arrived in July 1645, shortly after the shock of the news of the Royalist defeat at Naseby (seekers for portents had not very far to look). Beginning at the two principal inns of the city, it spread rapidly and by August had caused sufficient alarm for Sir Richard Dyott and his family to seek refuge in the Close. Others, no doubt, took themselves off into the country.

William Bennet and Talbot Edwards, the two Bailiffs, ordered the High Constables of the city to keep an account of every house and every person visited with the pestilence, so that provisions brought in from the country could be carefully distributed to those in need. From these returns[1] we learn that 821 persons died of the disease (probably bubonic plague). The population of Lichfield at that time was around 3,000, so well over a quarter of the inhabitants died. Comparing this with the Great

Plague of London, twenty years later, in which one inhabitant in seven died, we can appreciate the severity of the Lichfield epidemic. In the main it was confined to the city; the garrison in the Close remained, with one or two exceptions, free from infection.

At the beginning of March 1646, while the plague was still rife, Lichfield found itself once again embroiled in warfare when a Parliamentary force under the command of Sir William Brereton arrived to conduct the mopping up of Lichfield Close.

A native of Cheshire, where he took his name from the village of Brereton, Sir William owned considerable property in that county and represented it in Parliament before the war. He was created a Baronet by Charles I in 1629, when he was 22 years of age. As with Lord Brooke, his strong feeling against the crown was mainly a religious one, for he had had a Puritan upbringing, reinforced by his first marriage to a wife of similar strongly-held views. When she died he married a second time, in 1641, to Cicely, widow of Edward Mitton of Weston-under-Lizard, thus aquiring property in Staffordshire.

On the outbreak of war he supported the cause of Parliament and was commissioned as colonel with command of all Parliamentary forces in Cheshire. The county was at that time almost entirely Royalist, but in January 1643 he attacked and captured the town of Nantwich, where he set up his headquarters and maintained them for the rest of the war, together with a Parliamentary County Committee.

As we know, in the spring of 1643 he moved into Staffordshire and was present with his Cheshire troops at Hopton Heath, shortly afterwards capturing the town of Stafford and Eccleshall Castle, the home of the Bishops of Lichfield. This latter operation must have afforded much satisfaction to Sir William's anti-episcopal feelings. He regarded Eccleshall almost as his private castle and installed there as Governor one of his right-hand men, Captain Stone, a Walsall merchant.

Another of his right-hand men was his Serjeant-Major, James Louthian. Here it should be mentioned that the rank of Serjeant-Major in seventeenth century military usage had a different significance from that of today, corresponding instead to the appointment of adjutant — a commanding officer's administrator.

Administration was the field in which Sir William Brereton excelled. He was a competent, but not outstanding military commander. He lacked the dash and spirit of a Bagot or a Tyldesley, nor had he the tactical genius of Cromwell or of Fairfax. He never took part in any of the great battles of the war, but as the governor of a military district he did well. He was a methodical man, a fact for which historians must be grateful. Throughout the war he kept a letter book, consisting of several leather-bound volumes, much as a businessman of his time would keep a record of his business.

As with a business, he entered copies of all the letters he sent out, and all those he received. But unlike a business, there was a third category — letters intercepted, giving an interesting insight into what the enemy was thinking. Add to these copies of his orders, and transcripts of the interrogations of prisoners taken, and the whole gives a vivid picture of the campaign. One of these volumes, covering a large part of the third siege of Lichfield, has survived and it is on this source that most of this chapter is based.

On April 4th, 1645, the Self-Denying Ordinance came into effect, preventing Members of Parliament from holding commissions in the Parliamentary army. Sir William Brereton dutifully hung up his sword and resumed his legislative duties, but the following year Parliament decided that they had need of him once more in a military capacity. On the 22nd of January 1646 the following instruction[2] was published:

> Ordered by the Lords and Commons in Parliament assembled that Sir William Brereton be continued in the place of Commander of all the forces before Chester for 40 days with the like powers and in the same manner as he was formerly appointed and that his service in the House of Commons in the meantime be dispensed withal.

The forces referred to were those of Staffordshire, Shropshire, Worcestershire, Warwickshire, Derbyshire and North Wales, and as their commander Sir William Brereton had been promoted to the rank of Major-General. He took down his sword and recalled his right-hand men. Serjeant-Major James Louthian was promoted to be Adjutant-General and took charge of Sir William's staff, which included Captain Stone, released from his duties as Governor of Stafford.

The tasks give to Sir William were threefold. First, he was to capture Chester, thus denying the Royalists their last remaining port; then he was to follow and destroy the army which Sir Jacob Astley was trying to re-group. When both of these were accomplished he was to set about reducing the strongholds of Lichfield Close, Tutbury Castle, Dudley Castle and Hartlebury Castle, Worcester.

His first two tasks he accomplished with commendable speed. Chester fell on February 3rd, and on March 21st he defeated Sir Jacob Astley's force at Stowe-on-the-Wold. On March 23rd the Committee of Both Kingdoms was able to write to congratulate him and add 'there is now no force in the field to disquiet or interrupt your design against Lichfield.'[3]

At Lichfield his force consisted of Staffordshire troops (from Stafford and Tamworth) and contingents from Gloucestershire, Shropshire and Cheshire. These last were Sir William's own men from Nantwich.

From the beginning he had trouble over the matter of pay, for none of the county committees was willing to pay its own troops when they served outside the county boundaries. That, they considered, was a matter for the committee of the county in which they were serving. So at Lichfield, while the Staffordshire men were paid, those from Gloucestershire and Shropshire were not. As for the Cheshire men, they just dug in their heels and refused to march from Nantwich without back pay which was owed to them.

It was these same Cheshire troops who, the previous year, had mutinied over lack of pay. In Nantwich there was a branch of the Sequestration Office, responsible for administering the sequestration of estates in Cheshire and collecting the resulting monies. The civil servants working in this office were seized by the rude soldiery and imprisoned in St. Mary's Church where, to their horror, they had to mix with 'cavaliers, horse thieves and common felons'. They were offered their freedom in return for the soldiers' arrears of pay, and eventually order was restored.

Now the Cheshire troops were demanding money once again. There were 656 of them, in ten companies, one of which, commanded by a Captain Clegg, appears to have been the most contumacious, for they were the last to leave for Lichfield. At the end of March General Brereton had written to the Cheshire Committee about Captain Clegg and his men, and at the beginning of April received the following reply:[4]

Sir,

Wee have used our utmost endeavour concerning the March of Captain Cleggs companie (and soe hath he likewise). We have borrowed for the souldiers one months pay but cannot pay them any more, neither will they march until they have the one months pay promised upon the surrender of the cittie [Chester]. Wee are therefore necessitated to desire you to take course there [i.e. at Lichfield] for the satisfying of the engagement according to your promises, so that you may have them ready to be commanded and obey your orders, which otherwise thay will not (for anything wee are able to doe at present) and soe leaving it to your consideracion wee humbly take leave and remaine,

Ready to be commanded by you to our power,

| | |
|---|---|
| Henry Brooke | Roger Willbrooke |
| Thos. Stanley | John Bryen |
| Phil. Mainwaring | Jo. Wetenhall |
| Ed. Hyde | James Garfylde |

Chester,
4th April, 1646

It would appear from this letter that Sir William Brereton had rather rashly entered into some sort of agreement with the Cheshire Committee to try and obtain money from Parliament for the payment of the Cheshire troops, should the county be unable to pay them. They were now taking him up on his promise.

Sir William had two particular friends in Parliament, Mr. Ashurst and Mr. Swinfen*. He now wrote to them,[5] soliciting their help and enclosing the letter of the 'Cheshire Gentlemen'.

---

*John Swinfen was M.P. for Tamworth throughout the Long Parliament.

*Personal Standard of Robert, Lord Brooke*

*Cornet of Colonel Bagot's*
*Regiment of Horse*

"Three blue cornetts without any
manner of badge, motto or distinction"
*(Richard Symonds, Diary)*

*Colour, 1st Company (Capt. Dyott)*
*Bagot's Regiment of Foot*

"Azure, a mullet or, on a canton a cross"
*(Richard Symonds, Diary)*

*(Captured at the Battle of Naseby)*

*Colour, 3rd Company (Capt. Glasier)*
*Bagot's Regiment of Foot*
*(Captured at the Battle of Naseby)*

*Colour, 4th Company (Capt. Swift)*
*Bagot's Regiment of Foot*
*(Captured at the Battle of Naseby)*

DEUS NOBISCUM

*Personal Standard of Sir William Brereton*

Sirs,

The inclosed will imparte to you what the soldiers here may expect out of Cheshire. And impossible it is to obtaine soldiers to continue upon service without money. Those that came first are, not without cause, impatient as may appear from their petition. Captain Cleggs and Captain Walleys men are in Cheshire, but will not march without money. Had I not, for the Parliaments advantage, husbanded the last money sent downe, as well as to draw on and encourage the soldiers for the service as to discharge part of the engagement of the Cheshire Gentlemen, there had been no siege maintained here. I am sending to Coventrie upon my own Credit to take upp some money upon Bond.

Such I cannot doubt but the Parliament will consider, for you know well there was £6,000 ordered for this service and the Enemys strength and obstinaciousnes in the Close (wherein are acknowledged to bee more than 1,000 feighting men enlisted) requires a suitable strength to be applied to reduce them. This £6,000 is otherwise disposed of, but I cannot doubte that the Parliament will be wanting to make necessarie supplys for us, who I hope may without ostentacion and offense affirme that what they have allowed my forces from the beginning of this warre to the end hath not exceeded (nay, I believe not equalled) the chardge of the Train of Artillerie whereof also wee have not been unproved nor unserviceable and unsuccessful (through Gods Blessing) in the use thereof; as also the chardge of Newarke hath also doubled the chardge of Chester; and yet unreduced, and Banburye hath (the tyme considered) cost you much more than double what Lichfield hath, and yett I believe thay are much stronger in Lichfield than in Banburye. These thing considered I cannot doubt but that wee shall be provided for, and the Horse that were with me at Stowe Battell* may share proportionately with the rest, otherwise seeing they performed as good if not better service as the rest. Differenceing and Laying them aside may be imputed rather to their misfortune in beeing under my command than to their undeserving, which I am not willing to believe, and have therefore ordered Mr. Worral to take care of and convoy downe what is appointed them. I have appointed him to observe your orders and desire your Assistance whereby you shall much engage.

Your most faithful friend to serve you,

Will Brereton

Lichfield
11th Aprill, 1646

While Sir William was thus trying to advance the claims of his forgotten army, the Staffordshire and Gloucestershire troops had moved into the area and taken up positions in and around the city, General Brereton setting up his headquarters at Beacon Hill, a high point about 400 yards to the north of the cathedral.

The reply[6] to General Brereton's letter came a week after he wrote.

April 16th, 1646.

John Swinfen to Sir William Brereton.

I have lately written to you by two several messengers. This bearer brings you a letter from the Committee of Both Nations to inform you that £3,000 is assigned for the support of the leaguer and because it may only be paid where it is most necessary either to provisions or to forces not provided for, and not upon a general dividend to all, which way it would be little serviceable to any. The direction of the payment is 'for forces not otherwise provided for' as you will understand by the letter of the

---

*The fight with Sir Jacob Astley at Stow-on-the-Wold on March 21st.

committee. My desire now is, if you send directions to Worral, who is now in town, to continue here to attend the borrowing of the money for the present, and the returning thereof to you as it can be gotten. If you please to order your forces according to my advice in my former letters, so that this money may supply the greatest exigencies, I hope we may by the strength thereof continue until the work be ended, or if it prove very long our good account of the provident spending of this will procure us more. I send enclosed a copy of the order I have promised for 60 barrels of gunpowder with match proportionate, which you will have in a fortnight, meanwhile I hope Coventry will supply your wants.

In due course Sir William got his £3,000, brought from London by Mr. Worral. With him came one Richard Stelfox, agent for the Parliament, who kept a strict account of how the money was spent. His record of the transactions, under the title of 'The Lichfield Accounts'[7] can be seen today in the Public Record Office. From it we learn that most of the money went on pay for officers and men, the names of the recipients being given down to the rank of drummer. This gives valuable information about General Brereton's staff. Under the heading 'Fireworkers, Petarders and Engineers' appear the names of Captain Coldhurst, Bartholomew Kelcher (also spelt Celsher), Captain Millington and Captain Buchanan (Eng.). Captain Coldhurst was in charge of the mortars, for in one of Brereton's reports he refers to him 'playing his mortar pieces with singular judgement'. Bartholomew Kelcher was probably a Dutchman; both sides employed specialist officers from Holland.

Other staff appointments were Lieut. Colonel Robert Hunt, Muster-Master; Mr. Gelson the Quartermaster and John Fox, the gunner, of whom we shall hear more later.

The accounts also tell us that £50 10s (a fairly considerable sum) was disbursed under the heading of 'Intelligence', in other words payments to spies. Both sides employed these freely.

Lastly, on a more personal note, there is an entry, 'Payde Lieutenant Turner, who lost his sword in service against the enemy leading in to possess the enemys works before the Close, towards buying a new sword, £1 0s 0d.' Lieutenant Turner served in Captain Gimbert's Company of the Cheshire Regiment of Foot. One is left wondering how he came to lose his sword.

*     *     *     *     *

The first of Sir William Brereton's troops entered Lichfield on March 9th. They captured the town with the loss of three killed and several wounded.

In the usual pattern of tactics, Sir Thomas Tyldesley had withdrawn his troops inside the Close fortifications. For the first time in three years Lichfield people found themselves living under the occupation of Parliamentary troops, who billeted themselves in the house of the the citizens and collected the supplies, both in money and in kind, which hitherto had gone to the Royalists.

*Major-General Sir Thomas Tyldesley*

(William Salt Library)

Inside the Close preparations had been made to withstand a long siege. Stocks of food and ammunition had been built up, the fortifications strengthened by earthworks and gun positions created by building platforms inside the steeple of the centre tower. From here the Royalists had an excellent observation post from which they could follow enemy movements all around them, as well as fire positions for small arms from which they could harry and annoy the attackers.

Like many other Royalist strongholds all over the country, Lichfield had become isolated from the King and his cause, unaware of what was happening elsewhere and thrown entirely on its own resources.

Sir William Brereton, appreciating this situation, decided not to attempt to take the Close by storm. Time was on his side; there was no possibility of a relieving force coming to the Royalists' help and at this stage in the war his men were not over-anxious to risk their lives in an assault.

So he decided to surround the Close, cut it off from supplies and wait for General Tyldesley to surrender. He doubted he would have long to wait.

With this end in view he set his troops to work under the guidance of Captain Buchanan to surround the Close with earthwork fortifications, designed both to keep the Royalists in and also to defend his own troops from attack. These consisted of a trench running from Stowe Pool to Beacon Street, and from Beacon Street to the Bishop's Fish Pool, a stretch of water west of Minster Pool.

No details of the size of this trench are recorded, but a similar trench constructed around Bristol was four feet deep and six feet wide. The earthwork behind it was five feet high and three feet thick, and the side facing the enemy had a wooden frieze of sharpened stakes to deter cavalry. The works at Lichfield were probably similar to these, and had at each end a "mount", a raised defensive position which could contain cannon and act as a small fort. In addition, a third mount, just north of the Close, was adapted to the same use and named "Gloucester Mount", being manned by the troops from Gloucestershire. The Staffordshire troops were responsible for the other two mounts, but these do not seem to have been given names.

General Tyldesley was not the man to let this sort of project go on unhindered. Soon after work had commenced he mounted an attack on the Parliamentary forces on the west side of the Close, sending out a strong force through the West Gate to attack the Staffordshire troops engaged in the construction of the trench. A reference to this operation is contained in the register of St. Editha's Church, Tamworth,[8] which contains the entry, dated March 21st, which reads, 'Buried the body of Richard Waughton of Cumberford [Comberford]; he was slayne by the enemy at Lichfield in fighting in the worke.'

It was probably on this occasion that the Royalist troops burnt down a number of houses in Beacon Street. One of the principal streets in the town, it ran right past the West Gate and west wall of the Close. The houses in it would have provided excellent cover for anyone attacking the Close on that side. Most of them being of timber-framed structure with thatched roofs, it would not have been too difficult, after clearing out the occupants, to set fire to them. But we know for certain that one building which escaped was the Women's Hospital, an almshouse on the west side of Beacon Street opposite the north-west corner of the Close. Built by Dr. Milley in 1504, a solid structure of brick and stone, it still stands today. One cannot help wondering what the old women who lived there made of all the fighting and especially of the blowing up of the tower, a few yards away, by Prince Rupert, during the second siege.

In addition to Sir William Brereton's trench and the three mounts already mentioned, he made a fourth mount in Dam Street, facing the South Gate, in order to meet any sally made out of that opening; and around the camp on Beacon Hill he constructed a "sconce", an elaborate system of earthworks in the form of a square with a diamond-shaped bastion at each corner. In this fort he installed his Cheshire troops, when at last they arrived. Perhaps he wanted to keep them under his eye.

By the 11th of April he was able to write to his two friends in Parliament, John Swinfen and Mr. Ashurst, as follows:[9]

Sirs,

Touching the state of affairs in these parts, you will receive an account at large by Colonel Bowyer*, Mr. Vernon and Andrew Miller who all went from Tutbury on Tuesday last, whence myselfe also after I had setled the Leaguer† there, went, and am now returned back to the Leaguer att Lichfield, where we are in verrie good forwardnes with our workes and have not only erected several mountes and sconces on each side, but if Pyoneers come in we shall finish our trench from Mounte to Mounte and from the Water to the Water rounde about the Close at a verrie near distance so as it will be impossible for any to escape. Our Mortarpeeces and granadoes are also in as goode forwardnes to be played, and now I am preparing a summons to send within a day or two which I have foreborne the longer, to the end [that] the enemy may first bee made sensible of the improbabilitie of reliefe or of escaping; and if that receive not a satisfactory answer, to proceed to use of all means possible to reduce them otherwise. The Cheshire men are now come upp to the number of 700 and are very willing to do service. But I feare (unless speedily prevented by a supply of money) there may be an evill president given for those that came upp first beginning to murmur and threaten to go home if they receive not money, money, speedily; for they must have none out of their own County for the service they doo here. I have here inclosed sent a letter to the Committee of Both Kingdoms to be delivered if you think fitt and it may avail for the encouragement of those who were in the last Battell if our soldiers might receive the encouragement of some certaine constant pay.

---

*Colonel Bowyer was in command of the force beleaguering Tutbury.

†A "Leaguer", in the military jargon of the period, was a force besieging a stronghold.

It would much Enable and Encourage us not only to carrie on this worke and that against Tutbury, But likewise the designe against Dudley and Worcester which service shall bee by no man more Endeavoured than myselfe who am and always will remayne

your verrie faithfull friend to serve you

Wm Brereton

Lichfield
11th Aprill 1646

This letter to Mr. Swinfen was not sent off immediately but was delayed two days so that the letter to the Committee of Both Kingdoms could include the news of Sir William Brereton's summons to surrender sent to Colonel Tyldesley. Late on April 13th Sir William sat down and wrote as follows:[10]

Letter to the Speaker of the House of Commons and to the Committee of Both Kingdoms, sent inclosed in a letter to Mr. Swinfen by Sir William Brereton.

Sir,

These lines may give you this account touching on further progresse in our Engagement against Lichfield. Now that the full number of Cheshire men are come upp we have inclosed the enemy on Bacon Street syde and have perfected three Mountes upon the same syde and have Efficiently Entrenched and secured our Cheshire campe soe that I hope (by Gods Assistance) it will be a strong reserve for them all. Wee have also drawn a line and made a trench (which is almost finished) from Stowe Poole to Bacon Streete which is intended to bee made Goode to the poole over against Sandford Streete where wee [have] erected another Mounte for the securing of our men in that part of the towne.

Until these works were finished I did not apprehend it reasonable to summons them. But now that the same are brought into such forwardness, this inclosed summons was this day (by the advice of a Councell of Warre) sent into the Close and an answer returned which you will likewise herewith receive.

When wee have made tryall of all the Mortarpeeces that wee could possibly secure (although wee could not obtain the great one from Belvoir nor that from Shrewsbury, the one being employed at Newarke and the other at Bridgenorth) wee shall be able to give you a further accompt of the Effects thereof (those that wee have being in readiness to bee made use of) and noe other endeavour shall be omitted that may condues to the shortening of this worke which is not more desired by any man than by

Your most humble servant

Wm. Brereton

Lichfield
13th Aprill, 1646

This was the summons that Brereton sent to the Royalist forces in the Close:[11]

Aprill 13th 1646
Sir William Brereton to Sir Thomas Tyldesley and Colonel Bagot.
Gentlemen,

I have hitherto forborne to summons you, to the end that you might as much despair of escape as of Reliefe, and have not before tenders of mercie put in execution any destructive attempt, knowing the Parliament whom I serve desires rather your Reducement than your Ruine. It can bee noe news to impart to you the total defeate given to your only field Army in the Kingdome (late under the command of

*Major-General Sir William Brereton*

(William Salt Library)

Sir Jacob Astley) within a short time after the submission of Sir Ralph Hoptons Army to Sir Thomas Fairfax in the West, besides the surrendering of Exeter which (though perhaps unknown to you) is most true, whereof I make mention not to adduce Triumph over you but to bring you to a right understanding of your present condicion. I have now sent this summons to demand for the use of the King and Parliament* the Close of Lichfield with all Armes, Ammunition and other Warlike provisions, your speedie surrender whereof will prevent further effects of hostilities. And yourselves and those gentlemen of qualitie and others with you may receive Honourable condicions. But if your obstinacie deprive you and them thereof, the guilt (which must necessarily be answered for) is your owne and you must expect worse conditions hereafter. Your positive answer is Required by 4 of the clock this Afternoon.

Your Servant,

Wm. Brereton.

From our Camp,
On Beacon Hill, Aprill 13th.

The answer to this summons came the same day. It was short and to the point.

To Sir William Brereton,

Though your summons has long been expected the Answer shall be shorte.

Wee will keep this Garrison, (God Willing) with our lives and fortunes for the King, our Liege Sovereigne by whom wee are entrusted. This is the Resolution of the whole Garrison.

Your Servants,

Thomas Tyldesley
Hervey Bagot

Lichfield Close,
Aprill 13th, 1646.

And to emphasise his answer the Royalist commander mounted a sally out of the Close the same day, killing 30 and taking 50 prisoners.

Sir William Brereton, in giving the reason he did for delaying his summons to Sir Thomas Tyldesley, was to some extent bluffing. He was hampered from mounting an offensive on the Close, not only by lack of money to motivate his troops, but also by lack of ammunition for them to use. He had already taken this matter up with John Swinfen, and on April 17th he wrote[12] to two more of his colleagues in the House of Commons, Messrs Vane and Strickland, as follows:

Our line is now round about the Close and almost finished, and the enemy invested. Our mortarpeeces have done some execution and our cannons are ready for batterie. But want of ammunicion disables us for progress, whereof when we are supplied I hope we shall give you a good accompt of this stronghold.

Help, however, was already on the way. The proceedings of the Committee of Both Kingdoms, dated April 15th,[13] contain the following:

Ordered that 60 barrels of gunpowder be provided for the force at Oxford, and 60 barrels of powder for the force before Lichfield, and match and bullet proportionately.

---

*The phrase "the King and Parliament" was always used in such circumstances by the Parliament, even though they were fighting against the King; by so doing they emphasised their claim to be acting constitutionally.

This information was communicated to Brereton in a letter from John Swinfen[14] a few days later. The powder would arrive in about a fortnight, he promised, and then went on, in the manner of politicians, to suggest to Sir William how he should use it.

By now both sides had settled down to a state of siege warfare. The Parliamentary forces had dug in sufficiently far away from the Close to be out of musket range, making it difficult for the Royalists to mount an attack. So, following the accepted practice of the time, they commenced digging "sallieports" with trenches from which they could move nearer to the enemy while remaining under cover. The construction of one of these is recorded in the following letter sent at the end of April to Sir William Brereton, who had taken himself off to Dudley to see what was happening in that part of his command. The writer of the letter was Lieut. Colonel Gilbert Gerrard, Commanding Officer of the Cheshire Regiment, who usually took over command in the absence of Sir William Brereton.

Honoured Sir,

Wee were fully resolved to give your Honour an Accompte of the Campe yet wee protracted the tyme until wee did really apprehend the workes nearly made by the enemy and to what end it was done. Upon Munday our Centinells [sentinels] at the pitt discovered them working at the Edge of the feild over against them by the Railes nearest there own trench, yet could wee not conceive what his intentions might bee except to cast up a breastwork to annoy us in the setting up of our own mounte, it being directly opposite. That night wee had tryed for certaintie but that our Carpenters and Pyoneers would have failed us had there bene anie shot, soe wee resolved to gaine tyme in erectinge our own Mounte and performed it, blessed be God, without loss of blood.

The same night there came a souldier from the Close and wee straitlie examined him what there worke was. Hee answered, about a weeke since, they began the making of a new sallieport under the Pallace wall and from thence a runing trench to the edge of the hill, and there they made a work to secure there Trench. Which wee conceived to be true in regard wee see the work like a Horne formeinge to either side of there Trench.

Yesternight wee went [on] with our Mounte and rought it verie stronge, and before this night there is liveing and foot space which will be perfected and wee intend to have a strong guard therein.

Theire worke is not anie disadvantage to us in the least particular, neither can wee take it from them without loss of many men tonight, but it beeing soe neere they will regaine and repayre theire grounde tomorrowe. If they come on with anie other worke, through Gods assistance weele use our best endeavours, that prevention may be given. Till then, you intending neither myne nor Battery, and they being potent within, they will make a worke at there own doore and wee cannot possibly prevent them. Wee conceive, whilst wee keepe our guard secure and our Enemys from getting relief or breaking through us, wee discharge the duty of your Honours engagement. Myselfe and all others shall most cheerfully obey your Honours further commands.

Your Honours servants

G. Gerrard
Wm Daniell

From Beacon Hill Campe
April 29th, 1646

The letter gives an interesting insight into the actions of the Royalists in the Close, who were following the dictum that 'the best defence is attack'. They dug a trench in the garden of the Bishop's Palace leading to a short tunnel under the east wall of the Close. This would bring them into the dimble or dingle, a dry moat, at a point about half way along the east wall. From here they made a trench large enough, as we shall see later, to contain four men marching abreast. Once into the field outside (this being the Mill Crofts which Colonel Bagot had railed off to provide grazing for his horses), the trench swung left through ninety degrees and pushed north towards Beacon Hill on which the Parliamentary forces had their camp. As the letter makes clear, they were building a 'mounte' or little fort as a defensive position in front of their lines, and the Royalist trench was aimed at this. When it reached the rails on the south side of Gaia Lane, a cross trench with breastwork towards the enemy (the 'horns' as Colonel Gerrard called it) was constructed to protect any troops using the main trench.

To anyone familiar with this area today, the trench must have followed the line of the pathway now known as the Bishop's Walk.

The work, on both sides, would of course be done at night under cover of darkess and it is not difficult to imagine the atmosphere of suspense on both sides as the sounds of spades clinking or a hammer's knock set eyes straining through the blackness to see what was going on. Under the circumstances one would expect a commander to institute some system of night patrolling to keep his enemy on their toes, but Colonel Gerrard appears to have preferred to leave well alone.

The 'souldier from the Close' mentioned in his letter was one William Pearson, and the transcript of his interrogation appears in Sir William Brereton's Letter Book a page or two later, reading as follows:

Intelligence Out of Litchfield.

Bacon Hill, April 28th, 1646.

Wm. Pearson, born in Bedfordshire and a souldier in the Close of Litchfield under Major Harsnett, running voluntarily from the Enemie and examined, sayeth:

That the commanders in the Close did cause a new sallieport to be made and began the worke about a weeke since and have already perfected a runing trench towards the rayles on Bacon Hill that foure men may march abreast and, soe the againt [agent] did confidently report, and sware, they were fully resolved to make a desperate sally to attempt one of the mountes and he beleeves it is that wee call Glauster [Gloucester] Mounte and the tyme would either bee Munday night past or Tuesday night tomorrow.*

[Sayeth] their allowance in the Close is halfe a pounde of bread and halfe a pound of cheese a day, or halfe a pound of beefe.

[Sayeth] there is one family shut up of the sickness and a sentinel set at the door and noo person as yet dead.

---

*April 28th, 1646, was a Monday.

Sayeth that Granadoes have broken six severall times into the church but neither man nor woman harmed that he knowed of.

[Sayeth] that the enemie doe not now make any gunpowder.

Sayeth that upon Saturday next they have resolved to make a sally into the cittie at the main-gate causeway at a fitt tyme in regard they beleeve that the souldiers will be disordered by reason of the fayre.

[Sayeth] that he verilie beleeves they will within a short tyme turn out all theire Horses.

Sayeth of late they have not had any Intelligence and alleges that their officers tell them Montrose is in England and the Scotch Army joined with him, yet they [i.e. the soldiers] give not credit to them and soe [he] doth beleeve that a small continuance in the Close will weary the souldiers of theire engagement.

Quite a number of interesting points emerge from this statement, assuming, of course, that William Pearson was a genuine deserter telling the truth and not a captured messenger trying to deceive his captors, as any good soldier should.

General Tyldesley obviously intended to fight an offensive campaign; hence the need for sallyports, i.e. points in the defences from which the defenders could make a sudden surprise attack. The two which already existed, the West Gate and the South Gate, were now covered by two of Sir William Brereton's mountes, or forts. A new one was needed, and the garrison appears to have been engaged in making the one on the east side of the Close.

Conditions in the Close at this time were still reasonably good, with no shortage of rations, sickness confined to one house, and even the dreaded granadoes causing no harm. Possibly this was due to the fact that the fuse was so inaccurate that the bombs did not explode or else did so after a long delay that enabled people to take cover.

If this was so for humans, it was otherwise for horses. The 200 cavalry chargers within the Close would be running out of fodder and there was nowhere for them to graze — every blade inside the walls must have been turned over by now, with the ceaseless activity of throwing up earthworks. It was a case of turning the horses out of the Close or letting them starve, and a starving horse is of little use in combat. So, on the appointed day the drawbridge outside the West Gate would be let down, the gates flung open and a stampede of hungry horses issue forth, to be captured, no doubt, in due course by Sir William Brereton's men for remounts. One is glad for the horses' sakes.

The manufacture of gunpowder in the Close had probably come to an end with the cutting off of supplies of sulphur, or possibly of supplies of coal to make saltpetre. Either way, it emphasised the state of siege and the increasing sense of isolation that the garrison must have felt. Another factor was the lack of information on what was happening elsewhere on the country. The news from their officers that the Duke of Montrose was in England with the main Scottish army was quite untrue; in fact

Montrose had been defeated at the Battle of Philiphaugh, near the border, by forces from the main Scottish army, the same army that now held King Charles a prisoner at Newcastle.

Perhaps the most surprising information in William Pearson's statement is the garrison's decision to mount a sally into the city in the belief that 'the souldiers will be disordered by reason of the fayre.'

Lichfield had a number of Charter Fairs at this time, including a May Fair, the right to which was granted by a charter of James I. This lasted for two days, and in 1646, in the fourth year of the war, with the city beleaguered and plague raging, it still appears to have gone ahead. Perhaps it was a gesture of defiance to the Puritans amongst the Parliamentary troops, for May Day celebrations and merrymaking were one of the things they condemned as evil. As far as the Royalist garrison was concerned, this was certainly true. On the morning of May Day the sun rose to show the four remaining Colours of Bagot's Regiment of Foot flying from the centre tower of the cathedral, while from every window of the spire there fluttered in the breeze numbers of red sashes worn by officers of the Royalist army.

If the object was to annoy Sir William Brereton and his men, it certainly succeeded. For them the cathedral spire now assumed not only the identity of a military objective, a place from which the Royalist sharpshooters harried them in all directions, but also the character of a symbol of many of the things against which they were fighting — the pomps and vanities of this wicked world and all the sinful lusts of the flesh!

For the moment there was little they could do, but from that hour the centre spire of the cathedral was marked down for destruction as soon as the necessary ammunition arrived. In preparation the two heavy guns they possessed (a demi-culverin and a demi-cannon) were brought into action in the emplacements specially prepared for them on the mount in Dam Street, and John Fox, the gunner, set them up to fire at the steeple.

In the meantime they continued to harass the Close with mortar fire, reported as follows in one of the Diurnals:

Thursday May 6th.
This day letters came from Litchfield certifying that we have played all our Mortar peeces against the Close and tore some Howses, especially with the great peece on the backsyde of the George in the towne which hath played well upon the Howses about the Minster, but they are still stubborn within and do not come out to capitulate . . .
(Perfect Occurrences, etc.)

By May 7th the promised sixty barrels of gunpowder had arrived, and the bombardment commenced. It continued for five days, during which time each gun fired about forty shots — ten pounders from the demi-culverin and thirty pounders from the demi-cannon. In all, about three-quarters of a ton of metal was hurled at the spire, and if one assumes that the aim was good, as it should have been at that short range, it says a great deal for the workmanship of the cathedral's mediaeval builders that the spire resisted attack for so long. Of those shots which scored a hit, one of each kind can be seen on view in the cathedral today.

The end came on May 12th at about 11 o'clock in the morning. A shot at the base of the spire struck home and the whole structure crashed to the ground, part of it falling into the choir and part into the nave. There was jubilation in the Parliamentarian camp and Sir William sat down and wrote a second summons to surrender to Sir Thomas Tyldesley.[16]

His clerk turned to a new page in the letter book and wrote:

The rest of the page was left blank — perhaps for a description of the great event which he never got around to writing. However, shortly afterwards there is the text of a letter from Brereton to his two friends in the House of Commons, Mr. Ashurst and Mr. Swinfen, 'touching battering down the greatest of the three steeples of the Minster at Litchfield'.

Sirs,

Soe soone as we were Furnished with any Considerable proportion of Ammunition which was noe more but a Tunne of powder and a Tunne of Match, Wee made the best use thereof erecting a Batterie neere unto our next Mounte to the Close, and plaid for five dayes freely upon their highest Spire steeple out of which that had most galled and annoyed us, even from the very highest Windows (which were not many yards belowe the Weather Coke) whence they had done much execution both in the Town and Camp and elsewhere, noe lesse than 8 or 10 slayne and wounded uppon May day last, which was their Fayre day, though it is true most of them were their owne Friends.

This was that Spire which was most beautified and adorned with Coulours, Scarves and other Ornaments on all Sydes even from the Belfrie to the Toppe all most of the Spire, especially on May day last. Herein their Ladyes and Grandees (as was reported) were accomodated with Lodgings, not knowing where to bee soe much secured from the danger of our Mortarpeeces, which begin to bee more formidable among them. And this was conceived to a most safe and Convenient place for their Magazine.

Wee had noe more than two Gunnes, a Demi-Cannon and Demi-Culverin, both which had noe more than 60 Shott apeece or thereabouts; when 20 for each were remayning, and with the expence of less than 7 or 8 Barrells of powder, wee brought down (May 12th, about eleaven of the Clocke) this lofty proud spire which was the highest and most Comaunding of those three stately Spires which did belong to this Minster which (it is believed) were erected in resemblance to the Pope's triple Crown, and if soe this downefall may be omen and Prognosticke of a further downefall; The effect whereof was almost like that of Sampson's pulling down the House (with great execution) at his death. Soe here the fall of this Spire did mightie execution as well uppon the Chauncel [Chancel] wherein was their Quire Service and Organs placed, as alsóe on the other syde of the steeple upon that parte of the body of the Minster wherein the Pulpit stood, and wherefrom sermons were made, into both which there are great breaches as though the Lord were purposing Reckoning for that Hypocrisie, prophanesse [profaneness] and Ignorance which hath been therein nourished and practiced. This Spire was the greate ornament of that Cross Structure which now looketh nakedly bare.

It was conceived that this downefall would also humble their loftie proud Spirits in the Close, upon which consideracion I sent this second Summons herein enclosed, whereunto I Received this Answer, whereby you may perceive that they doe still obstinately persist to the further chardge of the Country and to bring uppon themselves Certaine Destruction.

The Lord direct and guide you in all your great Transactions and send you a speedie and blessed Peace, for which noe Man desires to be more thankfull than,

Your verie faithfull Servant

to serve you,

Wm. Brereton

Lichfield,
May 14th 1646.

Sir William Brereton's allegation that the 'Grandees' and their ladies had taken up lodgings in the centre spire to escape the granadoes strikes one as being rather far-fetched. Theoretically, they would be safer at that height above ground against all but a direct hit, but the inconvenience attached to such a lofty and windswept accommodation, together with the danger of sharing it (according to Sir William's account) with the powder magazine, must surely have rendered it highly unlikely.

The second summons[17] to Sir Thomas Tyldesley read as follows:

Gentlemen,

Your rejecting my first somens at such tyme as you could not but behold the hand of God everywhere against you might justly have deprived you of further tenders of mercie; But such is the Clemencie of the Parliament whose Servant I am that to prevent the further effusion of blood and the Ruine of yourselves and all those Gentlemen and others with you I nowe send this second and last somens, and hereby demand and Require you to surrender the Garrisoned Close of Litchfield, with all Ordinance, Arms, Ammunition, Provisions of Warre and all other goods whatsoever into my hands for the use of Kinge and Parliament.

What I informed you in my last summons concerning Sir Ralph Hopton and his Armies submission to Sir Thomas Fairfax, the defeate of Sir Jacob Astley and the deliverie of Exeter I cannot now doubt but you believe.

It is as true that since that tyme the Garrisons of Barnstaple, Dunstar [Dunster], Woodstock, Ruthin, Bridgenorth, Aberistwithe, Tutbury, Banbury, Newarke, and others are delivered and Dudley Castle agreed to be yielded upp tomorrow, and

Oxford with the rest either straightlie Beleaguered or blockt upp, and his Majestie in Person come to our Armie; You cannot therefore but apprehend yourselves in a desperate Condicion, and that as there is a vast Difference betwixt the Condicions you might have expected when I first Somoned you and and these I can now grant, soe the longer you persist in your obstinacie (adding to the expence of tyme, income and blood) the greater will be the Accompt and Judgement upon yourselves and those with you.

I give you untill foure of the clocke tomorrow afternoone to advise, at which tyme I expect your finall Answer.

Remayning,
Your Servant

From Our Campe on
Bacon Hill
May 12th, 1646.

Wm. Brereton.

## The messenger returned with a brief note:

Sir,

You shall tomorrow receive an Answer from:
Your Servants,
Thomas Tyldesley
Hervey Bagot

## When it came the next the reply was a letter of some length.[18]

Sir,

Yesterday the 12th of May Wee Received your second Somens Wherein you Require us partely by persuasions and partely by Menaces to surrender into your hands the Close of Litchfield with all Ordinance, Armes, Amunition, Provisions of Warre and all other goods whatsoever for the use of the King and Parliament, but neither produce nor affirme that you have any Warrant or authoritie from the King or Parliament to enable us to deliver it, or you to receive it, which you might easily have procured (if the King and Parliament had been thereunto Consenting) since the King (as you write) is come in person to your Army, and you have dailie intercourse of intelligence with the Howses of Parliament; unless perhaps the Kings Consent bee little regarded by you whoe in your letter professe yourselfe (only) Servant to the Parliament without any mencion of dutie or acknowledgement to your lawfull Sovereign.

For our Partes as wee know that noe Governor of Commander of any of the Kings Forces Canne without Manifest guilt of High Treason deliver upp the same without His Majesties Consent, unlesse they bee thereunto forced or necessitated, (which thanks bee to God wee need not to fear) Soe being as sensible as yourselfe of the miseries of a Civill Warre, wee shall not keepe this Garrison an hour after wee are assured it is his Majesties pleasure it shall bee delivered, And wee must tell you nothing makes us more diffident of your Relation of the accorde between the Kings and your Partie than your outrages and Barbarous vyolence utterly to deface and destroy the Lords Howse, one of the most Auncient Monuments in this Kingdom, being a thousand yeares ould within eleven and the Cheife Ornament of this Countrey, which being no way advantageous to your designe, Renders you odious to all Men. As for the submission of the Lord Hoptons Armie, and the surrender of the many Garrisons mentioned in your letter, wee know not upon what ground or reason it was done; let them answere for themselves, if they have done anything unworthilie (which wee canne never believe especially of so gallant and honorable a Person as the Lord Hopton) they shall bee examples for our detestation, not imitation, whoe had Rather suffer for our loyaltie than prosper by perfidy.

The expence of Blood and Treasure must be cast uppon your Account whoe are the Assaylants, doe the violence, and endeavour the Ruine of his Majesties Loyall Subjects, not uppon ours, whoe stand onlie uppon a juste defence of our Sovereignes Righte, our own persons and estates, a defence which the Lawe of God and Man Comaunds and wee must observe unlesse wee will bee Accessaries to the Ruine of our Maister and ourselves.

And what heavie Judgement you intend against us and those with us for our Constant Loyaltie which you term Obstinacie; Know Sir, it is our Resolution rather to suffer evill at your hands than doe it with our own, Rather to bee Martyrs than Traitors, and Rather to offend them that canne but kill the Body than Him who Canne destroy both soule and body in Hell.

Whereas you say wee Cannot but behould the hand of God every where against us, Wee conceive Fortunate successe to be noe good Argument of a juste Cause, for he that hath Right hath many tymes sinnes for which God justly permitteth him to bee scourged by his enemies, and at last Casteth his scourge into the Fire, as he oftimes did to his owne people by the Philistines, and to the Christians by the Turks and Saracens. And though afflicitions bee many tymes the Portion of Gods Children, yett this is our Comfort, that Gods Judgemente beginnes in the Howses of his Servants and ends in the Howses of his enemies. And wee heartily wish that a true sense and sight of your errours may avert Gods Judgement from you, whoe imply the efficiency of that to the God of Heaven, which rightly belongs to the God of this world, who hath blinded your minds and is the Author of Averice, Ambition, Disloyaltie, Crueltie etc.

Sir, the many particulars of your letter and weight thereof occasioned this length, which wee hope you will pardon in them who have no other end than to aquitt themselves and satisfy you (as well as they could) and to expresse themselves as indeed they are,

His Majesties Loyall Subjects and,
Your Servants,
Thomas Tyldesley
Hervey Bagot

By now it must have been obvious to Sir William Brereton that the siege of Lichfield Close was going to be a long drawn out affair. Writing, on May 15th, to his commander-in-chief, Sir Thomas Fairfax, he refers to the 'obstinacie' of the garrison of the Close which prevents him from moving any of his forces to Worcester. He goes on to mention:

some say they were in a high Mutiny the last night in the Close, but I cannot give the certainty thereof, but doe confidently beleive the Comon Souldiers have been kept in subjection by meere falsities and untruths.

There may have been an element of wishful thinking in this last statement, for at this moment Sir William had an incipient mutiny on his own hands. On May the 13th, the day after the battering down of the spire, the following letter[19] arrived on his table:

(from) The Cheshire Commanders at Litchfield touching want of
Moneys for their Soldyers there.

Honourable Sir,

Were wee not absolutely inforced by the necessitie of our Soldyers, wee should very unwillinglie have given you these ensueing expressions of our Condicion, and were wee not assured that your Honor is fullie acquainted how long wee have been engaged under your Comaund, and what Continued subsistance our selves and

Soldyers have Received this paper had been too little to sett downe, and your Honors affairs too weightie to look over.

Wee have been imployed in this Leaguer of Litchfield Close, and the tyme of our Respective engagements, as also our duty and extraordinary workeing, is fully known to your Honor. Wee have not allottments as divers here, soe wee cannot in the least particular furnish our Men with present necessaryes. Our Comaunds are uncomfortable and performed with a great deal of trouble, and wee Reallie acquaint your Honor that some of our Men have deserted our Coulours, the Rest in a Mutinous Condition because their cloathes are worn and they have noe assurance of subsistance to furnish themselves for the future. Wee desire your Honor to take what we speak into your thoughts, and supplie our Companies with Moneys very speedilie, least our utmost endeavours prove ineffectuall for the keepeing our Soldyers dilligent and observant to your Comaunds in this service. Wee leave it to your Honors discretion, Remayning,

Your Honors humble Servants,

|  |  |  |
|---|---|---|
|  | William Daniell | Edward Glegg |
|  | Godfrey Gimbart | Symon Finch |
| Bacon Hill Camp | John Rathbone | Thomas Walley |
| May 13th 1646 | John Leadbeater | Hugh Bertles |

The signatories to this petition were all but two of the company commanders of the Chesire Regiment of Foot. Captain Booth and Captain Monke did not sign. Whether the letter was addressed to their regimental commander, Lieut.-Colonel Gilbert Gerrard, or whether (heinious crime!) they went over his head to Major-General Brereton is not clear. Nor, unfortunately, does the Major-General's letter book contain any reference to his reaction to their request. The reference to men deserting, however, moved Sir William to issue instructions to his Muster-Master, Lieut.-Colonel Hunt, to muster the Cheshire Foot. This, accordingly, was done on May 23rd, with the results shown in the accompanying muster-roll.

It was certainly not a propitious moment to launch any new offensive against the Close, and the destruction of the cathedral spire not having had the desired effect of bringing the garrison to the point of surrender, Sir William Brereton now took the only course left to him, tightening his grip on the beleaguered fortress and waiting for the supplies to run out. In the meantime Captain Coldhurst was ordered to keep up his bombardment of the garrison as far as his limited supplies of gunpowder permitted.

On May 19th Brereton's men captured another deserter from the Close and his examination was recorded[20]. John Bust, a common soldier, had served at Naseby, and when examined said:

That the last sumons sent to the Governour was not read or made known to the Soldyers;

That the allowance to the soldyers is not lessened to them above half a pound of bread in a Weeke since the beginning of the Leaguer.

That it is reported that there is betwixt seven and eight hundred Soldyers in the Close beside Women and Children.

That there are three Sally Ports beside the great Gate [i.e. the South Gate] which

254)

May the 23: 1646./

An abbreviate of the Names of the severall Cap[t]
their L[ieutenant]s and Ensignes, with the Number of the
other Officers and whole Companies whoe are nowe
engaged in the Seige against Litchfeild Close,
Mustered by L[ieutenant] Col[onell] Hunt on Cheshire syde the
Leaguer the day abovesaid.

92.    Major Danyell, L[t] Heath, Ensigne Witter, 3 Serjeants
2 Drums, 3 Corporalls, 1 Gentleman of Armes and
92 Comen Soldyers./

18.    Captaine Booth, 1 Serjeant, 1 Drum, 2 Corporalls
and 18 Comen Soldyers./

32.    Captaine Leadbeater, L[t] Norbury, Ensigne Bunnell
1 Serjeant, 1 Drum, 2 Corporalls & 33 Comen Soldy    { These two
make but one
Company and
Officers are
allowed accord[ingly]

60.    Captaine Rathbone, L[t] Browne, Ensigne Wellmough
3 Serjeants, 1 Clarke, 2 Drums, 3 Corporalls &
60 Comen Soldyers.

36.    Captaine Walley, L[t] Bostocke, Ensigne Bradford 2 Serjeants
1 Drum, 2 Corporalls & 36 Comen Soldyers./

76.    Captaine Chinch, L[t] Adlice, Cornett Sydes, 2 Serjeants
1 Drum, 3 Corporalls & 76 Comen Soldyers./

65    Captaine Gimbert, L[t] Surner, Cornett Yrmson, Quartermaster
Bentley, 2 Serjeants, 1 Drum, 3 Corporalls & 65 Soldy[er]s

52.    Captaine Birtles, Ensigne Cartwright, 2 Serjeants, 1 Drum
2 Corporalls, 1 Clarke & 52 Comen Soldyers./

69    Captaine Glegg, L[t] Snellnham, Ensigne Ball, 3 Serjeants
1 Clarke, 2 Drums, 3 Corporalls & 69 Comen Soldyers

36.    Captaine Menke, L[t] Pargiter, 2 Drums, 2 Corporalls and
36 Comen Soldyers./

           The number of Cap[t]s other Officers & privates Soldyers

564.    Cap[t]s 10, L[t]s 8, Ensignes 8, Serjeants 22 Clarkes and
Quartermrs 4, Drums 19, Corporalls 25 Comen Soldy[er]s 564./

is barracaded upp; one into the Mounte before Damm Street, One neere the Drawe Bridge goeing towards the Swan [i.e. the West Gate], the third leading into the newe Worke next Bacon Street.

That the Newe Worke is Triangular and with Pallasadoes about, saving the end next Stowe Church which is not yet finished.

That the Enemy hath Intelligence of the bringing upp of our great Gunnes, and thereupon are lining the Walls about tenne foote thicke, the whole Wall being distributed among the Companies for the effecting of it.

That it is not yett finished within the Close.

That the hand Granadoes shott by them were shott by a Mortar-peece made of Leade, and that the Enemy hath gathered some of our Granadoes about 40 pounds weight which burst not, and are casting a Mortar of Leade to Returne them uppon us.

That the Granadoes have ruined the Howses of the Lord Aston, Henry Hynde, Mr. Martins, Mr. Turnpennyes, Mr. Williams, Mr. Robinsons, One neere the Vicarage, One Gentlemans neere the Ashtree, The Garden Howse neere the Pallace, Morris his howse, the Smith, a Smiths Shoppe neere Sir Thomas Leighs, and parte of Sir Thomas Astons Stables.

That yesterday the Gentlemen were borrowing Moneys from the Inhabitants and the Citizens for the satisfaction of the soldyers.

(signed) John Bust

The picture painted by John Bust was certainly not that of a garrison about to capitulate. Rations were still good, troops were even being paid to some extent and considerable ingenuity was being expended to carry the fight into the enemy camp.

The manufacture of the lead mortars is an intriguing example of this. There is no doubt that the granado, fired from a mortar, was the most successful artillery weapon of the Civil War. At Lichfield, as elsewhere, ordinary cannon firing solid shot had little effect against mediaeval stone walls, banked up behind with earth. But granadoes, lobbed over the walls, not only caused death and destruction (when they exploded) but also had a profound psychological effect. The sound of the mortar firing, the whistle of the projectile in the air (and possibly the sight of it) for what seems like an age and the feeling that the projectile is coming straight for the observer, all combine to produce a traumatic experience, as the writer can testify. In the Civil War there would be the added suspense, following the thud of the granado landing, while one waited to see if it would explode. With the crude form of fuse then in use (a length of smouldering match) many did not go off, and the desire to give the enemy a taste of his own medicine was understandable. Hence Sir Thomas Tyldesley's experiments with lead mortars. Brass he had not, but there was a plentiful supply of lead on the roofs of the cathedral. Lead is also easier to cast than brass or iron, and a lead mortar, strengthened with bands of iron, might just have provided the required weapon.

So first they made a small mortar piece to fire hand granadoes, and this being successful they attempted one to fire 40 pound shells. This was a medium-sized weapon, firing a granado half the weight of those used in the first siege in 1643. Whether they succeeded in this attempt is not recorded.

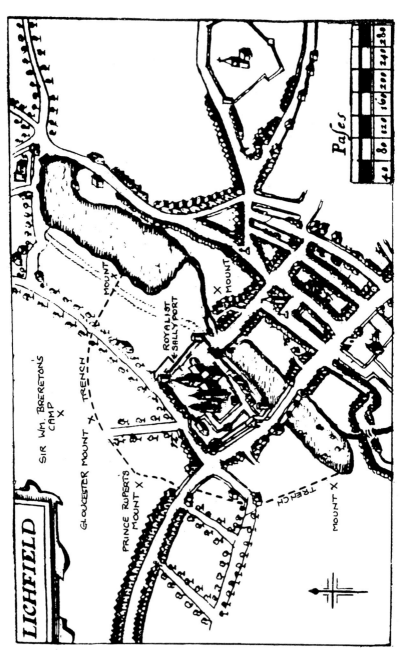

*The Third Siege, showing fortifications*

The internal defences of the Close, as described by John Bust, are also of great interest. It would appear that although the main gate, that is the one to the south, leading into Dam Street, had been barricaded up, a new sally port had been made near it, 'into the Mounte before Damm Street'. The precise position of this mount is not clear, but it was probably to the south-east of the gateway, close by the mill. 'One neere the drawbridge goeing towards the Swan' must refer to the West Gate and is a reminder of how much in this country we use inns as direction marks; one could still give the same direction today, and no doubt many people do.

'The Newe Worke' referred to must have been outside the walls of the Close; 'next Bacon Street', 'triangular in shape' and with one end 'next Stowe Church' points to the area lying between Beacon Street, Gaia Lane and the Close wall. It is understandable that any commander in the Close would want to hold this area; it was built-up and thus provided cover for attackers to approach close to the north-west corner of the walls. This was where Prince Rupert had exploded the mine which breached the walls in the second siege, and probably the defences here were still weak. The 'Newe Workes' therefore would provide an advanced line of defence as well as a sally port to the north.

The month of May passed without any further military action, both sides content with lobbing granadoes at each other. Among the civilian population of the city and the close, however, much was afoot, and these matters are dealt with in the next chapter.

# SOURCE NOTES

*Chapter VI*

1.  Harwood, History of Lichfield, p.306
2.  Calendar of State Papers, Domestic Series, Charles I, Vol. 21
3.  Ibid.
4.  Sir William Brereton, Letter Book, March-May 1646
5.  Ibid.
6.  Calendar of State Papers, Domestic Series, Charles I, Vol. 21
7.  Ibid.
8.  Staffordshire County Record Office
9.  Sir William Brereton, Letter Book, March-May 1646
10. Ibid.
11. Ibid.
12. Ibid.
13. Calendar of State Papers, Domestic Series, Charles I, Vol. 21
14. Ibid.
15. Sir William Brereton's Letter Book, March-May 1646
16. Ibid.
17. Ibid.
18. Ibid.
19. Ibid.
20. Ibid.

*Chapter VII*

# A Matter of Human Relations

UNLIKE wars between nations, in which the combatants may be separated by differences in language or culture, civil wars breed strange and tragic confrontations in which friend fights against friend and brother against brother.

Nowhere was this more true than in Lichfield, and during the four months of the last siege many strange situations arose. The letter book of Sir William Brereton reflects many of these human relationships; letters between the two commanders, between civilians and military, between citizens and governor and, perhaps most poignant of all, between a serving soldier inside the Close and his wife in the city. Such letters tell us more about people's true feelings in this conflict than all the official accounts could ever do.

We have already seen something of the correspondence between the two commanders and it is a reminder that in those days war was still conducted on a very formal basis. There were strict rules which each side adhered to, and protocol governed the way in which combatants must address each other. Both Sir William Brereton and Sir Thomas Tyldesley were acting as mouthpieces for the politics of their respective parties as much as voicing their own thoughts on the situation. Sir Thomas, for example, could hardly have meant what he said when he accused Sir William Brereton of profaneness in battering down the great spire, when his troops had been hard at work shooting their enemies from that same vantage point. In this as in other matters both sides pursued their own party line.

But now and then the mask dropped briefly to disclose something of the man behind it, as in the following letter[1] from Sir Thomas to Colonel Bowyer who at this time was commanding the Parliamentary forces besieging Tutbury Castle. The Colonel had been Governor of Stafford during the time that Tyldesley had been a prisoner under him at Ecclshall Castle, so they were well-known to each other.

Sir,
    According to your desire Mr. Terrick shall meet Mr. Birche at the place appointed by you; There is now a Drum with us, upon a proposition that Colonel Snead [Sneyd] should meete Major Daniel this afternoone, to which I have given my Consent, and upon Receipt of Mr. Gerrards Passe they shall all come together. I am as desirous to meete you, but this scurvy punctilio of Governorshipp will not give leave, but I can truly subscribe myself,
                    Your Friend and Servant,
                    Thomas Tyldesley.

16th May 1646
P.S. Remember mee to Mr. Birche and give him thanks for his Civill visits to mee when I was in Eccleshall.

The identity of Mr. Terrick is not known, though he was obviously one of the garrison. Mr. Birche would be one of the officers of the Parliamentary force; Major Daniel, we know, was second i/c of the Cheshire Regiment, and Colonel Gilbert Gerrard its Commanding Officer. Colonel Sneyd, a member of a well-known Staffordshire family, was also one of the garrison. What all these people were meeting about is not clear, but the letter illustrates the relatively amicable relationship which existed between the two sides in the early part of the siege, the tone of which is evident in two postscripts to letters exchanged between the two commanders. The first, from Sir Thomas Tyldesley, reads 'You will pardon our scarcety of paper, it is one of our greatest wants'. The reply from Sir William Brereton was brief and to the point, 'By the next I will send you some paper, and do believe before long you will be sensible of greater wants than paper.'

A supply of paper followed on April 18th.

Meetings between representatives of the two forces over the matter of the exchange of prisoners were quite common. In this category came the negotiations over the release of Captain Antony Dyott, taken prisoner at Naseby. On April 16th Sir William Brereton wrote to Sir Thomas Tyldesley as follows:[2]

Sir,
    I have received your letter that Major Bywaters may be permitted to come upon his proll [parole] to you, whereunto I shall give way this afternoone, as also that the Governor of Stafford may come into the Close to Confer with Sir Richard Dyott about his sonne who is a prisoner with us, provided in the meantyme that you send a suitable [hostage?] to our camp on Bacon Hill with your engagement for their [i.e. Major Bywater and the Governor] safe returne unto,
                    Your Servant,
                    Will Brereton.

He received the following by return:

Sir,
    I give you thanks for permitting Major Bywater to come on his proll into this Garrison, but the other matter of the Governor is not thought fitting — But if you will send me your engagement for their safe return, I will send Sir Richard Dyott and Colonel Sneyd to meet Captain Stone and whom else you shall please this afternoone

in the field betwixt your leaguer and this Garrison* and I hereby engage my hand they shall return with safety.

I am,

Your Servant

Thomas Tyldesley

Also, early on in the siege, officers from inside the Close were allowed out into the city under escort to confer with their wives, and some of the civilians came out on parole to conduct their business. A curious example of this was the episode of Sir Walter Aston and his request.

Sir Walter had an estate at Tixall, near Stafford, and like Sir Hervey Bagot he had moved into Lichfield Close early on in the war after suffering the sequestration of his property. He joined the 'grandees' who had houses there, but were not part of the garrison. On May 1st he wrote to Sir William Brereton thus:[3]

Sir,

Your Centuries [sentries] having often this night tould the Centuries of this Garrison that Bridgenorth is delivered upp, Causeth mee, though a Stranger to you, to send this Letter to desire you to doe mee the favour to lett a Servant of mine passe with any Drum or Trumpett of yours to Bridgenorth to enquire if hee can find what is become of some Writeings of mine that were left in the Castle in Sir Lewis Kerkes tyme. Sir, they are writeings that only concern my Barrondry which cannot any way advantage anybody but my selfe and posterity; that which encourageth mee to desire this at your hands is that in the Instruccions for the Committee for Sequestration of Delinquents Estates the 12th Instruccion gives Comaund to all Sequestrators in these words, 'you are to take Care for the safe keeping of the Deeds, Evidences & Writeings of all Delinquents and for preserving their Howses, Tymber trees and Fruit trees from Waste and destruccon.' Sir, if you shall please to doe mee this favour, or to lett my Man goe to Stafford and acquaint Mr. Backhouse where he left these Pattents and give Mr. Backehouse leave to goe to take care of them, your Civilitie will much oblige mee, and I will passe you my honour & faith that my Servant, if soe licenced by you, shall neither carry Letter nor Message of any thing but Concerning these Writeings, nor Sir, shall I receive them into my hands but that they may bee in any Gentlemans hands if that should cause any difficultie; Sir, your care to observe the direccons of Parliament I doubt not will bee one motive to you to doe mee this favour. Sir, my Brother Benjamin Weston in being much your Servant may bee another motive, as likewise the Civilitie will oblige mee to be,

Your humble Servant,

Lichfield Close                                      Walter Aston

May 1st, 1646.

This interesting example of the old-boy network in action, had the desired effect. Sir William, with admirable forebearance, wrote back:

My Lord,

It is most Certaine Bridgenorth is delivered upp, and for your further Satisfaccon therein, as also if possible you can hear of these Writeings you specifie in your Letter, I shall send a Drum with your Lordships Servant, which if they may be found I shall desire your Lordship to nominate some Genetleman in whose hands you shall desire them Intrusted, which shall likewise be assented to by

Your humble Servant

May 2nd, 1646.                                      Wm. Brereton

---

*Probably the field known as The Mill Crofts, east of the Close.

So Sir Walter got his way, the precious title to the baronry was saved and in the following century passed to Sir Thomas Aston whose three daughters, the "Aston Sisters" achieved a touch of immortality as the friends of the great Samuel Johnson.

About the same time as the above correspondence was passing, an entry of quite a different kind occurs in the letter book. It is headed 'Letter Sent into the Close to Lady Dyott by All the Women of Litchfield'. It is not signed and no names are mentioned. From the fact that it appears in such a collection one would assume that it had been intercepted and therefore never reached Lady Dyott. But on second thoughts one cannot help wondering if the writers were some of those in the town who were sympathetic to the cause of Sir William Brereton and had collaborated with him to produce this piece of psychological warfare, making sure that it reached the intended destination. It went as follows:

Good Madam,

The miserable and vexatious Occurents, the woefull effects of warre, that hath of late befallne us are such as forceth us to make a Relation of them unto your Ladyship as to our noble and Compassionate friend that will commiserate though you cannot help us, for it will be some ease to our grieved minds if you will be pleased to entertain the unburthening of them into your Ladyships consideration and to take a view of our many Miseries being deprived of the fruition* of our husbands, the only stay and comfort of us and our families, and haveing our Howses filled with Soldyers, our land untilled that should mainteyne our Families for future and paying Weeklie soe great Assessments towards the Mainteyning of the Army as wee are not able long to subsist under; besides some of us having our Howses that were emptie defaced and pulled to pieces, in which manner the Glorie of our Cittie, wee meane your owne faire Habitation† doth exceedingly suffer, the Rooms being every day more and more pulled downe. Wee would not intimate these our griefs unto you were there either hope of helpe or Reparation, for then it would bee both Comfortable and honorable for our Men to continue in their Resolutions, but seeing we can expect nothing in the progresse but a Continuation of our miseries, nor any Reparation in the Conclusion, wee think it would bee happie for us if the tyme of a good agreement might bee hastened, least deferring till necessitie cause it, the end as well as the progresse Concludes with our Ruine. Wee acknowledge it presumption in us to take upon us to give Councell to Men of Wisdom and in tymes of Warre, though that wise and valiant Warrior of God, the Prophett David, both accepted and pronounced a blessing on a Womans Councell at such a tyme.[5] And indeed our intentions thus farre extend to desire your Ladyship to intimate to such of our Husbands as shall at any tyme present themselves unto your Ladyship our present and much feared Miseries, especially to your owne most Worthy Husband whoe wee Conceive as best able in his wisdome to help us all and that both hee and they may use their best endeavours to free themselves and us from these Miseries which wee feare some Men from sinister ends and desperate engagements seeke to bring them to. And as a Notice further to engage your Ladyship to the more effectuall performance of our desires, Wee Represent unto you that Newarke, Banberry, Hartleberry, and Ludlowe are lately

---

*Enjoyment.

†This refers to the Dyott's house in Market Street which they had recently left to come into the Close.

surrendered, Oxford, Worcester and (for aught Wee knowe) all other Garrisons of the kings in England besieged, and soe farr off from any hopes of helpe from him that the king himselfe for safetie hath Cast himselfe uppon the affection of his native People. And wee Conceive it cannot bee against the Rules either of honour or Wisdome for us to followe his example and uppon good condicions to seeke our owne saftie alsoe, which hath been His Majesties Comaund to divers Garrisons that have sent to him, and whom hee hath been unable to succour. And wee Conceive his Action and Example herein carrie with it the nature of a precept, at least a Sufficient direction, but wee cease further to bee troublesome to your Ladyship, beseeching the Lord God soe to direct your Ladyship that by your means and some other happie Instrument wee may attaine some freedome from dailie Miseries and a happie end of them.

There is no indication as to who wrote the letter, nor as to the identity of the 'Women of Litchfield'. But it is difficult to avoid the suspicion that the substance of the argument, especially in the latter part, received some prompting from a member of Sir William Brereton's staff, if not from himself. The information of the surrender of the Royalist garrisons was premature, to say the least. In fact, Newark fell on May 8th, Banbury on the same day, and Ludlow not until May 29th. Although the letter to Lady Dyott is not dated, the one immediately after it in the letter book is dated May 4th, well before the incidents mentioned above.

The next letter, of May 4th, is of a very different kind. It is headed 'Letter out of the Close from Mr. Hill to His wife in the Fryery'.

John Hill was a Lichfield man, one of those who in 1643 had signed the letter from the Staffordshire Gentlemen to Prince Rupert. Born in 1612, he is described as an 'Utter Barrister of Grayes Inn'. He married Ursula, only daughter of Thomas Clayton of Lichfield, and they made their home in the ancient Franciscan friary which occupied a central position in the city. This foundation dating from the 12th Century, had suffered the usual fate at the Dissolution of the Monastries, the Friary church being demolished and the buildings sold for a private residence. It passed by inheritance to Thomas Clayton and thus to his daughter Ursula.

Although a supporter of Prince Rupert, John Hill was late in taking up arms, but by 1646 he was a Lieutenant serving in the Close garrison, and on May 4th he sat down and wrote to his wife in the Friary:

'In Deo spes Mea'*

My dere sweete Ursula

There Cannot bee a greater blessing on earth befall me than to hear of your welfare which would be Compleated to the highest pitch if soe God were pleased wee could enjoy one the others mutual Society; his leisure must be expected and I doubt not but hee will continue to give us more patience to endure the worst Afflictions which noe way shall move or stagger mee, and I hope your Resolves are Correspondent, and never grieve at but undergoe what cannot be altered.

Younge is not yet returned into the Close. The rest of the things you mention in the letter I have Received and somewhat else . . . The plague or any other disease

*'My hope is in God'

within us is not, about us it may bee. I am, and soe have been since my hither coming, in as good health as ever, and I hope shall continue; the heate of the weather will make me cautious in taking much Tobaccoe; God blesse with health and happiness you and,

Your truly loving Husband
John Hill

May 4th 1646          'Fato patientia Major'*

Younge, one imagines, was John Hill's servant who had been sent out of the Close as a messenger and possibly captured, If so, it was a fate that was to befall the bearer of the present letter, for it never reached Ursula, being intercepted by Sir William Brereton's men. The result, as we shall soon see, was tragic for the young couple.

As May passed without any sign of capitulation from the garrison of Lichfield Close, Sir William Brereton's irritation grew. Dudley Castle had surrendered and Colonel Bowyer had been successful at Tutbury, but Sir Thomas Tyldesley and his men continued to hold out and fight back with frequent sallies at Lichfield. Meanwhile Brereton's Commander-in-Chief, General Fairfax, was urging him to settle the matter so that his troops could be transferred to Worcester. In a move to hasten this he tightened up his restrictions on the garrison and on the morning of May 26th he sat down and wrote out the following two orders:[7]

Order to the Shropshire Foote.

It is ordered that Captain Haslam, Captaine Hunte, Captain Mainwaringe and their Companies of Shropshire Foote doe forthwith march to the Leaguer before Worcester to assist the strengthening of that Leaguer, and to receive orders from the Comander in Cheife till further order.

Litchfield, May 26th, 1646.                    Wm. Brereton.

Order to send all the Wives into the Close.

Whereas many persons have Come out of the Close to speake with their Wives and by that meanes gaine intelligence from them to the greate prejudice of this Leaguer, it is ordered therefore that for the future preventing hereof a List be taken of the names of all the Wives of those that are in the Close that they may bee specially sent into the Close to their husbands and not permitted to come out again and if they or any other shall dare to come out of the Close, the Officers of that Guard are required to shoote them, or otherwise be answerable for the same at a Counsell of Warre. Given under my hand the day above written.

Wm. Brereton

Postscript: The Major of the Towne† is to take care that out of every Company in the Towne one Officer be chosen to see this order bee speedilie put into execution, and that Care bee taken that under pretence hereof noe plunder be committed in their Howses, and to give an Accompt in writing of the Names of those that are sent in.

---

*'Endurance is greater through the will of God'

†The Town Major is the term used to denote an officer of the military who is responsible for maintaining liaison with the civil power in a town.

Both orders were put into effect the same day. The Shropshire Foote set out on their route march to Worcester and in Sir William Brereton's headquarters work began on drawing up a list of women in Lichfield who had husbands in the Close. It is perhaps not surprising that at the head of the list was the name of Ursula Hill, nor that in the course of the day armed soldiers called at the Friary and took her into custody. All over Lichfield the same process was taking place. Sometimes the women on the lists were not to be found — the word had got around and they had sought refuge with neighbours. But by evening eight women had been rounded up, some of whom brought young children with them. As darkness fell they were assembled in Bird Street and marched up towards the Close. When they came to the Roundheads' front line they were told to keep going and not to turn back or they would be shot. So they trudged on over the causeway and up to the great West Gate of the Close, where they asked for admission.

The Royalist Commander was faced with a dilemma. He could not send them back or they would be shot, but if he admitted them to the Close they would be extra mouths to be fed, and their places at the gate would be taken by more and more women and children. There was also the risk that they might bring the plague with them into the garrison.

The decision was hard, but the order was given that they were not to be admitted, nor any help or sustinence passed to them. And so for the rest of the night they sheltered shivering in the no-mans land between the two armies.

The following morning a letter was sent out of the Close, addressed to Sir William Brereton.[8] It contained a blistering attack.

> Sir,
>
> Your last nights nightworke (which might well be ashamed of the light) is an Act of soe much Barbaritie, so remote from natural lawes and Christianitie, and soe dangerous to your souls, that wee cannot suffer you to sleepe in it another, and pray you may not harden your hearts to Comsumate it; for our parts wee are secure that neither the blood of those Innocents (if shed) can bee layd to our Chardge, nor dare wee faile to lett you understand to whom it must be imputed . . .

After nearly a page of moralising on the danger to their opponents' souls the letter finished:

> Wee pray God to keepe you from soe Merciless, unreasonable and wilfull a wretchedness as you are acting uppon these innocent Women whoe (uppon our engagements as wee are Gentlemen and Souldiers) have not done anything in this siege prejudiciall to you Cause by intelligence or other that wee know of. If this may not satisfy you, wee shall send two or three Gentlemen to meete the like number of yours to discuss the business by word of Mouth, lest this extremetie should be occasioned by some mistake. In the instant tyme, Remayning,
>
> Your Servants,
> Thomas Tyldesley
> Her. Bagot

Litchfield Close
28th May 1646.

But Sir William Brereton was not there to receive the Royalist Commander's denunciations. Having issued his orders he had departed, probably with the Shropshire Foot, to visit other parts of his command, leaving his subordinates to carry out his instructions. Perhaps his conscience troubled him and he found it easier to remove himself from the scene. So when, the same day, Sir Thomas Tyldesley received a reply to his letter, it came from the hand of Lieut.-Colonel Gerrard, who wrote:

> Gentlemen,
> In the absence of my Superior Comaunder I have perused your letter of this day directed to my General or Comaunder in Chiefe of this Leaguer, which is full of the bombastic Language of one of you, much like a Wilde Bull in a nett, and (according to your accustomed manner) grosely abusing the Sacred Word of God, by which you and all your Complices must one day bee judged. And for soe much of your paper as is worthie to bee considered of, I return you this Answere. That if you soe farr wish the welfare of yourselves and those deluded persons with you as to Certifie mee that you desire to send two or three Gentlemen to meete the like number of ours for the surrender of Litchfield Close, and the submission of yourselves and those with you to the Justice of the Parliament, I shall then recommend your desires of that nature (if it bee not too late) to my Generall, and bee ready to doe you and all with you any friendly office therein; otherwise I shall rather supress your follie (in thinking wee will receive your Friends backe into our quarters, or Retaine those not yett sent in to you) than answer your expectations in the least measure more than to assure you that I am and will bee,
>
> Your dailie Watchman<br>in this Leaguer,
>
> May 28th 1646.                                    G. Gerrard.

While the above correspondence was being exchanged another letter[9] was brought to Sir William Brereton's headquarters, having been found in the towne by some of his men. It was wrapped around an arrow which had been shot out of the Close. Although unsigned, the handwriting was recognisable as that of Sir Thomas Tyldesley and the message it carried was addressed to the public at large.

> Whereas for our Constant persistance in our Loyalty in mainteyning and defending his Majesties Garrison of Litchfield according to our duety, Wee have visiblie seene the blessing of God in our protection against the fury of the Enemie hitherto, which hath soe farr enraged him, that not being able in a Cleanly way to prevayle against us, he hath betaken himselfe to Barbarous and Inhumane attempts in such as has never yett been practiced by Christians, bloodilie thrusting poore innocent Women and Children (noe way engaged in the quarrell) upon that danger which they dare not look uppon themselves, exposing them either to famine or their merciless Swords.
>
> Wee doe hereby desire the Countrey to take notice that the king is now in the head of a very powerful Army Consisting of 30,000 Men,* which by Gods Assistance may Resettle him and all his Loyall Subjects in their rights and wee doubt not but will speedilie Relieve us. If therefore the Country will suffer the Enemy to go in this Barbarous way and bring any more Women for their relation to us and a good Cause into this danger, or suffer those to continue in it whereby they may innocentlie perish

---

*He must have been referring to the Scottish army.

as is threatened, they must expect wee shall bee enforced to a course Contrary to our dispositions and if God shall enable us wee will endeavour to make all Men and their wives that consent to their proceedings, and endeavour not to hinder the same, to feele these miseries which are now so unjustlie inflicted upon us and ours, and this wee desire, that all that have any Relations in the Garrison to take notice and publish.

Signed by the generall Consent of the Whole
Garrison, 27th May, 1646.

This rather clumsy attempt at psychological warfare (the claim about King Charles and his army of 30,000 was so incredible that it would deceive nobody) must have infuriated Colonel Gilbert Gerrard. But before he could reply yet another written message was delivered to the headquarters. This took the form of a petition from the unfortunate women marooned between the Close and the town. By now they had spent two nights in the open, ostensibly without food, though it is hard to believe that those in the Close did not attempt to smuggle something to them over the wall. The petition had been drawn up the previous day, May 27th, probably by Ursula Hill whose signature appeared first. It read:

To His Excellencie Sir Wm. Brereton, Barronet and Major
Adjutant* Louthian,
The Humble Petition of the Miserable, Unfortunate Women
of Lich. whose names are subscribed.

Sheweth,

That by reason of your strict Comaund last night given to thrust us out of our Habitations uppon the Garrison of the Close of Lich. and the vyolent Carriage of your Soldyers to the great endangering of our lives Wee are enforced to lodge in the Cold open Ayre, and there likelie to perish for want of Reliefe to sustaine nature, which all the Garrison absolutely denying us either admittance, sustenance or other necessaries to defend us from the cold or hunger, whereby some of us are already much endangered in our healthes and likely to come to some untimely and miserable end, if not otherwise Remedyed and helped.

May it therefore please you out of your Christian Charitie to give us (Relying only uppon your mercie) Leave to Repaire into the Countrey to prevent perishing for lacke of food and lodgings, that soe our innocent blood may not untimelie bee taken away by this Lingring kind of death and most grievous suffering.

And wee shall ever pray for your health
and happinesse.
Ursula Hill
Anne Pyddock
Anne Cowsie
Elizabeth Baker
Judith Ballard
Katherine Burbry
Frances Sute
Elizabeth Stubes.

---

*The ladies had got their military ranks a little mixed.

Throughout the day of May 28th there was considerable activity at the Parliamentary headquarters on Beacon Hill, with messages flying to and fro. Early in the day Adjutant-General James Louthian sent his reply to the petition from the eight women. It was brief, and ran as follows:

> Gentlewomen,
>
> If your Husbands and their Comaunder in Chiefe will not showe you Mercie, you must knowe the greatest Mercie that can be showed from us is to execute Justice uppon you and all your Complices, which you shall find if you come within viewe of our Line, and they continue in their Rebellion and their obstinacie; only this for your Comfort that the Lady Bagot, Mrs. Snead [Sneyd], Mrs. Scrimshaw and Mrs. Archibald* [Archbold] with many more of your sex and opinion (soe soon as they can bee apprehended) shall be sent unto you for your Consort.
>
> Your Servant<br>James Louthian.

To this he added a postscript with a sting in the tail, adding a new dimension to the arguments with a suggestion of puritanical disapproval.

> I hope you will bee as deare to your husbands as Mrs. East was to hers, and as Mrs. Ward is to the Governor whoe would not suffer her to come forth to live with her husband, being one of your own Partie and late Comissarie at Tutbury, but after Conference had with him Caused her to bee guarded backe by two Captains into the Close.

There was indeed little for the comfort of the eight women in the Adjutant-General's letter, but as the day wore on they were joined by more wives including none other than the wife of the Deputy Governor himself. She got no more satisfaction from those in the Close than had her humbler companions. They were now ensconced in some of the abandoned works that lay between the Close and Minster Pool, and the Deputy Governor's wife joined them there and in desperation sat down and wrote 'to Sir Wm. Brereton or in his absence the next Comaunder in Cheife'[10]

> Sir,
>
> All the favour I can gett of the Close is this, to gett a Drumer to come to begg the favour from you that I may safe come to you my selfe with a drum to acquainte you with what answer I received from them.
>
> Your servant
>
> May 28th.                                    Arden Bagot

But the answer she got was little different from that extended to Ursula Hill.

> Lady,
>
> Your answer I desire not, you must remayne where you are till those within the Close submitt themselves to Parliament; yet if there bee a desire to meete uppon a treatie with three Gentlemen on either Partie, I will upon receipt of the names of such as Colonell Bagot shall nominate, send them safe passe, and the names of such as my Generall shall send to meete them, if I Receive the like from Colonell Bagot. And this never the sooner for Sir Thomas Tyldesley's false Rumor shott forth of the Close yesterday upon an arrowe, I have no more Madam, but that I am,
>
> Your Servant·
>
> May 28th.                                    James Louthian.

---

Lady Bagot was the wife of Sir Hervey Bagot and mother of Colonel Hervey Bagot; Mrs. Sneyd the wife of Colonel Sneyd; Mrs. Archbold the wife of Sir Henry Archbold, Chancellor of the Diocese of Lichfield. All of them had husbands in the Close, and presumably also Mrs. Scrimshaw.

No time was lost in passing this message[11] on to those in the Close. As a result Colonel Bagot penned a brief note to James Louthian:

> Sir,
>
> I understand by your Civill letter to my Wife (Which I received over the Wall) that you are willing to admitt of three Gentlemen, such as I shall name, to meete three others whoe shall be named by Sir Wm. Brereton. If you please to send mee your engagement for the Lord Aston, Sir Richard Dyott and Sir John Pate, I doe hereby assure you safe Conduct for such three Gentlemen as shall be appointed to meete them by you at our ould workes betwixt the Close Wall and your Lyne in Bacon Streete.
>
> Thus expecting your answer, I remayne<br>Your Servant
>
> Litchfield Close         Hervey Bagot<br>28th May 1646

The meeting was duly arranged, and sometime during the afternoon of May 28th Colonel Croxton, Lieut.-Colonel Gerrard and Captain Stone met Lord Aston, Sir Richard Dyott and Sir John Pate at a spot in Gaia Lane, between the opposing lines. While they were doing so, numbers of women were still being rounded up and sent to join the party in the old works. By now the Parliamentarians had given up any pretence of selecting relations of those in the Close; any women who came to hand were seized and impressed into the party. Under the circumstances it is hardly surprising that the meeting of the "Gentlemen" did not progress very far. Before long Sir Thomas Tyldesley and Sir Hervey Bagot were once again writing to Sir William Brereton, now returned to the Leaguer.

> Sir,
>
> The Gentlemen of our party have met with yours out of hopes to have Created a Right understanding concerning the Women forced by you within our Sleighted Workes, but your commissioners, pretending to have noe instruccions from you to agitate that business, made the Treatie short and fruitlesse. They seeme to make you a partie in this uncivill Act, where wee can hardlie persuade ourselves to fix it, unlesse you owne it yourselfe; Wee believe you to bee a man of soe much honour that you will neither begin nor Continue an Example which would imply soe great a thirst of Blood and produce Consequences of greater Inhumanitie than becomes Men (though of different persuasions in some things) yett linked together in many Common obligations and especiallie that greate one of Christianitie, which makes profession of better things. Wee have tried all other means, and they failing wee make this last particular Address to yourselfe as haveing the greatest Comaund of your Partie here, desireing you to understand that Wee are Resolved to defend this place like Men, and shall bee ready to encounter those Attempts that you shall make uppon us in a Manlike way. Wee cannot think ourselves bound either in honour, Conscience, or Reason to pester ourselves with these Multitudes of Women that you presse uppon us, Manie of them having noe Relation at all to us, and fewe or none to this place of our engagement. Besydes wee have noe entertaynement here but what is fitt for soldyers, and if we should receive them to a dyett soe unnatural to their weake bodies, wee should expose them to a destruction as inevitable as by famine. Wee are therefore Resolved that Wee neither Can nor Will admitt them, lest wee should Contract the guilt of their deaths uppon ourselves, and wee think our-selves bound to prevent it in you, and if it bee possible in all other, the ill consequences of it, by this timely premonition. Wee hope you will take it into your sad and serious

consideracion and since you are Resolved to bee our enemy, to have soe much regard for your owne honour at least, as to showe yourselfe a gallant one, and not to staine yourselfe with these inhumanities, which will render your Accompt greater at the Latter Day and lessen your esteem in the Reputation of the World, especially to us whoe (whatever opinion wee have of your Cause) will have a greater one of you if you prosecute it noblie.

Sir, since Captain Stone has left Civilitee soe farre, that he will not Answere a letter to a business wherein wee wholly relied uppon his word* yett wee are Confident that you will enforce the three ensigns to perform their perolles [paroles] which they cannot denie, and if Captain Hesketh be escaped, propose some faire exchange for the Prisoners wee released uppon your word. Resting,

Your Servants
Thomas Tyldesley
Hervey Bagot

Sir William Brereton had returned to Lichfield late on the 28th to find a sheaf of letters waiting for his atttention and everyone preoccupied with the affair of The Women. The next morning he sat down and wrote to his opposite number in the Close as follows:

Gentlemen,

Yours of the 28th I received and two former, soe full of impertinentcies and incivilities that I intended not to have vouchsafed any Answere, were it not that you might Conclude I had noe reply in Justification and Defence of that which you term Barbarous and Inhumane, which may bee most justly Retorted uppon yourselves for not admitting those access to their husbands whom the Lawes of God and Man have joined together, some whereof were never Ceasing to petition for access to them, by all or most whereof I Conceive you might Receive such abundent Informacion of the Condicion of your affairs abroad, as might bring you to a more Right understanding thereof, and teach you not to dispense such silly and senselesse untruths, as were those Papers shott into the towne and sayde to be signed by the whole Garrison, dated 28th of this instant May, a coppie whereof is inclosed, the first whereof (that I ever saw) was written by Sir Thomas Tyldesley (if wee know his hand) but signed by none wherein there is nothing more true than that which is most false, that the king is in the head of an Army of 30,000 Men, which you doubt not but will speedily Relieve you, and yett in the mean tyme you Refuse not only to give entertainment to the Wives of those with you (whose affections to you and your Cause so farre prevailed with them as to forsake their Wives, Families and Estates) but you doe also Retayne other mens Wives, (desired from you by their husbands), affirming your garrison to bee sufficiently able to entertayne whome you please at will.

You pretend this to bee an unparalled and unpresidented Act of Crueltie; wee can put you in mind of much more Crueltie practised by your Partie in Chester when the Wives and Children of those husbands with us were not only sent out before the cittie was besieged, but after the Suburbs taken, divers Persons sent forth, and their Howses and whole Estates of great value as well before the Siege as after the takeing of the Suburb seised uppon, which wee have not yett done to those wee have sent in to you, for their Families Remayne possessed of their Howses and Estates as when they left the same.

If there were any vyolence offered to any of these Women that were sent (for Children, none were sent but such as went on their owne accorde) wee must charge

---

*This last paragraph refers to an exchange of prisoners arranged with Captain Stone, whereby three of the Parliamentary ensigns in Royalist hands were to be exchanged for a Captain Hesketh in the hands of Parliament, on the basis of 3 Ensigns = 1 Captain.

the same uppon your score, whoe taking away all their provisions, left many of them to a mercielesse Enemy (as you term us), and disclaime any such thing to proceede from us farther than in sending those Wives to their Husbands whom God hath joynes together and were fitter to bee with them than with us.

You say Gods visiting hand* is uppon some of them. It is more than wee know or believe, but sure wee are that you or some of you did threaten and send amongst us some of those with you that were visited with the plague.

And whereas you lay to our Chardge the Barbarities and inhumanities Committed by us, I cannot but believe you have forgotten what hath been practised by yourselves in fireing all Bacon Street (whereby you advantaged us much but yourselves nothing, for you may see God hath made better provisions for us) and in Burneing and Ruining divers Families of your Friends in the Cittie nothing at all to your advantage or our predjudice.

You aggravate much the battering down of your Spire Steeple, not considering how much our Men were galled and annoyed from thence in severall places, and how much you had defiled the same with blood, what your selves had purposed and endeavoured by undermining and battering down the Chapple Steeple, (which still stands with its wounds) witnesse against you the little Respect you give to these places which you call the Houses of God, further than they may be serviceable to your owne needs.

You insist much uppon the defacing of the Auncenstral Monuments of Christian Piety in these parts of the Kingdom, and will not see the hand of Gods Justice uppon the same for the Ignorance and Superstition that hath been nourished and practiced in that place, the guilt whereof is further increased by being made use of to bee your only Refuge both for yourselves and those with you, and your Magazene, and therefore the most proper object to bee demolished by us, seeing it had been formerlie abused by others and none so much prophanely as by yourselves and those with you whom God, it seems, hath hardened because He hath purpose to destroy you, otherwise He would not suffer you to persist in your obstinatenesse when you cannot but knowe yourselves incapable of Reliefe and that the longer you hold out the worse Condicions you must expect, seeing you discover nothing at all but perversenesse and frowardnesse and cannot but know that it is as unsouldierlike as indiscrete for you to attempt to hold out that place now that you have no skeme of Reliefe since the king hath put himselfe wholly uppon his Parliament.

In your last you say you believe mee to bee a Man of honour soe much as that you cannot persuade yourselves to fix uppon mee this (as you say) uncivill act. And you Acknowledge mee the Comaunder of these Forces here, whereas formerlie, in your letter of 13th April directed to Adjutant-General Louthian, you speak scornfully and much more in your Answer to my first dated March 9th, which if you had remembered, might have spared you the Labour of reflecting that uppon mee which you then justified to bee souldyerlike in yourselves.

And whereas you desire I would take notice that you are Resolved to defend the place where you are in a Manlike way, you may hereby bee assured that by Gods assistance there shall bee as Manlike and Souldyerlike Attempts and Endeavours used for correcting your Insolences and Reducing you to obedience to the Parliament, if not makeing you examples to the Whole World for your desperate follie and obstinatenesse and impudence in mainteyning this Hould when you cannot but knowe there is no hope of Reliefe, and Render yourselves every day more uncapable of the Parliaments Clemencie, which you have soe often rejected, which if desired might have been extended to you. I shall therefore once more further advise you

---

*i.e. the plague.

forthwith to submit to the Mercie of the Parliament, so that Ruine which is otherwise inevitable fall uppon you, the prevention whereof (if you will yett embrace the same) is still desired by,

Your Servant,

Wm. Brereton

\*  \*  \*  \*  \*

At this point Sir William Brereton's clerk completed that volume of the Letter Book, just managing to squeeze in his Commanding Officer's name at the bottom of the last page. No doubt he opened another volume for the next letter, but that volume has not survived, and we are left wondering at the fate of the unfortunate women of Lichfield who were marooned, helpless between the two opposing forces. They are never mentioned in any of Brereton's despatches to Parliament, nor do they figure in the Diurnals (which were distinctly selective in their choice of news). What happened to Ursula Hill, Anne Pyddocke, Judith Ballard and all the others? One would dearly like to know, but history is silent on the subject. All one can do is to trace the subsequent movements of those members of the group whose lives are recorded for posterity. The only two who come into that category are Ursula Hill and Arden Bagot. Mrs. Bagot, wife of Colonel Hervey Bagot, survived the siege but died not long afterwards, in 1649. What happened to Ursula Hill is less certain. Her husband, John Hill, survived the war and in later years became Town Clerk and Coroner of Lichfield. His will, proved at the Prerogative Court of Canterbury in 1687,[12] makes no mention of any family, and the only reference to his wife is a note at the beginning to the effect that he wishes 'to be buried beside my dear wife Ursula in Litchfield Cathedral'. The Register of Burials of the Cathedral records John Hill was so buried on the 16th of March 1687, but nowhere is there any record of the burial of his wife Ursula. Unfortunately the register only runs from February 1664, anything which existed before that having been destroyed, so all we can say is that she died sometime before that date. It is likely that we shall never know what happened to the luckless wives.

How long the lengthy exchange of polemics between the two commanders continued (with an apparent indifference to the plight of the wretched women lying between them) is not recorded. But one interesting fact emerges from the correspondence. Sir William Brereton refers to the Royalists 'undermining and battering downe the Chapple Steeple (which still stands with its wounds)', from which we gather that the Parliamentary troops had taken a leaf out of the Royalists' book and had installed their sharpshooters in the spire of St. Mary's church.\*

As a result of the battering it received, the steeple of St. Mary's had to be rebuilt in 1682, at a cost of £35 8s 0d plus another £3 17s 6d for a globe on the top.

---

\*Until well into the 19th century St. Mary's was known as the 'Chapel Church', probably because it was formerly the chapel of the ancient Guild of St. Mary.

# SOURCE NOTES

## *Chapter VII*

1.   Sir William Brereton's, Letter Book, March 1646
2.   Ibid.
3.   Ibid.
4.   Ibid.
5.   I Samuel, v.25
6.   Sir William Brereton's, Letter Book, May 1646
7.   Ibid.
8.   Ibid.
9.   Ibid.
10.  Ibid.
11.  Ibid.
12.  Public Record Office, Chancery Lane

*Lichfield Cathedral after the siege*

*Chapter VIII*

# The Slighting of Lichfield Close

MAY turned to June, and June to July, and still Sir Thomas Tyldesley's garrison held out. With their lead mortars they returned Sir William Brereton's unexploded granadoes, and when all their iron cannon balls were expended they made these too out of lead from the cathedral roof with lumps of scrap iron in the middle. There are no records of any fighting during this period, but echoes of previous skirmishes occur in the pages of the register of St. Editha's Church, Tamworth, which records that on June 10th 1646 little Robert Lukin Brabin was baptised, the Vicar adding after the entry, 'his father was cruelly murdered by the enemy in Lichfield Close, after he was taken upon the enemies sally'. A few days later, on June 16th, he records the burial of Henry, son of Thomas Riccard of Comberford; 'his father Thomas was slain by the enemie in Lichfield Close'. The first entry suggests that at the time Sir Thomas Tyldesley's men were giving no quarter to prisoners.

All around Lichfield Royalist garrisons were falling — Bridgenorth, Ludlow, Tutbury, Ashby, and Dudley. One after another they succumbed, but still Lichfield held out. In the town the citizens must have wondered if the siege was ever going to end; but as they wondered events were gradually shaping themselves behind the scenes.

On June 6th, from Newcastle-on-Tyne, where he was with the Scots army, King Charles wrote a letter to 'The Lord Aston* and Sir Thomas Tyldesley'.[1] The messenger conveying it managed to get through to Lichfield Close and hand it the Governor.

> My Lord Aston and Tyldesley,
>     The greatest of my misfortunes is that I cannot reward soe gallant and loyall sub-jects as you are as I ought and would. For the present I must deal freely with you, and give you my condition, which is that I can give you no relief; but I desire you to hold out till Oxford bee rendered, which will be ranked amongst the rest of the good services done by you to your assured friend,
>                                         Charles R

---

*In his capacity as one of the King's Commissioners of Arraye.

The King's position was that, far from being at the head of the Scottish army, he was virtually their prisoner and as he said in the letter, could do nothing to relieve his loyal garrisons.

At Lichfield a council of war discussed the letter and decided that the true state of affairs concerning the King's cause must be ascertained. A parley was held with the Parliamentarians and permission obtained for Lieut.-Colonel William Hudson, one of the garrison, to go out of the Close and travel to Newcastle, returning to the Close when he had discovered the true state of affairs. This was granted and Colonel Hudson proceeded on his mission.

He returned with the news that the King had indeed no support, and carrying with him a letter[2] from Charles to all the governors of those garrisons which still held out. It read thus:

> Hudson,
>
> Not having time, I desire you to advertise all the severall loyall Governors of my remaining townes and forts that I wish them now to make their compositions, upon the best terms they may — for the truth is I cannot relieve them; but assure them, as their suffering is my greatest affliction, soe whenever God shall enable me, they shall reap the fruits of their fidelytye, nor shall ever grief go from my heart untill I have shewed by my successful accions that I am to all a real constant friend.
>
> Charles R.

On June 26th Oxford fell to Fairfax and his New Model Army, and it was apparent to all that the King's cause was utterly lost. The Lichfield garrison had fulfilled their final obligation to their sovereign, and they could honourably lay down their arms. Even so, there was a reluctance to take the final step, and it was not until the 10th of July that Sir Thomas Tyldesley finally surrendered the fortress of Lichfield Close to Parliament by handing it over to Adjutant-General James Louthian.

The Articles of Surrender[3] were negotiated on behalf of the Royalists by Lord Aston, Sir Joseph Pate, Sir Jervas Lucas, Sir Richard Dyott and Captain Thomas Glasier; on the Parliamentary side were Edward Mainwaring, Esq., High Sheriff of the County of Staffordshire, Lieut.-Colonel Gilbert Gerrard, Major Owen Cambridge, Captain-Lieutenant Stone and Captain Henry Slade.

The articles which they negotiated were as follows:

> 1. That because Sir Thomas Tyldesley and Colonel Bagot were satisfied, by the information of Colonel Hudson, (who having latelye gone out of that garrison, was permitted by the said Adjutant General to come in again), that the King hath no armie in the field to the number of one hundred men, nor any one garrison unbesieged, the garrison of the Close of Lichfield and all places whatsoever about it, with all the ordnance arms, ammunition, provisions for warre, with all magazines and stores thereunto belonging and all manner of goods whatsoever within the said garrison, (except what is allowed within the ensuing articles), shall be delivered to the said Adjutant General Louthian, or to whom he shall appoint to receive them, for the use of the Parliament, without any spoyle or embesilment, upon Thursday, the 16th day of the instant July, before eleaven of the clock in the morning.

2. That the said Sir Thomas Tyldesley, and Colonel Bagot, with all other following officers and souldiers, both of horse and foote, shall march out armed souldier-like, in such sorte as when they march towards an enemye, upon the said 16th of July, before the aforesaid hour of eleaven, unto such place at the end of Bacon Streete as the said Sir Thomas Tyldesley and Adjutant General Louthian shall appoint, and there draw up into one body of foote and one body of horse; and all and every of them (except such of them as are allowed horses and armes by virtue of these ensuing articles) shall then and there lay down their armes, and from them depart according to their several passes.

3. That the said Sir Thomas Tyldesley and Colonel Hervey Bagot, with field-officers, lords, baronetts, lieutenants, captains and gentlemen of quality, to the number of thirty-eight more, shall march forth of the said Close of Lichfield with forty horse and forty case of pistols and their swords; and the residue of the officers (reformed as well as others) with their swords onely; and all of them with their wearing apparell of what sort soever, together with their charters, evidences, and writings concerning their estates, dignityes or professions. And the said Sir Thomas Tyldesley and Colonel Hervey Bagot shall each of them have liberty to carry out twenty pounds apiece; the Lord Aston twenty pounds, and all colonells ten pounds apiece; the baronetts, captains lieutenants five pounds apiece; and all other gentlemen, clergiemen and officers not formally in this article comprised, three pounds apiece.

4. That all persons who were inhabitants in the Close before these warres (as well as members of the cathedral church as others) and all townsmen and citizens of Lichfield now in the Close, shall have liberty to carry all their goods to their own howses, and to the howses of their friends, the said goods being first apprised by such as shall be appointed by the committee of Parliament for this county to take an inventorye of them, and the owners giving public notice to the committee to be responsible for them, according to the ordinance of Parliament. And all such persons whose habitations were in the Close before these warres as aforesaid shall have libertye to remain there, submitting to all ordinances of Parliament. In habitants of the Close desirous to remain there, with their families and goods aforesaid, it shall be in the power of the said committee to suffer so many of them soe to do as they shall think fit.

5. That the above-named persons, as well as such as are excepted from composition (if any such bee) as others, shall have free passes to march to their places of abode (not interrupting the occupants thereof) or elsewhere within the kingdom of England (except to the place of his Majesties present abode) there to abide; as also to passe to and fro upon their occasions quietly and free from molestation for the space of three months next after the surrender of the said Close, engageing themselves by promise that in the interim they will not do anything prejudical to the Parliament or kingdom. And in case they do not perform their composition with the Parliament before the end of the said three months, then they to have safe passes (if they desireit) unto any port town, to be exported out of the kingdome, engageing themselves not to take up armes against the Parliament.

6. That all inferior officers and souldiers, and all other persons of whatever sort within the garrison, not comprised in the former articles, (except all Irish rebels who were in arms against the protestants in Ireland, and are to become prisoners) shall have free passe, without molestation, to march to their severall places of dwelling, or to their friends, and there to have libertye of abode and protection from time to time; conforming themselves in all ordinances of Parliament. And that so many of the said officers as desire to goe beyond the seas shall have safe passes to what port they shall nominate for transportation, and free quarter as well in their march home, as to the place of transportation if they soe resolve within one month after the surrender of the said Close.

7. That all ladyes, gentlewomen, and other women whatsoever, within the said garrison, shall have free libertye to go to their several places of abode, or to their friends, or else whither, with all their wearing apparell whatsoever, and two suites of bed linnen a-piece; and there to remain and be protected from violence or plunder of souldiers, doing nothing prejudicial to the Parliament.

8. That all persons comprehended in these articles who are unable by reason of sickness or wounds to march at the time aforesaid forth of the said Close, shall be allowed to remaine there until their recoverye, and then to have the benefit of these articles, according to their respective qualityes, and provision to be made in the mean time for such of them as are in want.

9. That all writings, evidences and charters belonging to the cathedral, as also the library thereto, shall be preserved and kept together in the Close, until the Parliament shall otherwise order; and it shall be lawful for every minister and other person in the Close (not formerly comprised in the capitulation) to carry along with them notes, writings and books; but their printed books are to be compounded for being first viewed and aprised by such as the committee of this countye shall think fit.

10. That if any souldier or other person, within the said garrison shall ignorantly, fraudulently or otherwise, break any of these articles, the offender onley to be punished therefore, and others not to be prejudiced by his offence, unless they were thereunto assenting or shall refuse (being requested) to do their best endeavours for his apprehension.

11. That upon the signing of these articles, each partye shall deliver hostages to the other, for the performance of them.

| Signed by us, in the behalfe of Sir Thomas Tyldesley and Colonel Bagot. | Signed by us, in the behalfe of Adjutant General Lowthian. |
|---|---|
| Walter Aston | Ed. Mainwaring |
| Jo. Pate | Hen. Stone |
| Jervas Lucas | G. Gerrard |
| Ric. Dyot | Henry Slade |
| Thomas Glasier | Owen Cambridge |

Thus, having resisted all attempts of their enemies to dislodge them, and having maintained the King's cause in the City of Lichfield with great gallantry and perseverance to the very end, on the morning of July 16th the garrison marched out of the Close for the last time, with drums beating, colours flying and armed 'souldier-like'. They turned right into Beacon Street and, watched by the townsfolk, marched to the end of the street to a place near by the camp of the Cheshire regiment and Sir William Brereton's headquarters. There they laid down their arms and went their various ways.

The party which Sir Thomas Tyldesley led out of the Close consisted of far more than just the two Bagot regiments. According to Sir William Brereton's report to the Parliament the garrison which surrendered mustered as follows:

8 Colonels
2 Lieut.-Colonels
9 Majors
31 Captains

15 Lieutenants
10 Cornets
 9 Ensigns
700 Common Souldiers

while of civilians there were 6 Commissioners of Arraye and 20 esquires.

It would appear from these figures that for a considerable time Lichfield had been a rallying point for any one wanting to carry on the struggle on behalf of the king. (Sir Jervas Lucas, for example, had come here from Belvoir Castle after its surrender, with 100 men). This would account for the relatively high number of senior officers in the garrison. Possibly this was a result of a decision made when Sir Jacob Astley, the Royalists' Sergeant Major General of Foot, had visited Lichfield in January. It is significant that in the Articles of Surrender Sir Thomas Tyldesley is described as 'Deputy Governor to Sir Jacob Astley', who although he was not present at Lichfield, had assumed the nominal governorship. Lichfield was central geographically, it was well fortified, and it was an obvious place for making a last stand. This would explain why the garrison had held out so long, while others around them were surrendering.

When they marched out they left behind them, reported Brereton,

5 pieces of ordnance
800 muskets
100 cases of pistols
4 months provisions and
'a small quantity' of powder and match.

The news of the surrender of Lichfield was received by Parliament with great rejoicing. Meeting on July 19th, the House of Commons resolved that the Articles for the Delivering up of Lichfield Close, together with additional information on the surrender, should be printed and published. They further resolved that orders should be given to Sir William Brereton to demolish the walls of Lichfield Close forthwith, and that Tuesday, July 21st should be a National Day of Thanksgiving for the surrender of Oxford and Lichfield, Members of Parliament attending their own thanksgiving service in St. Margaret's, Westminster, at which Dr. Smith would preach. It is interesting to surmise on the form a Puritan service of thanksgiving would take; since music was forbidden, Te Deums and psalms of praise would definitely be out. Perhaps Dr. Smith, after preaching for sixty minutes, turned over his hour-glass and continued for a second spell.

So the slighting of Lichfield Close began. Technically, slighting of the walls of a fortification meant simply removing the battlements, but those at Lichfield were razed to the ground so thoroughly that little of them was left. Only in the north-west and south-west corners of the Close do any traces remain. The two gateways were allowed to stay, but the portcullises and the gates themselves were removed.

The document published by Parliament,[4] entitled 'ARTICLES For the Delivering up of Lichfield Close' is an interesting communication. It begins with the following preamble:

To the Honourable
WILLIAM LENTHALL Esq;
Speaker to the Honourable House of Commons.

Honorable Sir,

It hath pleased God, after a long siege, to deliver this stronghold into our hands; there hath not been any Omission of our utmost endeavour to have expedited this work sooner: wherein the Care, Courage and Industry of Adjutant General Louthian hath been very helpful to us. But the strength of the place, both in fortifications, in Provisions of men, Armes and all other respects is such that it was not possible for us, either by Battery, Mines or assault to have reduced it, so that we were necessarily enforced to make tryal of this way by Composition to take it in. The Enemy hath long persisted to make very high Demands (as the bearer hereof can inform you) and of our resolutions not to hearken to large terms, which inclined them to surrender upon the Articles here enclosed, which he have made bold absolutely to conclude upon, in regard there is nothing (as we Concieve) contrary to any Ordinance of Parliament, nor in any way prejudicial to your service, or dishonourable to be yeelded unto (in our judgement). We are now in very great straits how to satisfie the Forces that have assisted us, which are about two thousand, so they may return to their respective Counties without spoiling this Countrey, [County] which is not able to pay them. We hear of moneys which you have been pleased to assigne us out of the Excise, at the first return of these Forces from the Defeat of Sir Jacob Astley, and since out of lands of Sir Robert Wolsley and Mister Warner; but neither of these afford us any present supply; which the Souldiers must have, or they will presse this County above what it is able to bear. We have entered into verie great Debts for the carrying on of this service hitherto, and we have now treated with the several Forces to understand what present moneys will content them; and they have agreed to march off to their own Counties upon the receipt of a month's pay, which amounts to Three Thousand Pounds. Therefore for the preservation of our County, and for the satisfaction of those who deserve more than they demand (if it were in our power to give them) we have (notwithstanding our former engagements) taken this debt upon us, and have given them assurance, to their content, to pay it in short time. We do therefore make it our humble suit, that the Honourable House will please to make the former ways you have been pleased to think of for our repayment effectual, for our speedie discharge of those great debts we are forced to make for your service. What further particulars the House desires concerning this service, this bearer, who hath been present in the service, is able fully to impart. For the condition of this County and Forces thereof, we take leave to refer you to another letter here enclosed; humbly desiring it may be read; whereby we shall be obliged to remain Your humble and most obedient servants

|  |  |  |
|---|---|---|
|  | E. Mainwaring | Leicester Barboure |
|  | Phil. Jackson | Joseph Whitehalgh |
| Lichfield Close | Hen. Stone | Will. Bendy |
| July 14th 1646 | Edw. Broughton | Joseph Simcox |

This letter, from the Committee for the County of Stafford, throws some light of the difficulties experienced in funding the war on the Parliamentary side and also explains what had been going on behind the scenes during the period since June 26th. Sir Thomas Tyldesley had been driving a hard bargain over the surrender and as a result had been able to obtain terms far better than those with which Sir William Brereton had been threatening him throughout the siege.

The pamphlet then went on to give the terms of the Articles, which we have already seen, followed by a list of the 'Commanders, Officers, and Gentlemen of quality that were in the Close of Lichfield at the Surrender thereof.' It is interesting to look through the list of officers for the names of those who were serving in the garrison when it was formed in 1643. In Bagot's Regiment of Horse, only two familiar names remain, that of Captain Will Ridgley [Ruggely] who must have commanded his troop right from the beginning to end, and Lieut. Walmsley.

With Bagot's Foot, however, it was a different matter. Their Commanding Officer, Colonel Hervey Bagot, is still at their head, though his second in command, Major Harsnett, no longer appears in the list. We know he was still serving on April 24th (William Pearson, the deserter, describes himself as serving under him), so he must have been a recent casualty.

Of the company commanders we still find the names of Captains Thomas Glasier, Badderley, Turnpenny, Dier [Dyott?], Collier, Johnson [Johnston?] and Startin (promoted from Lieutenant). Under them were still Lieutenants East, Robinson and Blenkhorne. None of the eight cornets and nine ensigns have familiar names.

The publication ends with a statement by Henry Stone, one of the County Committee who acted as a Parliamentary commissioner for the negotiation of the surrender. He was also, it will be remembered, a captain on Sir William Brereton's staff. The statement reads as follows:

The Information of
Henry Stone

—

I, having some private discourse with Sir Tho. Tyldesley, about a week before the surrender of the Garrison, he told me he had an order from the King, that when he heard Oxford was surrendered, he should make his Conditions for the surrender of the Close, and reserve his Forces in their several Counties as privately as might be, till there were an opportunity.

He further said that the Parliament should have all the Garrisons, but when we thought all was our owne, we should see a force which would cut our throats: and this would be done before the next spring.

He also said the King, he thought, would come to London and speak you faire and seeme to comply, but he will not sit downe so, but take his advantage when time serves, and so would he [Sir Thomas] and many more.

These words, or to this effect, being delivered to me, I thought it my duty to declare it.

July 16th 1646

Hen. Stone.

In the event, Sir Thomas Tyldesley's prophesy was not far wrong. King Charles was kept at Newcastle by the Scots army and for the next year kept up a tenacious bargaining on the national issues at stake. He hoped to profit by the differences between Parliament and the Army as well as the differences between the English and Scottish governments. In the end the Scots handed over the King to the Parliamentary Commissioners in return for an installment of the money due to their army for the service performed in England. In due course he was seized by the Army, tried and found guilty of treason, and executed on January 30th, 1649. Four days later his eldest son was proclaimed King Charles II in Edinburgh.

\* \* \* \* \*

After the surrender of Lichfield Sir William Brereton's force stayed on to demolish the walls of the Close, and Parliament voted £5,000 for their pay. Then they marched back to their home counties and shortly afterwards to demobilization. Sir William hung up his sword once again and resumed his duties in Parliament, living in Croydon where a grateful Parliament bestowed on him, for his services, the former Bishop's Palace. He died there on the 7th April, 1661.

Two members of his force deserve further mention. John Fox, the Gunner, who had been responsible for shooting down the centre spire of the cathedral, came to an untimely end. In September 1651, when he was stationed in Stafford, he was charging his piece to fire a salute on the arrival of Major-General Harrison in the town when he 'was shot in pieces with that cannon, which accidentally took fire. His chin and one arm being shot off, he died a day or two after.' From this account[5] it would appear that the charge exploded when he was ramming it; not surprisingly there was no shortage of people to claim the occurrence as an act of Divine retribution.

But the one who carved for himself the biggest niche in history was Captain Henry Stone, former merchant of Walsall, right hand man to Sir William Brereton and member of the Parliamentary Committee for Staffordshire. In 1651 Charles II was in Scotland and led an expedition south to recover his kingdom. On September 3rd he fought and lost the Battle of Worcester. The events which followed; his hiding in the oak tree as Boscobel, his adventures at Moseley Old Hall and his escape to Bristol in the guise of a groom escorting Jane Lane and riding pillion on her horse; all these are well-known. The part played in this drama by Captain Stone was an unwitting one, but it was he who, as Governor of Stafford, signed the authority which permitted Jane Lane, accompanied by her groom, to travel to Bristol to attend the lying-in of her sister. In doing so, his signature on that piece of paper had a profound effect on the course of English history.

Among those who rallied to the aid of Charles II in his march south was Sir Thomas Tyldesley. After the surrender of Lichfield Close he had returned to his native Lancashire where he continued to work for the Royalist cause as a secret service agent, there and in Ireland. In August 1651, when the Royalist forces were passing through Lancashire, he met his end in a typical fashion, leading a cavalry charge against Parliamentary troops in Wigan Lane, Leigh. His horse was shot from under him, and while still on the ground he was pistolled by a trooper. He ended his life as he would no doubt have wished to, fighting valiantly for his sovereign. He was buried in the parish church of St. Mary, Leigh, the burial place of his family, where a well-tended brass plaque bears record to him in these words:

> At the east end of the Tyldesley Chantrey of St. Nicholas, within this ancient parish church, resteth the body of Sir Thomas Tyldesley, of Tyldesley, Moreleys and Myerscough in this county, Knight, a Major General in His Majesty's army and Governor of Lichfield, who was slain fighting gallantly for his Royal Master under James, Earl of Derby, in the Battle of Wigan Lane near this place, on the 25th day of August, 1651.

The plaque would appear to be of 19th Century origin, but an older memorial was erected in Wigan Lane near the spot where he met his end, with the following inscription:[6]

> An high act of gratitude erected this monument, which conveys the memory of Sir Thomas Tyldesley to posterity. Who served King Charles I as Lieutenant Colonel at Edgehill Battle, after raising forces of horse, foot and dragoons. And for the desperate storming of Burton on Trent, over a bridge of 36 arches, received the honour of Knighthood. He afterwards served in all the war in great command; was Governor of Lichfield; and followed the fortunes of the Crown through the three kingdoms; and never compounded with the rebels though strongly invited. And on the 25th of August was here slain, commanding as Major General under the Earl of Derby. To whom the grateful erector, Alexander Rigby Esq. was cornet. And when he was High Sheriff of the County, A.D. 1679, placed this high obligation on the whole family of the Tyldesleys.

Sir Hervey Bagot also carried on the struggle against Parliament. As late as 1659 he is reported as taking part in an abortive rising of Royalists under Sir George Booth in Cheshire. For this he was indicted, but got away with being bailed for £2,000, and survived the wars.

For Lichfield people hostilities ended with the close of the third siege. Subsequent fighting did not affect the city, but several of those who had supported the King suffered for their loyalty, having their estates sequestrated. Some of them compounded and took off their sequestration by payment of a lump sum. Among these were Michael East who paid £35 15s 0d and John Hill who had to hand over £270 0s 0d.[7] Others, such as Jeffery Glasier, hung on in the hope that a change in government would restore their estates to them without any loss. Sir Richard Dyott, who had a large amount at stake, appealed against his sequestration.

The basis of the appeal makes interesting reading. It has been suggested that it shows up Sir Richard in rather a bad light, as one who was trying to run with the hare and hunt with the hounds, but it should be remembered that he was a lawyer by profession, and in his appeal is pleading a case for himself before a court of law.

The appeal[8] begins with a statement by the sequestrators:

> To the right honourable the Barrons of Exchequer, Commissioners for appeals in case of sequestracion.
>
> The Certificate of Us of the Committee of the County of Stafford, whose names are hereunto subscribed.
>
> According to an order of 29th *Seprembris*, 1646, made of the Committee of Lords and Commons for sequestracions, and another order of 6th *Junii* 1649, made by your Lordships (both which are hereunto annexed) for the examination of the matter and cause of Sir Richard Dyotts sequestracion, we have given him the heads of his charge, and that he might certify the true state of his cause (as we are thereby required) have received his allegacions made for his defence and discharge wherein he doth in effect confesse the whole matter of fact layed to his charge, but endeavoureth to excuse and avoyd it: which charges and allegacions, together with the depositions of his witnesses taken upon oath, and the interrogatoryes upon which they were examined, we return sealed up with our seales to your Lordshipps and submit to your grave judgement.
>
>                              Tho. Crompton      Hen. Stone
>                              E. Mainwaring      Leicester Barbonel

The sequestration against which Sir Richard Dyott appealed was as follows:

> August 16th, 1646.                    By the Committee of the County of Stafford.
>
> These are to certify, to all whom these may concerne, that the estate, real and personal, of Richard Dyott is sequestrated. His personall estate is very inconsiderable. And as touching his lands, these are the particulars as they were in tyme of peace:

| | | |
|---|---|---|
| Certain lands at Freeford, per annum | | £60 |
| In the parishes of Whittington | | 40 |
| In the Constablewick and Towneship of Streethay and Morghull | | 50 |
| In Stichbrooke | | 30 |
| In Chorley | | 30 |
| In Stafford | in leases for years | 30 |
| In Lichfield | | 10 |
| | | £250 |

Out of this the Committee allowed him to keep £100 for the maintenance of his family, the rest being sequestrated. It was also certified that his house at Stafford, a very fine stone building, had been altogether demolished and his house in Sadler Street, Lichfield, very much defaced. This last house was the one, it will be recalled, which the women of Lichfield had referred to in their petition to Lady Dyott during the siege.

The charges made against Sir Richard[9] then followed, and after them the 'allegacions' or defence which he submitted.

The Heades of the Charges against Sir Richard Dyott.

I. That the sayde Sir Richard Dyott was at Edgehill battel on the late King's side in the yeare 1642, that he was taken prisoner and committed to the Marshalsey in Coventrie, where he was detained divers months.

II. That in the yeare 1645 he left his dwelling house in the citty of Lichfield and removed with his family into the Close Lichfield, which was garrisoned with the forces of the enemy, and there continued until it was surrendered to the use of the Parliament, and treated for the delivery thereof.

Sir Richard Dyotts Allegacion for Himselfe.

He confesseth it to be true that he chanced to go to Edgehill that day that the battel was there fought, and to be on the late Kings side *in place* but not *in action*; for he sayeth that he went *not with any purpose* to fight, *nor with any knowledge* that there would be fighting, neither did he take up arms on either side; but went thither on another occasion *as a messenger sent* by the citty of Lichfield with a letter of denyall to his late Majestie, who formerlie by his letter had earnestly requested the sayd citty to lend and deliver unto him money, plate and armes; which request they denyed and caused a civil answer to be drawne up by the sayde Sir Richard, expressing the causes of their denyall, which the sayde Sir Richard, with many others, subscribed; and afterwards he and John Burns Gent., deceased, (the most ancient Maister of the citty and a person known to be well affected to the Parliament) were entreated by the chiefe officers and inhabitants of best ranke in that citty, to carry and present the same unto his Majestie. And that this, and none other, was the cause of their going to the sayde King at that time, whome they accidentally found at Edgehill, but expected to have found at a nearer distance.

And the sayde Sir Richard confesseth that he was taken by a party of horse which came from Coventrie, in his inn at Southam, when he was preparing for bed, conveyed to Coventrie and there confined in the Marshalsey; but he verilie believeth *that his restraint was rather out of suspicion that was had of him in reggard of his relation to his late Majestie* (as having had the honour to be of his late counsel in the North than of any offence he had actuall committed against the Parliament, and rather for prevencion than punishment.

He likewise sayeth *that he never went to any of the late Kings garrisons, but that some of the late Kings forces came to the citty of Lichfield, where his dwelling house was and is, and there settled themselves and garrisoned the place; that the citty of Lichfield, as well as the Close, was garrisoned with the sayde Kings forces;* that he and his family continued at the sayde dwelling-house in the city of Lichfield until the month of August 1645; at which time the sickness was grown soe hott, and so much dispersed in the sayde citty that he was constrained together with his family, to remove for the safety of their lives; *that as his removal was not voluntary, but necessary, soe it was but out of one part of the garrison that was infected to another that was cleere.*

That he never did beare armes, or in any sorte act against the Parliament, but imployed his best endeavours to right, releive and help those who were imprisoned, vexed or troubled for their good affecions and services to the Parliament: and namely (amongst others) Major Foxe, Mr. Allen of Frodley [Fradley], Mrs. Swinfen, Lieutenant Sheldon, divers other prisoners and his neighbours in the town and country, which brought him into such suspicion and hatred amongst many of the soldiers that would publiquely rayle against him and threaten him, as being in hearte a Parliamentarian (as they put it).

Lastly, that he persuaded many, and particularly his own sonnes, to take the National Covenant and Negative oath,* and was present at the treaty for the delivery of the Close.

The fourteen years of the Interregnum was a bad time for Lichfield. The Monarchy, the Lords and the Church of England had each disappeared; now the Commons were to follow them as Cromwell dissolved the Rump and ordered his men to remove the Mace with his famous remark 'What shall we do with this bauble?'. There followed the period of dictatorship by Oliver Cromwell, the Lord Protector, a period which the Churchwardens of St. Mary's Church, Lichfield, referred to in their account book,[11] in 1653, as 'Ursupante Olivero Tyranno' [during the arrogation of the Tyrant Oliver], a comment made not without risk to themselves.

Economically, the city suffered badly. Since its foundation it had depended on the presence of the cathedral and all the activity that went with it as the centre of a large diocese. The Bishop of Lichfield and the Dean and Chapter had received their revenues from a wide area of the country in the form of rents and tythes, while the various parishes of the diocese sent their 'Chad's Pennies' towards the upkeep of the cathedral. A large number of the inhabitants of Lichfield earned a living from these sources. The Dean and the Canons had their stipends; so did the lay officials such as the Chapter Clerk, Diocesan Registrar, Master of the Choristers, Lay Vicars and the Proctors who worked in the Bishop's Courts (including the Probate Court). Many artisans such as stone masons, carpenters and plumbers, candle makers, scriveners and parchment makers derived their living from the Close, and finally there was the large contingent of domestic servants who found employment in the homes of the wealthier of the above list.

Now, under the Commonwealth, all this disappeared. There was no longer a Diocese of Lichfield and the cathedral was in ruins. The clergy had no stipends, not even one-fifth as their brother priests ejected from the parishes had. Some managed (Zachary Turnpenny stayed in Lichfield and even managed to become Sheriff of the City in 1658) but others lived as beggars, relying on charity. There was no longer work for artisans or domestics, producing an unemployment problem in a city already decimated by the plague in which over 800 died.

Some idea of the loss of revenue can be gathered from the following list of lands belonging to the See which were sold during the time of the Commonwealth, the proceeds, of course, going to Parliament.

---

* The form of this oath taken in the City of Lichfield was as follows:[10]
Civitas Lichfeldensis                                                          May 31, 1650
These are to certify that Will. Parrice of Wall in the Countie of Stafford, hath taken the Engagement to be true and faithfull to the Commonwealth of England, as it is established without a Kinge or House of Lords, and hath subscribed his name before us, the Day and Yeare above written.        Richard Drafgate ⎱ Bailiffs
                                                                    Nicho. Deakin ⎰

Lands belonging to the See of Lichfield sold during the Commonwealth:[12]

|  | £ | s | d |
|---|---|---|---|
| 1647. Prees Manor, Salop, sold Dec. 18th to Enoch Smith | 1121 | 16 | 0 |
| 1648. Prees Manor, &c. there sold April 21 to Thomas Harper | 866 | 5 | 0 |
| Sawley Fee-Farm rent sold March 20, to Nathaniel Hallows | 4 | 0 | 0 |
| Fee-Farm rent of Itchington, of £82 per ann. | 866 | 15 | 6 |
| sold to N. Taylor and William Brudges | | | |
| Fee-Farm rent of Lichfield City, sold, September 18th, | 700 | 0 | 0 |
| to Alderman Andrews | | | |
| 1650. Burton in Wirral Manor, sold, March 22nd to | | | |
| William Steel, for | 5340 | 0 | 0 |
| Farndon Manor, sold March 23rd, to Nehemiah Massey | 118 | 16 | 8 |
| Knutshall Manor, in the county of Stafford, sold | 833 | 9 | 9 |
| March 23rd to Sir Ar. Haslerigg | | | |
| Eccleshall Manor, sold Sept, 28th to John Holland, | | | |
| Nathaniel Andrews and John Bowles | 14224 | 3 | 10 |
| Coventry palace, sold Jan 1st to N. Lacey, | 105 | 0 | 0 |
| Samuel Palmer and Obadiah Chambers. | | | |

£29180  6  9

All of this represented capital and income lost to Lichfield, with the possible exception of the Lichfield Fee-Farm purchased by Alderman Andrews.

To this must be added the physical damage caused to the whole city by the war, and in particular by the last siege. Outside the Close, practically the whole of Beacon Street had been burnt to the ground by the Royalists and the northern part of Dam Street had also suffered in the fighting. The area around the George Inn, from the 'backsyde' of which Captain Coldhurst had played his mortars with such effect, had probably suffered much from the counter-battery fire from inside the Close. So, too, had the steeple of St. Mary's Church.

A total casualty, in the first siege, was the Market Cross erected by Dean Denton (c.1470-1522) by St. Mary's Church 'for market-folk to keep dry in'; it was composed of eight arches supporting a vaulted roof and was decorated with two crucifixes and figures of the apostles, a feature which guaranteed its destruction by Lord Brooke's soldiers.

Apart from damage caused by gunfire, all the churches suffered from the ravages of Parliamentary troops carrying out the destruction of anything contrary to Puritan principles — the tearing down of communion rails, the breaking up of fonts and the smashing of statues, painted windows and organs. St. Chad's suffered greatly in this respect for it had Parliamentary troops billeted in it in both the first and third sieges. Yet in its plate the church has a fine example of a silver communion cup, bearing the inscription 'St. Chadds in Lichfield. The gift of John Hammersley, 1632'. Somehow it escaped the despoilers; perhaps, like the St. Chad Gospels at the cathedral, it was carefully hidden. Another church which suffered badly was the chapel of St. John's Hospital. The Master of St. John's (the incumbent), John Macon, took himself off to Durham at the beginning of the war, leaving his old men to fend for themselves. He never returned, and while he was away the chapel and the Master's house fell into disuse so that in 1662, when Bishop Hackett visited the place the Almsmen complained to him that 'Our mansion house, (wherein formerly hath been kept good hospitality) is now become a cage for owls', while John Macon, writing from Durham to the Bishop's Registrar, admitted that 'The ruins of the House and chapel . . . are a common object of pity and compassion'.[13] It is likely that much of the damage to both buildings was the result of action by Parliamentary troops.

With the advent of the Commonwealth one change to the interior of every church was the removal of the royal arms from the chancel arch. At. St. Mary's this did not occur until 1650, the entry in the Churchwardens' Accounts reading, 'To washing [i.e. whitewashing] out the Kings arms, five shillings.'

On April 6th, 1648, Parliament published an 'Ordinance of the Lords and Commons, assembled in Parliament, for the Maintainence of a Ministry in Lichfield.'[14] The following citizens, who between them represented the Parliamentary interest in Lichfield, were named: Michael Biddulph, Michael Noble, Richard Pyot, Richard Swinfen, Zachary Babbington, Esquires and Menry Mott, Thomas Saxon, Richard Drafgate, Thomas Minors, Thomas Caterbanke and William Hammersley, of the City of Lichfield Gents, and were appointed to organise the spiritual welfare of the citizens of Lichfield. To this end they were required to sequester,

> the houses, rents, revenues, books, deeds, evidences and all writings and records belonging to the Dean, Dean and Chapter, Canons, Prebendaries, Vicars Choral, Officers or Ministers belonging to the Cathedral Church of Lichfield; as likewise all moneys, goods and materials bought or given, for repairing the said church, in whose hands soever the same remaineth; together with all arrearages of rents, pensions and moneys due and not yet paid; and all that out of the said revenues &c. they pay unto two such able and godly ministers, appointed by the Committee of Plundered Ministers and approved by the assembly of Divines, for their present maintainence and encouragement in preaching the word and dispensing sacraments and ordinances in the several congregations and parishes within the said city of Lichfield, the sum of three hundred pounds per annum, viz, to either of the said two ministers the sum of one hundred and fifty pounds per annum to be paid at the end of every quarter of the year; the first payment to begin the five-and- twentieth day of March 1648 and to continue during their natural lives; and that they do also set out and deliver to the said ministers, so approved, two good and convenient dwelling houses, belonging to the said Dean, Dean and Chapter &c, now sequestered, or to be sequestered, by reason of the delinquency of the owners thereof; to wit, to either of the said ministers one house for his dwelling, well repaired and fitted for his use, with gardens and other appurtanances.

The first two men to be appointyed under this ordinance were Thomas Miles, who took over the ministry of St. Chad's parish, and William Langley, who was installed in the vicarage, or to be more exact the 'lectureship', as it was now called, of St. Mary's. Miles was a Puritan, but Langley had been in orders of the Church of England, though he had accepted the Presbyterian practices now required. Even so, his churchmanship did not satisfy the committee who appointed him, and in due course he was accused of preaching on Christmas Day and also of administering the sacraments according to the Book of Common Prayer. For this he was ejected from his ministry and his place taken by Nathan Butler, his assistant. Langley published a pamphlet entitled *The Persecuted Minister*, in which he related his experiences.

Only at St. Michael's did the old order prevail. There, Thomas Hubbocke was curate from 1638 to 1676, though his position did not go unchallenged. An entry appears in the church accounts for 1653, 'Payde to a strange minister that staid two or three days in hope to be admitted here, — 1 shilling 6 pence.' Mr. Hubbocke and his congregation appear to have been successful in persuading the stranger that he was not wanted at St. Michael's.

In common with the rest of the country, Lichfield felt the stern hand of Puritanism. Christmas became a fast instead of a feast, the May Fair and the Shrove-tide Fair were abolished, and such pastimes as 'promiscuous dancing, maurice-dancing*, tipleing, gameing, quarrelling and wantonesse' could result in the offenders finding themselves before the justices.[15] As always happens under a repressive regime, there were persons ready to pay off old scores on their neighbours by reporting them to the authorities.

For nearly fourteen years England experienced this unaccustomed hegemony, first under Parliament, then under the dictatorship of Oliver Cromwell as Lord Protector and lastly for a short time under his son Richard. During this time the city of Lichfield slowly returned to normal, though it remained a poor community without the economic benefits of the ecclesiastical establishment; for the Cathedral Close remained a devastated wasteland around the ruins of a noble building.

Something of this desolation is conveyed by a number of surveys carried out during the Interregnum and shortly after the Restoration. The first of these, a survey of the property of the Dean and Chapter and the Vicars Choral,[16] was carried out in 1649 in accordance with the Act for the Maintenance of Ministers already mentioned. The surveyors were George Smith, John Fisher and Samuel Foxcrofte. That part of the survey which covered the property in the close (other property covered a wide area) took place in July. Starting by the West Gate and going into the first court of Vicars' Close, the surveyors mention each house, its owner and its

---

*Lichfield had its own particular form of Morris Dancing, different from that practiced elsewhere.

occupier and the state of it. The first one was owned by William Lambe, probably the one we know as blacksmith and soldier in the citizens' company. This house was in good repair, but next door but one, the house of Mr. Hind, was 'all torn to pieces by granadoes, and much of the materials carried away'. Most of the damage in the Close appears to have been caused by granadoes (mortar bombs); certainly the most effective weapon used in the sieges.

Other houses damaged were that of Zachary Turnpenny, Subchanter, which was described as 'defunct', and two little houses next to it 'void and much ruined', The Vicars' Hall was 'much demolished and spoiled; not worth repairing', and, unkindest cut of all, the Vicars' Boghouse and the chamber over it was 'utterly ruinated'!

Outside Vicars' Close, among the houses of the Dean and Chapter, that of the Precentor, Canon Higgins, was described as 'exceedingly ruined and demolished', while that of Mr. Hipps, Prebendary of Freeford, was 'all ruined and pulled to pieces', as was the Deanery next to it. On the south side of the Close, where they were within sight of and easy range of the mortars across the pool, nearly every house was badly damaged, being described variously as 'broken and torn with granadoes', 'ruinated and spoiled' and 'much out of repair'. So, too, were both gatehouses.

Of the cathedral church, the surveyors had this to say,

> The ground of the open space of the Close we valued not, most of which is the churchyard belonging to the cathedral. Nothing about the cathedral church valued. The whole fabric of it is exceedingly ruinated; much lead and iron was taken away whilst it was a garrison, and much lead and other materials is taken away since and is continually by evil persons taken away by night. A great part of the roof uncovered. If some course be not taken to preserve it within a little time, the lead will be all gone and the whole fabric fall to the ground.

In spite of the surveyors' warning, nothing was done about the cathedral roof until October 1651, at which time the Parliamentary Committee at Stafford sent a Colonel Danvers with troops to finish off the stripping of the lead from the roof. This was sold, together with the metal from the bells which had been broken up. With the mediaeval timbers of the roof now exposed to the elements, these rapidly decayed and the whole structure assumed even more the character of a ruin.

The first survey had dealt only with the property of the Dean and Chapter, and the Bishop's Palace was not included, being covered by a different Act of Parliament. The second survey, to value what was left of the Palace, took place in August 1652. It makes dismal reading.

> The materialls belonginge to the said Pallace . . . we value as followeth:
> The lead remaining upon the said Pallace and the gentlemens lodgings within the courtyeard, they beeinge very much ruined, and beeing about 32 tunns 8 hundred and 3 quarters, we esteem to be worth att
> 9s 6d per centum . . . . . . . . . . . . . . . . . . . . . . . . . . . . . . . . . . . . . . . . . . . . . . . £308 2s 9d

Item, ould ironworke  . . . . . . . . . . . . . . . . . . . . . . . . . . . . . . . . . . . . . . . . £1   0s 0d
Item, oulde glass worth . . . . . . . . . . . . . . . . . . . . . . . . . . . . . . . . . . . . . . £2   0s 0d
Item, windscott [wainscot] worth  . . . . . . . . . . . . . . . . . . . . . . . . . . . . . £3 10s 0d
Item, paveinge, tyles, brickes and shingles worth . . . . . . . . . . . . . . . . . . £6 13s 4d
Item, tymber belonginge to the Pallace, gentlemens
lodgings, stable and barn worth  . . . . . . . . . . . . . . . . . . . . . . . . . . . . . . £140   0s 0d
Item, the stones, beinge little worth in that place, and
consideringe the charge in takinge of them down  . . . . . . . . . . . . . . . . £30   0s 0d

<u>Memorandum:</u> The said Pallace and buildinge were very much ruened by the
soldiery when it was a garrison and alsoe, since the late warr, by some of the inhabitants
. . . the orchard and gardens are destroyed soe as there is not any trees remaining
there . . . There was within the wall, until this warr, a garden with a stone wall about
it and lyeing right before the Pallace; but during the tyme the Close was made a
garrison by the Kings partie the wall was demolished and the garden spoiled, beinge
digged upp to make workes and trenches* within . . . The Pallace is very much ruinated by the warr, much lead, iron, windscott and tymber stollen away by the souldiers
since it was in the Parliaments hands . . . The whole Close is very much defaced and
spoiled, the Cathedrall Church much ruined, part by granadoes and great shott, and
part by the dishonesty and carelessness of officers entrusted by the County of
Stafford since the enemy left it. The cisterns of lead were taken and sould, the pipes
of lead digged upp and cutt off, great quantities of lead imbesled and sould from the
cathedrall Church, the bells some broken and others conveyed away.

The third survey is a document entitled 'A list of such persons as have
possessed themselves intrusively of the church and sundry other houses
within the Close of the Cathedral Church of Lichfield in the county of
Stafford since the late unhappy war ended there etc.' Probably drawn up
for the Dean and Chapter soon after the restoration of the monarchy in
1660, it paints a sorry picture of a Close in an advanced state of decay and
squalor.

Most of the houses appear to have been occupied by squatters, usually
listed by name, as in the following examples:

In the deanery
    One Cope, his wife and children, a gardener.
    William Lindon, Junior, a weaver, and his wife.
    Samuel Sault and his wife, a letter-carrier.
    Willian Lindon senior, a weaver, with his wife and children.
In the house of Mr. Robert Hill, one of the Prebendaries
    Thomas Lindon, a weaver, and his wife.
    John Davis, a weaver, and his wife.
    Henry Davis, a labourer (a desperate, quarrelsome fellow) and his wife and
        children.
    Widow Terry with three children.

It was the same in the Vicars' Hall, the houses of the Chancellor, the
Precentor, and the other Prebendaries. The Bishop's Palace was occupied
by a miller and two tailors with their families; the Porter's lodge of the
Palace by a basket-maker. Even what remained of the cathedral was made

---

*This refers to the sallyport described by Colonel Gerrard in his letter of April 29th, 1646, to Sir William Brereton.

a habitation; in the south trancept lived Daniel Morgil, labourer, and his wife and children, while below them, in a vault under the church, lived 'Two women with children, both bastards, and one there lately brought to bed of a bastard and affirmed to be still there'.

The surveyors finished their report with the following note:

> The number of persons one hundred and eleven or twelve.
> We say nothing of gentle or honest families in other canonical houses not ruined.
> [Foul*] dunghills are made everywhere up and down the Close.
> Swine that were never formally permitted in the Close daily root in the graves of the dead . . .

There followed a list of the owners of swine, and the number each owned. Out of a total of nineteen, most were owned by the squatters named by the surveyors but two, rather surprisingly, belonged to 'the Lady Wolsley'.

The report ended with the comment that there were now six alehouses within the Close, where none had existed before.

*   *   *   *   *

Such was the state into which the City and Close of Lichfield had descended as a result of four years of war and fourteen years under the Commonwealth. Had affairs not changed there is little doubt that Lichfield would have finished up as just another Rotten Borough, in literal as well as political fact. But things were changing. By 1660 Cromwell was dead and his son Richard who succeeded him as Lord Protector was unequal to the task. The country was weary of dictatorships, and early in 1660, when General Monck marched on London from his headquarters at Coldstream, on the Scottish border, with 7,000 troops including his own regiment of foot, he met with no resistance. He dissolved Parliament and invited Charles to return to the throne.

In May, Charles Stuart returned to England as Charles II and General Monck's Regiment of Foot, under their new name of the Coldstream Guards became his personal bodyguard, a duty they have performed for successive sovereigns ever since.

---

*Deleted in original.

# SOURCE NOTES
## *Chapter VIII*

1.  Lord Bagot, Memorials of the Bagot Family, 1848. A copy of this letter and the succeeding one, both written on a scrap of paper (presumably the original) was found loose in the above book by the present Lady Bagot and deposited by her at the County Record Office, Stafford.

2.  Ibid.

3.  Printed copy, County Record Office, Stafford.

4.  Ibid.

5.  Shaw, History of Staffordshire, p.242.

6.  Young, Brigadier Peter, Edgehill, 1642, p.193.

7.  Harwood, History of Lichfield, p.35.

8.  Ibid. p.35

9.  Ibid. p.36

10. Ibid. p.39

11. St. Mary's Church, Lichfield, Churchwardens' accounts, Lichfield Joint Record Office.

12. Harwood, History of Lichfield, p.127.

13. Victoria, History of Staffordshire, Vol.14.

14. Harwood, History of Lichfield, p.458.

15. County Record Office, Stafford, Q/SR M16 f.9.

16. Lichfield Joint Record Office, D/30/LIV ff.92-9 (Printed in Transactions of South Staffordshire Archaeological Society, 1986, in article by Dr. Nigel Tringham).

*The Ashmole Cup, 1666*

(Courtesy Lichfield City Council)

*Chapter IX*

# The Restoration

ON the evening of Thursday, January 17th, 1666, a party of some
thirty gentlemen assembled at the George Inn in Bird Street. They
were all members of that group which the press of today invariably refer
to as "civic dignitaries". The two Bailiffs of Lichfield, John Burnes and
Henry Baker, were there with the Sheriff, William Bennet, supported by
members of the Corporation and members of the Grand Jury. An
unusual visitor was the Steward of the City, the Earl of Southampton,
appointed to this post by the recent Charter of King Charles II.

It had been the custom in Lichfield for many years (and still is today),
for bodies such as the Corporation, the Conduit Lands Trustees, the City
Companies and other such groups, to meet together at this time of the
year for their annual Feast. These are usually convivial occasions when
members who throughout the year may have fought wordy battles in
session chambers relax and enjoy the good companionship engendered
by food and wine.

The present occasion, the Epiphany Feast of Lichfield Corporation,
was one such, but it had more than the usual air of excitement about it, for
during the course of the evening there was to be an event which, while of
some moment in itself, was significant also as a recognition of a great
change in the life of the city.

This event was the handing over by our old friend Zachary Turnpenny,
now Sacrist of the Cathedral, of a gift which he had brought from London
of a large chased silver cup and cover, presented to the Corporation by
Elias Ashmole, Windsor Herald to Charles II.

Ashmole (1617-1692) was a Lichfield man. His grandfather, Thomas
Ashmole, was a saddler, but as we saw in Chaper I, a person of some
importance in the city, being successively Sheriff, Junior Bailiff and twice
Senior Bailiff.*

---

*Thomas Ashmole was illiterate, signing his name with a cross.

Thomas Ashmole's eldest son, Simon, was brought up to be a saddler, but was instead attracted to the more adventurous life of a soldier, serving in Ireland and on the Continent. He left behind him in Lichfield his wife Anne and their son Elias, who was thus brought up by his mother for most of his childhood.

Anne Ashmole came of good stock, being descended from the Bowyers of Knipersley, through whom she was related to many of the old families of Staffordshire and Cheshire. She was careful to give Elias a good upbringing. He attended Lichfield Grammar School, and when he was old enough became a chorister at Lichfield Cathedral under the direction of Michael East, who also instructed him in the virginals and organ.

At the age of sixteen, Elias Ashmole was enrolled as a freeman of the Lichfield Company of Saddlers, Glovers, Whittawers and Bridlemakers. No doubt his grandfather hoped that he would follow him in the family business, but an opportunity arose for Elias to leave Lichfield for London, to stay in the household of a relative of his mother. James Pagit, Puisne Baron of the Court of Exchequer. Here, with his cousins, he was given the opportunity to study mathematics and law, becoming a Solicitor in Chancery in 1638.

On the outbreak of the Civil War, Elias aligned himself with the Royalists and in 1644 was appointed by the King's Government at Oxford as a Commissioner for the Collection of Excise in the County of Stafford and the City of Lichfield. His fellow commissioners were James Povey and John Hill,* of the Friary, Lichfield, and at the end of 1644 Ashmole and Hill had to visit Oxford to invoke the help of the King's Parliament against Colonel Richard Bagot, Governor of Lichfield Close, who had obstructed them in the gathering of excise in the City of Lichfield. It will be remembered that in December 1644 Richard Bagot had petitioned the King regarding the cost of funding Lichfield garrison, and his dispute with the Commissioners of Excise probably was connected with this.

Ashmole stayed on at Oxford after Hill had returned to Lichfield and in addition to his duties as a Commissioner of Excise he became one of the four Gentlemen of the Ordinance in Oxford, in charge of the eastern artillery defences, while at the same time he entered Brasenose College to continue his study of mathemetics.

From an early age he had shown an interest in astrology, which at that time still carried a certain amount of intellectual respectability, and during his time at Oxford (which he described as some of the happiest days of his life) he put this knowledge to good use. Such spare time as he had from study, supervising artillery and collecting excise, he used in pursuit of sundry unattached ladies residing in Oxford. His method of

*See Chapter VII.

introducing himself on these occasions was to offer to cast their horoscopes, a ploy which could lead to all sorts of possibilities.

From these facts it will be evident that Elias Ashmole was a man of wide interests. Another of these was the use of ciphers, a subject which appealed to his mathematically-trained mind, and during his time at Oxford he devised the codes which were used for the messages which passed between the Royalist Headquarters at Oxford and the Lichfield garrison where they were received and deciphered by John Hill.*

Ashmole visited Lichfield in July 1646, only a few days after the Close had been surrendered. He found a city battered and scarred by war, the population decimated by the plague. Worst of all, he found that his mother had died from the plague only three weeks before. In due course he returned to London and resumed his legal practice.

It was during the years of the Interregnum that Ashmole began to work on his book, *The Institution, Laws & Ceremonies of the most Noble Order of the Garter* which was to bring him fame in the future, but which in the beginning caused him much expense and danger. He had the assistance of Dr. Christopher Wren, Dean of Windsor and Registrar of the order who had purchased the registers of the Order at the sale of Charles I's property. In the work on this book he developed further interests in genealogy and antiquarian research which led him to become one of the foremost authorities of his century in these subjects. It led also, when Charles II was restored to the throne in 1660, to Elias Ashmole, the saddler's son of Lichfield, being appointed Windsor Herald to King Charles. As such, he took part in the various proclamations, on March 9th 1661, of the impending coronation.

In August 1662 Ashmole accompanied William Dugdale, Norroy King of Arms, on his Visitation of Derbyshire and Nottinghamshire and during this visitation he renewed his acquaintance with an old friend, Zachary Turnpenny, now once again Subchanter of the Lichfield Cathedral. Earlier in the year he had written to him as follows:[1]

> For my honoured friend, Mr. Zachary Turnepenny, Subchanter of the Cathedrall Church of Lichfield, at his house in the Close of Lichfield (carriage of the box paid for). Mr. Subchanter,
>
> I have now sent downe by Mr. Rixham, your Lichfield carrier, the Sett of Church Services and Anthems, for the use of your Quire; with two Bookes of ruled Paper, wherein to prick the Organ parts for both; in all 12 Bookes, and well bound, having the Episcopall Armes of your See imprest on the foreside, and my owne upon the other. This is my first Free-will offering, which with a cheerful and willing mind I dedicate to the service of your Temple; and may as pious use be made of them, in sounding forth the praises of the Almighty, as the Donation hath sincerity of heart.
>
> from your real friend and most humble Serv.
>
> May 3, 1662.                                   E. Ashmole.

---

*This probably accounts for the reason why John Hill entered the Close to reside there just before the siege by Sir William Brereton's forces.

For this gift to Lichfield Cathedral he paid £16 — a fairly substantial sum in those days.

The following year he accompanied Dugdale on another visitation, this time of Staffordshire, beginning at Lichfield. This time they took with them a young clerk, Gregory King, whose home was in Stowe Street, Lichfield. A boy of fourteen at this time, he was later to beome Lancaster Herald and to make a name for himself as a statistician, enumerating the population of the country from the Hearth Tax returns.[2]

It was probably during this visit to Lichfield that Ashmole decided to make his gift to Lichfield Corporation — his *Tina Argenta* [silver wine cup] as he called it. There was more to this than just the desire of the local boy who has made good to remember his home town. Like his gift to the cathedral, it was to be a symbol of the new Lichfield which was arising out of the chaos of war, as well as a reminder of the part the "Loyal and Ancient" city had played in the struggle between King and Parliament. In that struggle the city had lost all its "evidences" that proclaimed its true status; the charter granted by Edward VI which with all the other muniments had been taken into the Close by the Town Clerk, Michael Noble, only to be destroyed by one side or the other in the fighting. Also lost were the two maces granted under the same charter, which had been presented to Charles I after his defeat at Naseby. Nobody knows what happened to these; they are never referred to again. Under an order of Parliament made in 1649, all maces belonging to corporations had the royal ciphers and badges removed and replaced by the arms of the Commonwealth with the inscription 'The Freedome of England by Gods Blessing Restored',[3] but in the case of Lichfield the two maces just disappeared and history is silent as to their fate. Similarly, any plate which the Coorporation may have owned was lost without trace. It may be that the maces and plate were confiscated by the Parliamentary forces, as was the Cathedral's communion plate, or they may simply have been looted in the aftermath of the war. It is doubtful if we shall ever know.

In November 1664 the city was granted a new charter[4] by Charles II which renewed all the previous rights, including that of appointing two Serjeants at Mace, 'who shall bear gilded or silver maces before the Bailiffs everywhere within the city and county of Lichfield'. A new silver mace was purchased in the same year. It bears the cipher of Charles II and the date 1664, and is one of the two still in use today*

The rehabilitation of the city's 'evidences' had begun, and Elias Ashmole was moved to make his contribution. It was to be a piece of plate, the first since all had been lost in the ravages of war, and so the oldest in the city's possession today. He referred to it as 'a large chased silver bowl

---

*This mace was gilded in 1690, when a second, similar mace with the cipher of William and Mary was purchased. A sword, dated 1684 (James II) completes the regalia in use today.

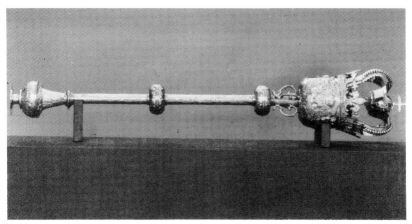

*Civic Mace granted to Lichfield Corporation by Charles II, 1664*
*(Courtesy Lichfield City Council)*

and cover, which cost me £23 8s 6d', but in fact it is a very fine silver loving-cup, ornamented with chasing and repoussé work, with a lid having a cherub for a handle. On the side of the cup are three panels with representations of the three slain kings which appear on the city seal. The cup is inscribed 'The Guift of Elias Ashmole Esq., Windsor Herald at Arms, 1666'.

In the course of the evening of January 17th the gift was handed over to the Senior Bailiff by Zachary Turnpenny who had brought it from London. The feelings of the assembled company were expressed in the following letter of thanks to Ashmole from the Bailiffs.[5]

For the truly honoured Elias Ashmole Esq., at his chamber in the Middle Temple, over Serjeant Maynard's Chamber. In his absence, to be left with the Butler or Porter of the Middle Temple, London.

Honoured Sir,

Upon Thursday, being the 17th day of this instant January (a day ever to be rubrical among our City Remembrances) we received your *Tina Argentea*, your munificent silver bowl, cloathed in its delivery with all those rich circumstances of advantage, that could possibly either enable the gift to bespeak the goodness and prudence of the giver, or invite the fairest acceptance in the receiver. For we consider the person from whom:- It is the gift of an *Elias*, a herald, not only proclaiming, but actually contributing good things to our city; and that by the hand of *Zacharias*, a faithful messenger, who with the gift did emphatically communicate the sense and good affection of the giver. And if we consider the time it was presented; it was the day of our *Epiphany* Sessions of the Peace for this city, where our Bailiffs, High Steward, Sheriff, Grand Jury and the rest of the Body Politic of this ancient and loyal Corporation, together with other persons of quality, both of the Clergy and Laity, were convened together and so became present at this great offering: as if some propitious stars arising in the East had, (at this time) gone before our *Magus*, steering its course to this our city of

Lichfield, (the *Sarepta* of our *Elias*) and stood over the new-erected pyramids of our cathedral, (where as yet a star appears) darting its benign influence upon this poor and loyal city, inviting the *Magi* from afar, to offer some tribute to it: a city that hath nothing to glory in but its ancient and modern Loyalty to God and Caesar, evidenced by her ancient Bearing in the City escoteon, (three knights martyred) as ancient as the days of Diocletion,* and her name signifying a field of blood then spilt, which may well be her modern and unparalleled loyalty to that blessed Saint (now in Heaven), King Charles the Martyr; universally witnessed by those honourable marks, traces and wounds of Loyalty she yet bears upon her persons, temples, streets and walls; (Trophies of Honour) sufficiently blazing to the world the true Heraldry of her ancient Arms; nor have you only given us this great *Cratera* [wine bowl] (upon which you have wisely impresst our City-Arms) to solace the best of the City, after their time of suffering, but like one of those true *Magi*, that offered to Christ in his poorest condition, you have largely offered to the repair of his Church, our ruined Cathedral, which by the unwearied labour, prudence, piety and charity of our good Bishop, a second Ceadda, and the charity of yourself and others, happily deposited in his hands, is, (almost to a miracle) so well and so soon restored again. But you have likewise annually and liberally offered, relieved and refreshed Christ in his members, the Poor of our City.† And as if you intended piously to ingross and cover all our necessities, under that warm and nourishing mantle of *Elias*, we have received intimation of your promises of greater good intended this City. Now, Sir, give us leave to conclude (having been already too tedious) by informing you that, according to your desire, (upon the first receipt of your *Poculum Caritatis* [esteemed cup] at the sign of the *George* for England) we filled it with Catholic Wine, and devoted it a sober Health to our most Gracious King, which (being of so large a content) passed the hands of thirty to pledge; nor did we forget yourself in the next place, being our great Mecaenus;‡ assuring you that (God willing) we shall take course that this great *Tina Argentea* shall, with our City Mace and other public ensignes of dignity and authority, be carefully transmitted by indenture, from Bailiffs to Bailiffs, in a continual succession, so long as this ancient and loyal Corporation, through the favour of princes (which, we hope, we shall never forfeit) shall have a Charter to give it life and being. For which end, your many other multiplied favours to this poor city We, the present Bailiffs of this City do, in the name and by the desire of our whole Company, return you most hearty Thanks, subscribing ourselves what we truly are,

Sir, your most obliged and faithful friends,

John Burnes<br/>Henry Baker

Lichfield,
26th January 1666.

Ashmole maintained his close relationship with Lichfield and its corporation throughout his life, visiting it on many occasions, especially after his third marriage in November 1668 to Elizabeth, daughter of Sir Thomas Dugdale of Blyth Hall, in Warwickshire. On one of these visits, in 1673, the Bailiffs and Corporation entertained him and his wife to

---

*The ancient seal of the City of Lichfield has a scene depicting three slaughtered kings or knights in armour (or possibly three martyrs wearing their crowns). It is supposed to represent a massacre which took place at the site of Lichfield in A.D. CCXCIII giving rise to the name Licidfield, or field of the dead. In choosing this scene for the decoration of his cup, Ashmole has shown the dead knights in armour of the 17th century, in front of a representation of Lichfield Cathedral.

†Ashmole made a bequest for the sum of £2 per annum for the Poor of Lichfield.

‡Gaius Cilnius Maecenas, Roman nobleman and patron of the arts.

'a dinner and a Great Banquet' to honour their benefactor. The future Bailiffs and Mayors kept the pledge contained in the letter of thanks, and the Ashmole Cup has remained to this day a symbol of the pride which Lichfield citizens keep for their 'Loyal and Ancient' city, being accorded a place of honour at civic occasions. For many years it was used as a loving cup, being filled with mulled port and circulated around the assembled company for the toast of 'Weal and Worship'.

The letter of the Bailiffs is interesting for the light it throws on happenings in Lichfield following the restoration of the monarchy. In 1660, on May 1st, Parliament had resolved 'that according to the ancient and fundamental laws of this Kingdom, the Government is, and ought to be, by King, Lords, and Commons'. Twenty-four days later King Charles II landed at Dover, and a new era of liberty began, especially for those who had supported the Royalist cause through all its vicissitudes. Not least among these were the citizens of Lichfield; for shortly after the King's arrival Elias Ashmole had an audience with him as a result of which he was appointed Windsor Herald. He took this opportunity to inform King Charles of the desolate state of the cathedral and close of his native city as a result of the civil war, and from then on the King took a personal interest in its restoration.

Ashmole was able to tell the King the news he had received that very morning from Mr. Rawlins* of Lichfield, that as soon as the Clerks Vicars of the Cathedral had heard of the King's return they had entered the chapter-house and there said service; this, with the vestry, being the only part of the cathedral that had a roof to shelter them.

Like all other bishoprics in England and Wales, the See of Lichfield had been abolished under the Commonwealth. Now it was revived, and those of its officers who had survived the Interregnum were reinstated. Jeffery Glasier, the Chapter Clerk, returned from Rugeley, where he had been living, and took up his abode once again in his house next to the cathedral library. Henry Archbold, Registrar of the Diocese, also returned to his former post and he and Glasier became the joint Treasurers of a fund to restore the cathedral church.

Among the clergy only William Higgins, the Precentor, and Zachary Turnpenny, the Subchanter, returned. They lacked a leader, for the Dean had died and the Bishop, Accepted Frewin, was living in retirement in Kent. He showed no interest in the See beyond accepting the Bishop's dues which now once more became available; fortunately for Lichfield he was removed by translation to the Archbishopric of York, and the way was open for a new Bishop of Lichfield.

---

*Town Clerk of Lichfield, 1678-1686.

The man chosen was John Hacket, a name second only in fame to St. Chad, the first Bishop. It can be said with truth that Hacket was the second founder of the See. He worked indefatigably to rebuild his diocese and cathedral, following in full his motto 'Inserve Deo et Laetare' [Serve God and be Cheerful]. He was appointed towards the end of 1661, and in January 1662 arrived in Lichfield. There is a story, probably apocryphal, that the first morning after his arrival he rose early, summoned his servants, and had his coach horses harnessed to waggons to start clearing away the rubbish from the cathedral ruins. True or not, it typifies the zeal he employed in organising the restoration of his cathedral. In a relatively short time he had raised £9,903 for this purpose, to which he added £1,683 out of his own purse. King Charles gave 100 timber trees out of Needwood forest for the roof, and in gratitude they put his statue on the West Front\* The Duchess of Somerset gave her late husband's library of 1,000 books to replace those destroyed by the Puritans and the faithful Dr. Higgins brought back from their hiding place the priceless St. Chad's Gospels.

So well did the work proceed that when the Bailiffs wrote to Elias Ashmole in January 1666 they were able to refer to the cathedral being 'so well and so soon restored again'. In the same letter they mentioned 'the newly-erected pyramids of our cathedral', from which it would appear that not only the central spire was rebuilt but also the two western ones as well. Although they were not shot down like the great spire, they no doubt suffered much in the bombardments.

The cathedral was re-consecrated on December 24th 1669, by Bishop Hacket at a service of great solemnity held in the presence of many of the nobility and gentry of the diocese, the Bailiffs and Corporation of the city and a great concourse of spectators. After the ceremony Bishop Hacket entertained separately members of the church, members of the nobility and gentry, and the Bailiffs and Magistrates of the city, in a new house which he built for his own residence on the south side of the cathedral, by the road leading to Dam Street.

One of the last acts of restoration of the fabric had been the siting, at the apex of the gable of the west front of the cathedral, of a statue of King Charles II, who, as already mentioned, had taken an interest in the restoration of the cathedral and had given 100 fair timber trees from Needwood forest to rebuild the roof. The figure was to remain there for the next 200 years until it was removed by Sir Gilbert Scott during his restoration in the 1860s and consigned to the interior of the north-west tower, being replaced by a statue of Christ in glory.

---

\*It can now be seen at ground level, outside the South Door.

The theological correctness of this move cannot be disputed, but there was probably more to it than that. Among the statues placed on the west front at this time was one of Queen Victoria, sculpted by her daughter. Her views on Charles ('We do not care for Charles II') were well known, and she would not have been amused by having to share a place with him on Lichfield Cathedral.

The bells were not replaced until 1670, and Bishop Hacket lived just long enough to hear the first of them rung; he retired to his bed after hearing it sound and died soon afterwards on the 28th of October 1670.

Gradually the Close was restored to its old place in the life of the city and to much of its former appearance as buildings were restored and new ones built. In 1687, a new Bishop's Palace was built by Bishop Thomas Wood, who has succeeded John Hacket. A man of very different calibre, he owed his preferment to his former mistress, Barbara Villiers, who had moved on to greater things as one of the mistresses of Charles II. She did not forget her old friend, however, and persuaded Charles to advance him to the See of Lichfield. A Londoner, he had no desire to venture so far north, and never came near his See during the rest of his life. The Palace was built at Wood's expense, as a fine imposed on him by Archbishop Sancroft for his waste of the woods belonging to the See. Today it forms part of the cathedral choir school.

The restoration of the monarchy brought a revival of military activity in Lichfield. Though Charles II had disbanded the standing army of 50,000 men on coming to the throne, the need for some sort of force to keep the peace throughout the country led to the introduction in 1661 of military associations entrusted with the task of raising volunteer forces in their areas. In Lichfield such an association was formed in order to raise a company of foot soldiers, and the sum of £38 3s 6d was collected for this purpose. The following list shows how the respective areas of the city contributed.

| | Inhabitants contributing | Sums |
|---|---|---|
| Sadler Street (in which Richard Dyott contributed £1 4s and Thos. Astle 5s) | 23 | £5 17s 2d |
| Conduit Street, and Dam Street, (in which Jos. Warder, Ensign, gave 10s and Richard Mason 10s) | 15 | 2 14s 6d |
| St. John Street, (in which Mr. Simon Martin gave £1 and Sampson Pott 6s 8d) | 24 | 4 9s 10d |
| Wade Street | 12 | 16s 6d |
| Bore Street (in which Mr. Ch. Chetwind, William Nichols, George Mason, and Thomas Marshall each gave 10s) | 29 | 5 8s 8d |
| Bird and Sandford Streets (in which Mr. John Rathbone, Joseph Dreng, William Tonks and George Smallridge each gave 10s) | 48 | 6 5s 6d |

| | Inhabitants contributing | Sums |
|---|---|---|
| Lumbard Street, (in which Tho, Harvey gave £1 and Mr. John Rawlins 10s) | 11 | £2 18s 6d |
| Stow Street (in which Mr. Christ. Thacker gave £1 and Francis Chaplain 12s) | 13 | 2 13s 0d |
| Tamworth Street (in which Mr. Thomas Dawes and Simon Hassell gave 10s each) | 27 | 3 16s 4d |
| Greenhill | 17 | 1 4s 6d |
| Bacon Street | 4 | 9s 6d |
| The Close | 11 | 1 9s 6d |
| Totals | 24 | £38 3s 6d |

Received at the hands of the above persons, (all of which are voluntary soldiers under the command of Captain Richard Dyott) within the citty of Lichfield, the several sums of money against their names exprest, which sums were subscribed as their free and voluntary present, given out of their great affection to his Majesty, in pursuance of an act of this Parliament. By me,

William Dugdale

30th October, 1661.                                Receiver of the City of Lichfield.

The company commander was Major Anthony Dyott, but after a very short time he handed over to his brother Richard, probably on account of ill health. A muster roll (unfortunately not dated) has survived, and this tells us that the company had three commissioned officers, four serjeants, three corporals, five drummers and one hundred and ninety-seven other ranks.

The officer commanding is shown as Captain Richard Dyott, his second in command was our old friend Lieutenant Michael East and the ensign, though his name is not shown, we know from the subscription list to have been Joseph Warder. The names of all the others are contained in the muster roll (Appendix A) and make interesting reading. Several Lichfield names of today such as Froggatt, Coxon, Williamson and Bull appear, while the list is also a reminder of how isolated the various regions of the British Isles were from each other in the 17th century; not a single Jones appears anywhere in the list!

The company was divided up into five 'divisions', three being 'divisions of shott' (musketeers) and two being 'divisions of pikes'. There was also a number of reserves, referred to as 'odd men of shott' and 'odd men of pikes'.

The overall command of all these volunteer companies in the county of Staffordshire was vested in the Lord Lieutenant, and by a curious irony of fate the Lichfield volunteers, commanded by a member of the Dyott family, found themselves serving the King under the leadership of none other than Robert, Lord Brooke — the son and heir of the Parliamentary general who had led the first siege of Lichfield and had met his end by a bullet fired by Dumb Dyott! History produces some curious paradoxes.

A year after their formation the Lichfield volunteers were summoned by Lord Brooke to carry out an important duty. The letter was addressed to Anthony Dyott, but by that time he had already been dead for a month, and it was Richard Dyott who carried out the order.

> For Anthony Dyott, Esq, at Lichfield, to be communicated to the rest of the deputyes of Lichfield, for his Majestys service.
>
> Gentlemen,
>
> The Duke of Ormond* being to lodge in your city on Monday next, I desire you would see your foot company and halbertiers gathered together and completely armed, to attend him at his entry into Lichfield; the ordering of which attendance I referre wholly to your discretions. I have ordered the horses that are to attend him to quarter in the townes about Lichfield, that his retinue may not be straightened for room in the city. I make no question but you will manage this business for your owne reputation and mine honour; in which confidence I rest,
>
> Gentlemen,
>
> Your very affectionate friend
> Robert Brooke.
>
> Brooke House
> 10th July 1662.

It is not recorded what other duties the volunteers performed, though no doubt they took part every year in the Court of Arraye and procession known as the Bower on Whit Monday. The Lichfield Military Association was still in existence in 1682, when records tell us that Michael Biddulph was appointed as Officer Commanding the volunteer company by the Lord Lieutenant of Staffordshire. It probably came to an end during the reign of James II (1685-1688), when a standing army made military associations and Courts of Arraye unnecessary. But musketeers and pikemen continued to form part of the Bower Procession, and still do today in the form of halbertiers.

By the end of the century Lichfield had recovered from the ravages of the Civil War. Rebuilding of the Close and city created an environment in which literature and the arts flourished, producing for the next century such great names as Addison, Garrick, Johnson and Darwin. But that is another story.

---

*The Duke of Ormonde was Lord Lieutenant of Ireland

---

SOURCE NOTES

*Chapter IX*

1.  Harwood, History of Lichfield, p.441
2.  Ibid p.447
3.  Cripps, Joseph, Old English Plate, 1878
4.  Harwood, History of Lichfield, p.347
5.  Ibid p.442

*South-east turret and remains of walls (Spite House centre) Lichfield Close*

*Remains of north-east tower and wall, with moat in foreground. Lichfield Close*

*Chapter X*

# Relics and Reminders

FOR a city which suffered so much during the Great Rebellion, Lichfield has little to show for it today. Time has erased most of the scars, but a careful search will still reveal traces of what must have been a catastrophic upheaval in the life of the city.

The cathedral, the centre of all the fighting, has undergone three major restorations since that time. As well as that of Bishop Hacket, carried out after the Restoration, in the 18th century the Dean and Chapter commissioned James Wyatt to carry out extensive works, following which nearly all traces of the destruction of the Civil War were obliterated. The few that remained finally disappeared in the 1860s when Sir Gilbert Scott carried out his exceedingly thorough overhaul of the fabric.

Today, the only reminders of a tragic period in the history of the cathedral are the memorial tablet to Colonel Richard Bagot, high up on the wall of the south choir aisle, unseen by most visitors, and a window close by which contains two stained glass lights of modern origin which depict Bishop Hacket directing the work of restoration, with the shattered building in the background.

To most students of this period the ancient mediaeval walls of the Close are a source of interest, but because they were so thoroughly slighted by the Parliamentarians little remains to be seen. A large-scale Ordnance Survey map makes a good starting point for an investigation. Two of the corner turrets of the Close are shown on the map as ancient buildings. Starting at the south-east corner, there is a small octagonal turret and portions of the south wall and east wall. These are incorporated in a building which is now the Lichfield Diocesan office; before that it was St. Mary's Vicarage, and originally was one of the Prebendal houses of the Close. It is probable that this building existed before the Civil War, for even by the beginning of the seventeenth century several of the prebendal houses had made use of the ancient mediaeval walls in this way.

On the map, the line of the east wall can easily be followed to the remains of the north-east tower. On the way the line passes through the front of Selwyn House, an 18th Century residence which folk-lore refers to as "Spite House" or "Hate House". There is a legend that one of the Aston sisters, who never married, built it to spite her two married sisters by spoiling their view of the cathedral from their houses at Stowe. Some years ago this story was demolished very effectively by the late Mr. Frank Marston who investigated the facts.[1] But the legend lives on.

Obviously the front wall of the house is built on the foundations of the mediaeval walls, the house itself occupying part of the former moat. Probably, also, the house is built around the foundations of a tower which projected into the moat, for it was in the basement of this house, in recent years, that the two wells previously mentioned were found.

The line of the east wall is followed by an 18th or early 19th Century brick wall, which runs into the tower at the north-east corner. On the inside of this wall, in the garden of the former Bishop's Palace, the rampart, or bulwark, of earth can still be seen, forming a terrace in the garden.

The north-east corner tower is again octagonal, but much larger than the south-east one, the sides being fifteen feet wide. Originally, this was part of the old Bishop's Palace, which occupied the north-east corner of the Close. It looks down, on two sides, to the dimble, or dry ditch.

Adjacent to this tower there still exists a section of the old mediaeval wall which protected the north side of the Close. It is about four feet thick, faced on the outside now with brick, but still showing the original stonework on the inside.

Again, the line of the wall can be seen and followed on the map, but when it reaches the north-west corner there is no trace of any corner tower. This was the one which was blown up by Prince Rupert's landmine and afterwards completely demolished at the slighting. Where the line turned southwards, therefore, its course can only be guessed by the position of the 15th Century houses of Vicars' Close; clearly it must have been outside them, and most likely they were abutting it.

Before reaching the south-west corner the line of the wall was broken by the West Gate, through which ran the road from Beacon Street into the Close. A small section of the gateway still remains on the north side of the road; a stone wall about twenty feet high and the same width.

The West Gate appears to have consisted of two towers, an inner one and an outer,[2] each containing a gateway with portcullis and gate. There was also a drawbridge over the moat. This form of construction, in which the gate house extended forward of the main walls into the moat, leading to the drawbridge, was known as a barbican, and was often found in mediaeval fortifications. The two towers were joined by high walls on either side of the roadway so that attackers breaking through the first set

*Remains of West Gate, Lichfield Close 1985*

of defences would be trapped between the towers and vulnerable to attack from above. The section of wall still remaining is probably the northern-most of these two walls.

From the West Gate the Close walls ran for only a short distance to the south-west corner tower. An interesting deed[3] in Lichfield Joint Record Office, dated 1718, records the lease from the Dean and Chapter of Lichfield to Mr. James Barrow, a tailor, of a house known as Westgatehouse, situated between the West Gate (then still in existence) and the site of 'the former tower of Lichfield Close'. Unfortunately the deed does not mention the size of the house, which would enable the exact position of the former tower to be plotted, but one would not imagine that an 18th Century tailor's premises would be very large, and the conclusion is that the corner tower was about thirty feet from the gatehouse.

An interesting clause in the deed is one whereby the Dean and Chapter reserve to themselves the right of 'ingress, egress and regress' to a dungeon carved out of the rock below the site of the former tower for 'their servants, prisoners and appointees'. That an 18th Century Dean should still require accommodation for his prisoners seems a little unusual, but is probably only a manifestation of the reluctance of lawyers throughout the ages to forego any right, however unlikely, for their clients.[4]

The West Gate (apart from the section of wall still remaining) was demolished in the year 1800 when Newton's College was built.[5]

From the south-west tower, along the south side of the Close, to the South Gate, there is little to indicate where the mediaeval fortifications ran. In 1977 an archaeological dig under the supervision of Mr. M. O. H. Carver of Birmingham University cut a trench southwards from the cellar of the former Theological College, starting from a point about 12.5 metres from the steps of the south door of the cathedral. The report of these excavations[6] states 'There was no trace of a defensive wall'. The earliest reliable plan of the Close is that of John Snape (1781), and from a scrutiny of this it would appear that all the houses to the south of the cathedral have their frontages along a common building line. Could this be the line of the wall? A sketch of the Close in 1646, attributed to Dugdale and taken from the south-west, seems to bear this out, for it shows some of the prebendal houses on the south side of the Close as being outside the wall. The most likely conclusion is that Langton's wall, constructed close to the existing roadway on the south side of the cathedral, was incor-porated in the 15th or 16th Centuries into the fronts of houses built along this road, just as was done with 'Spite House' in the 18th Century.

The South Gate again formed a barbican, projecting out towards the Minster Pool. On the east side of it was a building which, according to Charles Stringer, writing about 1800, was occupied by the gatekeeper.

From here the wall ran to the south-east corner, where we started, but on a line somewhat more to the south than that of the wall on the other side of the gate.

The Minster Pool was at the time of the sieges some distance away from the wall of the Close, though not so far away as it is today. Towards the end of the 18th Century, under the indefatigable leadership of Miss Anna Seward, who lived in the Bishop's Palace, the inhabitants of the Close carried out a scheme for "serpentising" the Minster Pool into its present shape, a process which involved taking soil from the bank on the town side and depositing it on the Close side. This extended the gardens of some of the Close dwellers and also removed the rather noisesome tanyards on the other side of the water.

Inside the walls of the Close all traces of the Civil War — the horse pond, the foundries, the mills and the trenches — have long since disappeared (with the exception of the bulwarks in the Palace garden). One hidden feature which did come to light some years ago, however, was the burial place of those killed in the fighting. In about 1955 the installation of a swimming pool on the north side of the Close required the laying of a new water main in the roadway which runs parallel to the west front of the cathedral. A route just outside the low wall of the graveyard was chosen, but when digging commenced human skeletons were found about two feet below the surface. They were close together, some lying on their backs, some on their sides. The trench was filled in and the water main re-routed, so a detailed examination was never made, but it seems likely that they were casualties of the Civil War, especially of those killed in Prince Rupert's attack on the Close. This took place at the north-west corner, not far from the burial place. Today, visitors park their cars on the site, unaware of what lies below.[7]

Outside the Close there still remain some slight traces of the earthworks thrown up by the second and third sieges. The most obvious of these is the site of Prince Rupert's battery on the side of Beacon Hill, shown on large scale Ordnance Survey maps as "Prince Rupert's Mound". Local people still refer to it, properly, as Prince Rupert's Mount. Although now enclosed by houses the site still remains as a piece of open ground with the horse-shoe shaped gun emplacement still easily recognisable. In the last siege this fortification was used by the Parliamentary troops under Sir William Brereton. From it one can still get the same view of the cathedral, about 200 yards away, as did the gunners and matrosses of three centuries ago.

The earthworks thrown up by Sir William Brereton's forces in 1646 are not so easily traced, though between them they must have shifted several thousand tons of earth. No names have survived to identify them. But again, recourse to the Ordnance Survey map of the area and to local folk-law is a help.

General Brereton's camp "on Bacon Hill" can be identified because it was on the highest point to the north of the cathedral. Until the beginning of this century his trenches and gun emplacements, like those of Prince Rupert, could be seen on this site; then the area was taken over for a covered reservoir for Lichfield's water supply and all traces of the fortifications obliterated. The reservoir has in turn been replaced by housing development.

It is possible to trace out on the map a line which may be that drawn by Brereton for his trench "from water to water". Even where no traces of the original earthworks remain, a study of boundary lines between plots of land will often give a clue to what was there in the past.

Brereton drew the line, in his own words, 'as near to the enemy as possible', and this would mean keeping it just outside effective musket shot, remembering that his objective was to reduce the garrison of the Close without a direct assault on them. One should look, therfore, for a defensive line at a distance of 100-200 yards from the Close perimeter. At about 200 yards, on the north bank of Stowe Pool, there is a footpath running northwards, past Parchment Cottages where Michael Johnson, father of Dr. Johnson, had his parchment factory. It could well be that this was the line of the trench; used after the war as a right of way from Gaia Lane to Stowe Pool until in the course of time it became the sunken footpath with banks on either side that it is today.

The path does not continue on the north side of Gaia Lane, but the line does on the map as a boundary between plots, curving around to the west until it becomes once again a footpath. This runs parallel to Gaia Lane, about 150 yards north of the Close, and then curves out to take in Rupert's Mount, forming a salient at this point. It then runs into the line of Gaia Lane near the junction with Beacon Street. On the far side (the west) of Beacon Street the fortified line extends along Shaw Lane. This may have already existed in 1646, but its sunken nature would have made it a natural defence. From the end of Shaw Lane a further trench across Beacon Park would take the line to the edge of the Bishop's Fish Pool, thus completing the defences 'from water to water'.

Sir William Brereton, it will be remembered, had four 'mountes'. The one in Dam Street, facing the South Gate, would not remain long after hostilities had ceased, but there were also three along the line of the trench. One of these was 'Gloucester Mount', which has just been described; the other two were situated at the ends of the trench.

At the Stowe Pool end a likely position would be the site of the present Parchment Cottages. On John Snape's map this is shown as surrounded by concentric circles which might represent a path, a ditch or a ramp. Possibly this was the remains of the mount. It would be the logical place for such a fort.

At the Sandford Street end of the line there was another mount, and this probably accounts for the mound known today as Bunkers Hill. From here there are still traces of a ditch across Beacon Park, marked today by a line of trees.

The last place to bear the marks of the war in Lichfield is St. Chad's Church. It was used for billeting troops in the first siege and again for the same purpose in the third siege. It suffered much damage in the war, the whole of the roof having to be repaired in the 1650s (hence the curious brick clerestory of today). The fabric of the church still has marks of cannon fire in the form of holes in the stonework filled up with bricks, so it is possible that the Royalists in the Close put in some target practice on it with their heavier cannon. The former pulpit, removed in 1916, had a musket ball lodged in its woodwork.

Relics of the war in the form of artifacts are few, and the most interesting are those connected with the death of Lord Brooke. The gun, reputed to be the one with which he was shot, is still in the possession of the Dyott family. It is a crude weapon of iron, about seven feet long with a calibre of one and a half inches. It was probably used originally as a punt gun, mounted on the front of a boat and used for shooting duck. When used at the cathedral it was loaded, not with birdshot, but with bullets of lead made from the covering of the cathedral roof. It has no sights, and one cannot help feeling, with all due respect to Dumb Dyott, that it was chance rather than skill that brought about the downfall of Lord Brooke.

The armour which Brooke was wearing on this occasion can be seen today in the great hall of Warwick Castle, where he lived and where his body was taken from Lichfield. It consists of his helmet (with a visor of three, not five, bars), breastplate, backplate and bridle gauntlet. The sword shown with it is not his, but is contemporary. The whole outfit, mounted on a figure, shows how a high-ranking officer of the Parliamentary army would be equipped. Until 1870 Lord Brooke's purple "cassock" or tunic, was there as well, still stained with his blood, but a fire in the great hall in that year destroyed it.

During the three sieges of Lichfield some 3,000 cannon balls of various sizes were fired, it has been estimated, and it would be surprising if a few of these had not been left behind. Some years ago, when Lichfield had a museum, there was a collection of these projectiles exhibited in it. As well as a number of solid shot of various sizes, there were two granadoes, quite intact, still filled with gunpowder and in one case even having the short piece of tow which had formed the fuse protruding from the touch hole. These had been recovered from the mud at the bottom of the Minster Pool by the Victorian engineers who drained the pool in 1856 in order to convert it into a reservoir. Obviously they were the ones which had fallen short during one of the bombardments of the Close; from their size (84 lbs) probably the first siege. Some solid shot were also recovered in the same way.

*Fragments of 84 lb granadoes. Lichfield Cathedral*

*Cannon balls from Civil War. Lichfield Cathedral*

These exhibits were weighed and measured by the author in 1965 and the details are given below. Unfortunately the collection has now been dispersed.

CANNON BALLS AND SHELLS FORMERLY IN LICHFIELD MUSEUM

| No. | Diameter (inches) | Weight (lbs) | Remarks |
|---|---|---|---|
| 1. | 3¼ | 3½ | Saker |
| 2. | 3½ | 4 | Saker |
| 3. | 4 | 9 | Demi-Culverin |
| 4. | 4 | 2½ | Stone or similar |
| 5. | 4¼ | 10 | Turned up by plough in Gaia Fields, 1946 |
| 6. | 5½ | 20 | Demi-Cannon |
| 7. | 10 | 84 | Mortar granado |
| 8. | 10 | 84 | Mortar granado |

The cathedral also has a collection of shot and shell, recovered at various times in that building. This included a fragment of a granado that **did** explode, and a ball from a cannon piece, probably one of those fired at the centre spire. There is also a small shot of very rough shape which could well be one of those cast by the foundry in the Close.

CANNON BALLS IN LICHFIELD CATHEDRAL 1985

| No. | Diameter (inches) | Weight (lbs) | Remarks |
|---|---|---|---|
| 1. | 2¾ | 3 | Drake |
| 2. | 3¼ | 4½ | Saker |
| 3. | 4½ | 14½ | Demi-Culverin |
| 4. | 6 | 29 | Demi-Cannon |

An interesting contrast with the rough-cast cannon ball of the cathedral is one found by Mr. George Deacon in 1946 in his garden on Beacon Hill, which was very well made indeed. From the position where it was found this shot could either be one left behind by Sir William Brereton's gunners or one fired at them from the Close. It has been the subject of a metallurgical examination, and through the courtesy of Mr. Deacon it has been possible to include the report in this book (Appendix C). From this it will be seen that the casting was of quite a high standard.

Lastly, there is in St. Mary's Church Heritage Centre at Lichfield, another cannon ball which could be of the Civil War period, but unfortunately no provenance is available.

One of the legacies of the Civil Wars in England has been the large number of stories of supernatural happenings connected with the struggle between Cavalier and Roundhead. Many houses have their reputed hauntings and perhaps the best known of all these stories is that of the ghosts of Edgehill where, at the scene of the battle there have been reports of strange happenings when people have heard the sounds of battle — drums beating, guns firing, the sound of men shouting and the clash of arms, though there is nothing to be seen. Lichfield, too, has such a story which might well be connected with one of the incidents mentioned in this book.

The story was related to the author some years ago, quite spontaneously, by Mr. and Mrs. Ted Simpson, both of whom were born in Lichfield and lived there for most of their lives. It begins in the summer of 1938. Mr. and Mrs. Simpson, recently married, had gone one Saturday afternoon to visit Mr. Simpson's parents at their home at the eastern end of Gaia Lane, near where it joins St. Chad's Road. The house, built at the beginning of this century, is one of several which at this point line Gaia Lane, with fairly long gardens stretching back behind them.

The only one at home was Mr. Simpson's younger brother who was working on his motor bike in a shed at the top of the garden. Ted Simpson stayed with him and Biddy went back to the house and sat in one of the front rooms looking out onto the lane and, in her own words, 'flipping over the pages of a magazine'.

It was a hot afternoon, the windows were open, and as she sat there she heard outside, approaching the house, the sound of men marching in step. There was nothing unusual in this: Lichfield has an army barracks and in 1938 troops still went on route marches. Mrs. Simpson put down her magazine and went to the window to look out. There was no one in the lane, but the sound of marching feet got louder and louder. Suddenly she was seized with a feeling of panic and ran out of the back door and up the garden to the shed where the two men were.

Her husband took one look at her face and before she could utter a word said, 'You've heard the marching men.' He then explained to her that the sound she had heard was well-known in his family, several persons having heard it from time to time. On one occasion a young girl who had come to work in the household as housemaid had heard the marching men and been so upset that she left immediately.

At the time Mrs. Simpson told this story to me and my wife, I had not started work on this book. When I did so, and came across the story of the event during the first siege when the storming party of Parliamentary troops marched from St. Chad's Church up Gaia Lane to attack the walls of the Close and walked straight into an ambush, I immediately thought of the marching men. At the first opportunity I questioned Mr. Simpson about his wife's experience. He confirmed her story and mentioned that on occasions human bones had been dug up in his father's garden. I then told him the story of the ambush, which he had never heard before, and mentioned the possibility that the bones in the garden were those of the soldiers killed in the ambush.

I should add that my wife and I have known Mr. and Mrs. Simpson as friends for many years and have absolute confidence in the veracity of the story. I have never myself experienced any supernatural phenomena, but it is hard not to be impressed by the story of the marching men.

SOURCE NOTES

*Chapter X*

1. Marston, Frank, 'Hate House', 1975
2. Glasier, Jeffery, Garrison Accounts, 1645
3. Lichfield Joint Record Office
4. Ibid
5. Harwood, History of Lichfield, p.293
6. Carver, M. O. H., Excavations South of Lichfield Cathedral, S. Staffs Archaeological and Historical Society Transactions 1980-81
7. I am indebted to Mr. Jack Salford for this information

# APPENDIX A

A List of the Officers and Soldiers names of the Volunteer Company
of the Citty of Lichfield under the command of the right
honble Robert Lord Brooke, Lord Lieutenant of the
County of Stafford and Citty of Lichfield.

Richard Dyott, Captain
Michael East, Lieutenant
[Joseph Warder] Ensign

| Thomas Horsman | | | Edward Carter | |
|---|---|---|---|---|
| Richard Sharpe | | | William Newton | |
| Richard Hill | } | Serjeants | John Collins | } Drummers |
| John Elliott | | | Edward Carter jnr. | |
| | | | William Elliott | |

### First Division of Shott
Humphrey Sutton, Corporall

| | | | |
|---|---|---|---|
| John Richards | William Lewis | William Langley | Ralph Nicklin |
| Thos. Johnson | Thos. Wright | Robt. Marrow | Richard Beardsley |
| William Bird | John Mayster | Richard Harvey | John Spencer |
| William Tayler | Richard Stubbs | Thomas Stone | Henry Allen |
| Thomas Allen | John Allen | Wm. Boddeson | Thomas Waite |
| William Draper | John Beardsley | Wm. Shelly | Peter Litton |
| Andrew Rooker | Thomas Hadley | Thomas Baker | Robt. Chapman |
| William Martin | Thomas Salt | Henry Rawleston | Richard Redding |
| Henry Evans | Thomas Burton | Michael Ryley | |

### Second Division of Shott
Thomas Winshawe, Corporall

| | | | |
|---|---|---|---|
| John Yates | Edward Sanders | William Sandler | John Burton |
| John Ryley | James Bullock | Gregory Evans | Edward Gossard |
| Anthony Rushton | Thomas Hull | Francis Coxon | Matthew Lapley |
| James Bradley | James Denston | Francis Vernon | Thomas Williamson |
| John Weake | John Pillsworth | Matthew Smith | William Bradbury |
| John Lambe | Thos. Holding | Thos Bellison | Richard Banks Snr. |
| Rich. Banks Jnr. | Henry Phillips | Mich. Hunnyburne | Hugh Shaw |
| John Taylor | John Loache | William Taylor | Thomas Allin |
| Nich. Brawood | Francis Ashbury | Thomas Morris | |

### Third Division of Shott
Erasmus Smith, Corporall

| | | | |
|---|---|---|---|
| John Littell | Samuel Morris | Thomas Allen | Thomas Reeve |
| Ambrose Bills | Robert Jones | Humphrey Hall | William Winfield |
| Robert Mason | William Gamble | Thomas Newell | William Webb |
| Edward Dilkes | Francis Fleming | Richard Pitts | Michael Salt |
| John Smith | John Grew | Thomas Humstone | William Lambe Jnr. |
| Thos. Bird Snr. | Thos. Bird Jnr. | George Newell | William Thorneworke |
| Thos. Reeve Snr. | Thos. Ashford | Thos Ashford Jnr. | Thos. Astle |
| George Mason | William Lambe | John Branton | John Branton |
| Samuel Keene | John Bull Snr. | John Bull Jnr. | Ffrancis Palmer |

## First Division of Pikes

| | | | |
|---|---|---|---|
| Henry Baker | Richard Caterbanke | Wm. Holmes | John Broadhurst |
| George Houlden | Richard Longshaw | Abraham Salt | Robert Baldwin |
| John Sharpe | Robert Bull | Henry Phillips | Daniel Braddocke |
| Thomas Clarke | Thos. Rawlston | Robert Wright | William Rowley |
| John Taylor | Walter Cotton | Richard Ingram | Thomas Clarke Jnr. |
| Joseph Clarke | Thos. Smalridge | Richard Deakin | Richard Grimley |
| Thos. Bennett | Thos. Martin | William Salt | John Paste |
| Simon Martin | Rowland Rawleston | Wm. Wright | William Chambers |
| Richard Hine | John Goodman | Richard Ward | |

## Second Division of Pikes

| | | | |
|---|---|---|---|
| Adam Froggatt | Richard Shaw | Rich. Broughton | Thomas Dawes |
| Dennis Napper | William Hill | Henry Bayliss | William Montford |
| Thos. Marshall | William Morgill | Thomas Alporte | Henry Browne |
| Thomas Booth | Thos. Kesterson | Wm. Halsall | Simon Ashford Jnr. |
| Thos. Northwood | Thomas Mott | Thomas Erpe | Thomas Bailey |
| John Bailey | Henry Meeson | Richd. Braddocke | Peter Alporte |
| Zachary Kirke | Edward Wilson | Thomas Astle | John Aldrid |
| Sampson Alsop | William Cotton | William Alsop | John Deakin |
| Simon Ansley | Robert Ward | John Hampton | Thomas Alton |

## Odd Men of Shott

| | | | |
|---|---|---|---|
| William Etheridge | Philip Godbehere | William Cox | Samuel Bliss |
| Job Bond | Thos. Blakesley | Wm. Kisse | Noah Potts |
| Robert Colston | ———— Needham | Isaac Scott | John Primrose |
| William Painter | | | |

## Odd men of Pikes

| | | | |
|---|---|---|---|
| Henry Vernon | ———— Glover | Richard Gilbert | William Hollis |
| William Byrch | Edmund Hector | Henry Charveatts | |

# APPENDIX B

The Last Will and Testament of Jeffery Glasier, Chapter Clerk
of Lichfield Cathedral, March 1647.

In the name of God, Amen.

I Jeffery Glasier the elder of the Cathedral Church of Lichfield, gent, being tired and
weake in body but of perfect and disposing memory and understanding, doe make and
declare this my last will and testament in manner and form following, viz.

First and principally I commit my soul into the hands of Almighty [God] trusting to be
saved by the atonement of my Lord and Savious Jesus Christ, and my body to the earth from
whence it came, to be interred probably in the Cathedral Church of Lichfield at the ffeete
of my dear ffather near the Chapterhouse doar. And as for my worldly estate which it hath
pleased God to bestow upon me, I give bequeath and dyspose as followeth:

Imprimis, I give and bequeath unto my dearly beloved and dearly loving wife Alice
Glasier, All my goods, cattell, chattells, household stuffe, leases, bills, bonds, plate and reddy
money for and during her natural life if she remains a widdow, soe long shee paying the
several legacies and bequests to the persons herein named according to the lynes herein sett
downe.

First, I give and bequeath to my eldest daughter Priscilla Glasier my best Bedd with all that
belongs to it and all the furniture that shall be in the Matted Chamber at the time of my
decease. And also two hundred pounds in money to be paid and delivered to her at such
tyme as my Executrix hereafter mentioned in her discretion shall think fitt.

Item, I give and bequeath to my daughter Alice Glasier my wrought bedd and two
hundred pounds in money to be paid unto her by my Executrix at such tyme as she in her
discretion shall think fitt.

Item, I give and bequeath unto my sonne William my best cloth suite and best stockings
and hatt and thirty pounds to pay for the annuity of the house he is to take. And after the
death of my deare wife I bequeath unto him the lease which I hold from the Dean and
Chapter of Lichfield of a certain ffarm called Shareshull Farm, nowe in the holding of
Thomas Ffletcher of Shareshull . . .

Item, whereas my kinsman Humphrey Bagguley* and myself are jointly possessed of two
several crofts of the severall prebends of Ffreyford [Freeford] and Longdon, the one
whereof is taken in his name and the other in my name, but for our joynte use as by accompt
betwixt us under both our hands appears; my will and mind is that my wife shall have and
during her life and widdowhood my moiety of one half of the yearly profitt which over the
rents and other dues shall from tyme to tyme accrew from both the said prebends leases, she
paying to my sonne Richard Glasier, who hath deserved nothing from me to maintain him
while he is out of employment, Tenn pounds a yeare if she think he deserve it, and if he
reforme and become a new man then I desire she will assigne and give him what further
portion she shall think fitt.

Item, I give and bequeath unto my sonne Jeffery Glasier my white doublett cloake and my
browne camlott coate, my riding coate, and all my books, and after the decease of my dearly
beloved wife I give unto him all the termes which shall be then unexpired of those severall
leases which I hold from the Dean and Chapter of Lichfield, of Kingsley Croft, Magdalens
Well Croft and ten acres of field land, the Dimbles, and the tythes of those places and divers
others lying in and about Lichfield which I hold of the Subchanter and Vicars Chorall of a
barn and croft at Greenhill, a house in St. John Street, the Bank Croft and a little croft in Gay
Lane, PROVIDED that he permitt and suffer my deare wife quietly and without the least
disturbance of him or any coming from him, to live and make use of the house, garden and

---

*Probably the same person as Lieutenant Humphrey Baguley who served in Bagot's Regiment of Foot (Chapter IV)

backsyde I now possess as if it were her owne and as freely as she now doth. And in case he shall any way disturb or molest her either by word or deed then he shall have noe benefitt of these leases but they shall goe and bee disposed of by her to such of my children as she shall think fitt to them.

Item, whereas my brother Sir Walter Littleton and myselfe are jointly possessed of a certain lease of the prebend of Aston my will and mind is that my wife shall have and enjoy to her selfe my moiety of one half of the yearly proffits thereof during her life, she paying to my sonne Goddard Glasier out of it forty shillings towards her providing his clothes until he be in a way of getting a handsome subsistance, and after the decease of my saide wife I then give and bequeath the remainder lease and interest which shall then be determined to my sonne Goddard Glasier for his portion he having beene already more changeable [i.e. biddable] to me than any the rest of my Children.

Item, my will and mind is if any doubt or question arise concerning any legacy herein given, that my worthy brother Sir Walter Littleton shall finally end and determine the difference between them. And of this my last will and testament I make, constitute and appoint my dearly beloved wife Alice as my sole executrix, in witness whereof I have hereunto put my hand and seale the twenty-fifth day of March in the year of our Lord God one thousand six hundred and fforty-seven.

Sealed, signed, published and delivered by the said Jeffery Glasier to be his last will and testament in the presence of Sir Walter Littleton Senior, Walter Littleton Junior.

Jeffery Glasier recovered from his 'weakness of body' and survived for another twenty years, his will not being proved until the thirtieth of December 1667, thus saving his wife Alice from having to make some awkward decisions, not to mention possible harassment by one of her sons.

# APPENDIX C

Extract from
## 'A Metallurgical Examination of a Cast-iron Cannon Ball'*

by J. E. Hurst, D.Met., F.I.M., J.P., and R. V. Riley, Ph.D., B.Sc., A.I.M.

During the Civil Wars the Cathedral Close of Lichfield sustained three sieges over the years 1643 to 1646. Garrisoned on behalf of the King early in 1643, it surrendered to the Parliamentary forces on March 5th of that year. In the following April, Prince Rupert, having taken the town of Birmingham, marched on Lichfield and laid siege to the Close a second time. Batteries were erected to the north of the Close and after ten days' ineffectual attack, he at length drained the moat and sprung two mines, one of which being successful enabled him to 'furiously storm the place.' The garrison surrendered on April 21st 1643, and remained in the King's hands until early in 1646 it was again 'harassed by the enemy' and surrendered to the Parliamentary forces on July 10th 1646.

From time to time cannon balls have been discovered in the neighbourhood of the Close, and one of these recently came into the possession of one of the authors. As a specimen of a casting approximately 300 years old it was considered of interest to submit this to a metallurgical examination, and particularly to examine and record, not only the residual elements present in its composition, but also the content of hydrogen, oxygen and nitrogen remaining after such a long period of preservation.

### Visual Examination

The ball examined had a diameter of just under five inches and was of iron. The surface was remarkably smooth and, although oxidised, was free from the thick layers of rust which might have been expected after 300 years. There still remained a very faint line running more or less continuously around a circumference of the ball, and this passed through a roughly circular area 2 in. dia., which was more pitted than the rest of the surface. If it be assumed that the ball was moulded in a two-part box which was subsequently placed on end for top pouring through a feeder/riser cut along the joint, this might account for the surface indications described. In the subsequent metallurgical examination this method of manufacture has been confirmed.

### Dimensional Accuracy

To the eye, the ball appeared truly spherical, and when rolled on the floor it showed little bias. Check measurements of diameter were made to the nearest five-thousandths of an inch along two circumferential rings. The readings obtained are given in Table I.

TABLE I.—*Measurements of Diameter of Cannon Ball*

|  | (a) Greek numerals | (b) Roman numerals |
|---|---|---|
| Diameter on circumferential line shown in | | |
| Position 1        ..        ..        ..        .. | 4.930 | 4.925 |
| 2        ..        ..        ..        .. | 4.925 | 4.945 |
| 3        ..        ..        ..        .. | 4.900 | 4.955 |
| 4        ..        ..        ..        .. | 4.910 | 4.945 |
| 5        ..        ..        ..        .. | 4.935 | 4.920 |

It is clear that the ball, as a casting, was to a tolerance of plus or minus twenty-five thousandths of an inch which, even on present-day standards, must be considered good. This assumes, of course, that there was no attempt at chipping or hand-grinding to shape, which on the whole is considered unlikely, especially in view of the prominence of the joint line and feeder/riser markings which were almost the only remaining blemishes apart from corrosion pitting.

---

*Paper read to The Institute of British Foundrymen, June 14th 1949.

### Density of the Ball

| | | |
|---|---|---|
| Weight of the ball ... ... ... ... ... ... | 14.25 lb |
| | 6,460 gms. |
| Average diameter of ball ... ... ... ... ... | 4.92 in. |
| Volume of the ball ... ... ... ... ... ... | 64.5 cub. in. |
| | 1,055 ccs. |
| Density ... ... ... ... ... ... ... ... | 6.13 gms. per cc. |
| Usual density of cast iron ... ... ... ... ... | 7.6 gms. per cc |

### Chemical Composition

By chemical analysis the cannon ball was found to be a phosphoric iron of similar composition to the iron used to-day for common engineering castings. The analytical results, shown in Table III, contain no unusual features except the sulphur which is probably lower than would be found in castings of this type to-day. The low sulphur may possibly be the result of charcoal smelting.

TABLE III.—*Chemical Composition of the Cannon Ball*

| | Per cent |
|---|---|
| Total carbon .. .. .. .. .. .. .. .. .. ... | 3.20 |
| Graphitic carbon .. .. .. .. .. .. .. .. .. | 2.76 |
| Combined carbon .. .. .. .. .. .. .. .. .. | 0.44 |
| Silicon .. .. .. .. .. .. .. .. .. .. | 0.80 |
| Sulphur .. .. .. .. .. .. .. .. .. .. | 0.056 |
| Phosphorus .. .. .. .. .. .. .. .. .. | 1.12 |
| Manganese .. .. .. .. .. .. .. .. .. | 0.48 |

### Gas Content of the Iron

The determination of the content of hydrogen, oxygen and nitrogen, was made by the vacuum-fusion method, and the results are given in Table IV.

TABLE IV.—*Gas Content of the Iron*

| | |
|---|---|
| Hydrogen .. | 5.2 mls. per 100 gms. or 4.5 parts per million. |
| Oxygen .. | 0.0032 per cent. or 32.0 parts per million. |
| Nitrogen .. | 0.0065 per cent. or 65.0 parts per million. |

### Concluding Remarks

If the specimen examined was typical of the round shot used for missiles in the 17th century, one must regard quite highly the skill of the iron-founder of that day. The ball was well within the tolerances of dimensional accuracy upon which it would be difficult to improve to-day. The shrinkage cavity, almost inevitable for a static sand casting of spherical shape, was normal and very centrally located.

The quality of the metal was good and in every way the equal of modern standards. In its comparative freedom from alloying elements (i.e. nickel and chromium) it was typical of an ancient iron, but somewhat surprisingly it contained definite small percentages of tin and copper. Could this be due to an accidental or perhaps intentional addition of a small amount of bronze cannon to the molten iron before casting?

The authors wish to thank the directors of the Staveley Iron and Chemical Company for permission to publish this Paper.

# BIBLIOGRAPHY

BAGOT, Lord, Memoirs of the Bagot Family (1848)

BRERETON, General Sir William, Letterbook (1646)

CLARENDON, Earl of, History of the Rebellion and Civil Wars in England, Ed. Macray (1888)

DENT, Robert, and HILL, Joseph, Historic Staffordshire (1896)

ERDEWICK, Sampson, A Survey of Staffordshire, Ed. Harwood (1844)

HARWOOD, Revd. Thomas, History and Antiquities of the City of Lichfield (1806)

HEWITT, John, Handbook of Lichfield Cathedral (1882)

HOGG, Artillery, Its Origin, Heyday and Decline (1970)

JOHNSON, Paul, British Castles (1978)

KING, Gregory, Staffordshire Pedigrees, Ed. Armytage & Ryland (1913)

PALMER, Tony, Charles II (1979)

PARKER, Alfred, A Sentimental Journey in and about the City of Lichfield (1925)

PLOT, Robert, A Natural History of Staffordshire (1686)

POPE, Dudley, Guns (1969)

REID, Stuart, The Finest Knight in England (Biography of Thomas Tyldesley) 1979

SHAW, Revd. Stebbing, History and Antiquities of Staffordshire (1801)

SYMONDS, Richard, Diary of the Marches of the Royal Army during the Great Civil War, Ed. Camden Society (1859)

TRINGHAM, Dr. Nigel, Two Seventeenth Century Surveys of Lichfield Cathedral Close (1986)

WARBURTON, Eliot, Memoirs of Prince Rupert and the Cavaliers (1849)

YOUNG, Brigadier Peter, Edgehill 1642 (1967)
                              Naseby 1645 (1985)

# INDEX

# INDEX

# INDEX

# INDEX

# INDEX